SECOND NATURE

SECOND NATURE

The Animal-Rights Controversy

Alan Herscovici

Published in 1991 by
Stoddart Publishing Co. Limited
34 Lesmill Road
Toronto, Canada
M3B 2T6

First published in 1985 by CBC Enterprises/
Les Entreprises Radio Canada

CBC logo used by permission

Canadian Cataloguing in Publication Data

Herscovici, Alan, 1948-
Second nature: the animal rights controversy

ISBN 0-7737-5498-9

1. Animal welfare - Moral and ethical aspects.
2. Fur trade - Canada. I. Title.

HV4708.H47 1992   179'.3   C91-095714-2

Cover design: Michael van Elsen Design Inc.
Cover photograph: R. Harrington for Hudson's Bay Company

Printed and bound in Canada

for Yetieve and Jack

The CBC Radio "Ideas" program, "Men and Animals: Building a New Relationship with Nature," on which this book is based, was produced in 1983. The executive producer was Robert Prowse and the producer was Max Allen.

CONTENTS

Preface

While preparing this book, and the radio series from which it grew, I crossed Canada and talked to many people. In Vancouver, in the cluttered, unpretentious walk-up offices of Greenpeace, Patrick Moore showed me a navigation map on which he plotted the daily progress of the *Rainbow Warrior*, which was en route to protest Soviet whaling in the Bering Sea. People bustled in and out, some wearing the distinctive yellow Greenpeace windbreakers with rainbow insignia at the shoulder. Plans were being laid to rush film from the *Rainbow Warrior* to the United States and Canadian media. Greenpeace was preparing another media coup. The room was filled with a spirit of joyful anarchism.

In Vancouver, too, I attended a symposium, where I met intelligent and articulate spokesmen for the animal-rights movement. Michael Giannelli, scientific advisor for the Fund For Animals, explained the theoretical premises of the animal-rights doctrine: that only irrational prejudice – "speciesism" – permitted us to treat animals in ways we'd never treat human beings. Donald Barnes, director of the Washington office of the National Anti-Vivisection Society, told me how he'd come to doubt the value of irradiation experiments on monkeys, which he had been doing for the United States Air Force. Robert Sharpe, a scientific advisor for the International Association Against Painful Experiments on Animals, explained that he, too, had given up research because the suffering inflicted on animals wasn't in the interest even of human patients, as it drew attention away from more organic approaches to medicine. All of them talked about reevaluating our place in nature and respecting "nonhuman animals," the fellow creatures with whom we share this planet. All these people were completely opposed to sealing, fur trapping and ranching.

Then I crossed the channel to Victoria, where Angus Matthews, manager of Sealand of the Pacific, told me that an apparent bid to "liberate" one of his young orca whales had resulted in the death of the whale. Matthews claimed that animal-rights activists were doing just what they accused others of: using animals for their own ends, in this case for publicity. After our interview, Matthews showed off a young sea-lion pup that had been found abandoned on a local beach. It was being cared for until it was old enough to fend for itself, when it would be set free. (Harbor seals that had been set free in the spring frolicked in the water around the visitors' entrance to the aquarium, reluctant, apparently, to give up the human companionship they'd become used to.) As the sea-lion pup rolled in Matthews' arms to have its belly scratched, I instinctively reached out to pat it. I pulled back my hand faster still as the pup swung around and snapped with small but efficient-looking teeth. In that instant I realized how much influence the media myth of cuddly "baby" seals has had on all of us.

My interview with Ray Demarchi, a British Columbia wildlife biologist, was recorded on a small island off Vancouver Island. While feral sheep grazed fifty feet away and chickens clucked noisily in the background, Demarchi explained why he's worried that "if we don't accept to use animals, we'll lose them." Instead of allowing wildlife habitat to be whittled away for agricultural and other purposes, he argued, we should recognize that wildlife can contribute substantially to our economy – whether through trapping, hunting, fishing or tourism. In an increasingly urban society, the occasional return to the land to harvest one's own food is "good for the soul."

Across the continent in the offices of the Grand Council of the Cree, in Val d'Or, Quebec, I met Thomas Coon, founding president of the Cree Trappers' Association. Coon, who is now director for traditional pursuits, had come off a plane that night from Quebec City, where he had met with government officials. The next morning he would fly into the bush for a meeting with James Bay chiefs. Patiently he told me about traditional Cree hunting practices, about how Cree "respected animals" and why they resented outsiders trying to impose foreign values on the Cree and other aboriginal peoples. When the formal interview was completed, he indicated with a sweep of his arm a long shelf of folio binders, thousands of pages of reports and testimonies that were produced for the James Bay negotiations. With these papers, Cree and other James Bay aboriginal people had proved their right to compensation for land flooded by Quebec's massive hydroelectric projects. Coon, like many of his generation, was taken away from his family as a child and sent to school in the south. The education he received has equipped him to fight the government and the outside society to defend the culture they were deprived of. Before his meeting in Quebec, he, his family and his parents had camped for a week deep in the bush, catching fish and drying them for the season. That was a good life, he said, and that was what he was fighting for. After the meeting of James Bay chiefs he would return to the bush; it would be time for the fall moose hunt.

In the summer of 1984, the founding meeting of the Aboriginal Trappers Federation of Canada was held in Toronto. Eli Weetaluktuk, of Inukjuak, told me that, during the negotiations for the James Bay

Agreement in 1974, Inuit hunters were brought to Montreal to testify. These men brought with them their own food, a whole harp seal, which they skinned one night in the bathtub of their hotel room. In the morning, the chambermaids saw the blood in the bath and the police were called in. After blood tests and translations everyone understood, what had happened, but the story illustrates how recent contacts between the many different realities of Canada are. It is really only beginning.

Some animal-rights campaigns show the dangers of one part of society interfering without comprehension of the lifestyle and values of other parts of society. The ecology movement – and, ultimately, much of the support for the animal-rights movement – stems from a growing conviction that we must learn to control the technological power we have unleashed before it devours us. Hunting societies have a lot to teach us about respecting the needs of wildlife; and where hunters and trappers are still out on the land, they can best monitor the impact of technological society on wildlife habitat. Alan Cooke, of the McGill Centre for Northern Studies, pointed out that, in the long run, the value of wildlife harvested by aboriginal hunters, for example, far outweighs the wealth of even the richest oil reserves or mining operation. And yet aboriginal peoples have been the hardest hit by animal-rights campaigns.

But finally, we must all ask how we will define our relationship with the natural environment in years to come. This is not an easy question, but unless we address it squarely it will be decided by other forces – forces of "circumstance" and market – and the result may not be one we would choose for ourselves.

The terms of the discussion must be broadened, for some of the conflicts we have seen are caused by inadequate or inaccurate information. For example, many animal-rights advocates claim that trapping and sealing are no longer important occupations. Discussions with aboriginal and non-native hunters and trappers, however, tell a different story, including the work that has been done to develop more humane trapping systems (with the active cooperation of trappers).

The adversarial stance that animal-rights groups have taken in recent years is not conducive to developing the understanding that will be needed to resolve these issues. It seems that many – often well-educated, well-meaning people – have donned blinkers just when we need to widen our vision. I hope the material presented in the following pages will help to make the argument more constructive.

I set out with little more than the certainty that, in the campaigns against sealing and trapping, the question of how we must redefine our relationship with nature was not being properly posed. It was gratifying to find an immediate and wholehearted response from knowledgeable authorities in fields in which I could claim little more than active curiosity.

Some of the people without whose help this book could never have been written include: Richard Van Gelder, curator for mammals at the American Museum of Natural History in New York; Bob Carmichael and Richard Stardom, fur-bearer specialists with the wildlife-management branch of the Manitoba Department of Mines, Natural Resources and Environment; Toby Morantz, George Wenzel and Alan Cooke, of the McGill Centre for Northern Studies and Research; Jack Ornstein, of the department of philosophy of Concordia University, Montreal, and German psychologist Harald Traue, on exchange at the University of Calgary.

I am especially indebted to Colin Scott for patiently submitting to long interviews, and for his enthusiastic support even when he was busy with work of his own. Mark Small, president, Kirk Smith, executive director and the late Captain Willie Deraspé, of the Canadian Sealers' Association; Bob Stevenson, of the Native Council of Canada and chairman of the Aboriginal Trappers' Federation of Canada; Mona Evans, policy advisor with the Department of Indian Affairs and Northern Development; Judith Swan, Brian Roberts and Greg Roger of Fisheries and Oceans Canada, who supplied the data I needed about the sealing industry and fishing in Canada; Ralf Winckelmann; Victor Topper, president of the Fur Council of Canada, Jordan Livingston, president, and Jack Hurtig, vice-president, of the Retail Fur Council of Canada, for information about the fur industry; Ron Daniel, executive director of the Fur Institute of Canada and Neal Jotham, chairman of the Canadian Federation of Humane Societies, for information about humane trap research in Canada.

Discussions with Arthur Frayling, chairman of the International Fur Trade Federation, and John Heppes, administrator of the Canadian representation to CITES, were very helpful; interviews were kindly granted by Harry Rowsell, executive director of the Canadian Council on Animal Care, Leo Bustad of Washington State University, Peter Hyde, of the International League for Animal Rights; George Clements of the Association for the Protection of Fur-bearing Animals; Patrick Moore, Robert Sharpe, Donald Barnes, and Thomas Coon.

Don McCrea, president of Manitoba Registered Trappers, and Norman Guilbeault, of Fort Smith, Northwest Territories, answered many questions about trapping. For information about the contemporary situation of aboriginal trappers and hunters I am indebted to Sterling Brass of the Federation of Saskatchewan Indians; Michael Amarook, mayor of Baker Lake, Northwest Territories; Jarvis Grey of United Native Nations, British Columbia; Joe Jacquot of the Council for

12

Yukon Indians; James Schaefer of Northwest Territories Hunters' and Trappers' Federation; and Jim Bourque, deputy minister for renewable resources in the Northwest Territories. Cindy Gilday of the Dené Nation National Office helped me locate photographs, as did George Wenzel, Lynn Whidden, Paul Wagner of Environment Canada, Richard Stardom and Colin Scott; also Leonard Werner and George Whitman of the Hudson's Bay Company.

I owe special thanks to Richard Salisbury of the department of anthropology, McGill University, for vital initial guidance and contacts. Dagmar Kafunke, of CBC Vancouver, helped with interviews in that city. Bob and Noella Cregheur on Lasquetti Island and Scott and Mary-Jane Terrill in Victoria offered help when it was needed. Michael Dorland allowed me to use him as a sounding board and throughout this project gave editorial advice that saved me numerous times when I lost track. Max Allen of the CBC radio program "Ideas" had the courage to produce the original radio series on what some considered "too controversial" a topic, because he believes that radio should deal with important questions. Greg Yarrow of CBC Enterprises has also been supportive. Bob Daley guided the book through production and Glenn Witmer, the publisher, has been enthusiastic and always patient with my often eccentric demands. Very special gratitude must go to Charis Wahl, who edited the book. Her encouragement and good humor were much appreciated as I worked through the long process of producing a manuscript, and her efficient blue pencil has eased the reader's job as well as forcing me to clarify some ideas that weren't sufficiently developed.

Three-year-old Jesse Jonah often kept me company as I wrote, sometimes curling up to sleep under my work table. To Liliane, I owe what only writers and their spouses can know.

PART ONE

THEORY

Animal-rights groups claim to represent a radical "broadening of our scope of moral concern." However, the western philosophical tradition is not quite so "anti-nature" as some would have us believe. Moreover, when the origins of animal-rights theory and the modern ecology movement are traced, some inherent contradictions are revealed. By contrast, the very different world-view of aboriginal Amer-Indian hunting peoples is described. According to this philosophy, using and respecting animals are not believed to be mutually exclusive. On the contrary, perhaps it is only when we recognize our dependence on other creatures that we truly respect them.

1

The Problem

As a species, our sense of belonging in nature, our sense of a place in nature, has been utterly destroyed ... this is the unilateral divorce from life and living that is the unique accomplishment of our civilization.
— John A. Livingston (*The Fallacy of Wildlife Conservation*)

As we hurtle into the final years of the millennium, riding a crest of unprecedented industrial and technological expansion, western civilization has been stricken with doubt. We've come only recently to understand the real costs of our new-found wealth. Few realize even today that our most impressive material achievements have been "improvements in the pump rather than the well."[1] Technology and geometrically increasing world population have resulted in apparently uncontrollable rising consumption and waste, depletion of resources, pollution and the specter of nuclear war.

How have we come to this? The Renaissance threw open the narrow horizons of medieval Europe. During the two centuries that followed, the discovery of new lands and the expansion of trade, the rise of urban merchant classes and the growth of modern scientific knowledge eroded the authority of church and landed gentry. Instead of faith, knowledge would save mankind. With the dawning of the Age of Reason, the "bonds of instinct" were loosened and limitless vistas beckoned. Through his ingenuity and toil, man might emerge from the shadows of famine and disease, and perhaps one day might conquer even death. In brief, he would free himself from nature, and fulfill the biblical promise of Dominion "over all the earth, and over every creeping thing that creepeth upon the earth."

Ironically, it is our very success that now menaces survival. World population was probably less than five hundred million in 1650, and it took *homo sapiens* at least three hundred thousand years to reach that density. By 1850, with the industrial revolution firmly established, population reached one billion. Since then it has quadrupled and, with a net gain of one million people every five days, it is expected to double each generation.[2]

Man is now the most numerous large animal on earth. Land has been cleared for cities and roads; more land is taken for agriculture and drenched with chemicals to protect the food supply of a growing population – all of which drastically reduces habitat suitable for wildlife. In Europe, where human population is most dense, few large wild animals have survived, and even in Africa, almost ninety per cent of the large mammals have disappeared, most of them during this century.[3]

The rapid rise of human population and, especially, the tremendous growth of technology, have so changed man's place in the ecological balance, it is argued, that they call for a fundamental change in our attitudes toward wildlife and life in general. "Our social and philosophical mind, as a civilization and as a species, simply hasn't been able to keep up with the physical and technological advances which have been made," says Patrick Moore, director of Greenpeace Canada, the environmental group that has actively called for a change in values.[4]

The ecological argument outlined by Moore runs something like this: for many centuries, man's ability to exploit nature was limited. The whole idea was to succeed in exploiting, and often you didn't. There was no question in the fifteenth century of causing the whales to become extinct; we couldn't have done it if we'd tried. But with the development, especially over the past hundred years, of technology that gives man the power to overexploit every living resource on earth, and in fact to destroy the whole thing fifty times over, man's ecological "niche" has been radically altered. "We are a different organism, a different entity," Moore says, "and to think that we can continue with the same values as we had a hundred years ago, while we are a radically altered phenomenon, is completely ridiculous."

Michael Giannelli, scientific advisor for the two-hundred-thousand-member Fund For Animals, agrees that what is required is nothing short of a thorough reappraisal of the traditional "justifications and rationalizations" of our relationship with nature, with which we've "gotten by" until now. The challenge is no longer the traditional Darwinian survival of the fittest, says Giannelli. We're "at the top of the heap," and now we must learn to control ourselves and our own aggression, and the terrible power of the technology we have developed. Giannelli explains, "This planet is a self-contained unit, and if we destroy the air, and the water, and the natural resources, in our mad rush to colonize, we're going to saw the limb right out from under ourselves."[5]

The word "ecology" was coined by the German naturalist Ernst Haeckel in 1866 to describe the interdependence of living organisms with their environment, which included each other.[6] The concept had little impact on laymen until a hundred years later, with the publication in 1962 of Rachel Carson's *Silent Spring*, an exposé of the indiscriminate use of pesticides. Pesticides made the interdependence of life deadly clear: DDT moved through the food chain, accumulating in higher concentrations as it went.

Carson's *Silent Spring* was a turning point and signaled the birth of the modern environmental movement. By the end of the 1960s, attempts were being made to assess the damage caused by a century of extremely rapid growth and to legislate controls. The realization that about half the animal species that had become extinct in the past two thousand years had disappeared during the first sixty years of this century, and that at least one-tenth of all remaining plant and animal species were endangered, led to the drafting of the Convention on International Trade in Endangered Species of Wild Flora and Fauna (CITES), in 1973, to monitor and regulate traffic in wildlife at an international level.[7]

As the naturalist John A. Livingston has argued, however, the "self-interest" argument alone is unlikely to restrain the ravages of an expanding industrial society:

> Having in mind the limits to ecological prediction, wildlife conservation can never present an airtight case. And of course industry, commerce, and the growth imperative are required to prove nothing. Their goals are part of the belief system. Wildlife conservation is not.[8]

Having asserted that all of nature is interdependent, and that the exploitive appetites of modern industrial society must be restrained, a militant edge of the environmental movement has gone a step farther. It is not enough to recognize that it's in man's interest to control his destructive tendencies, says Patrick Moore; the principle that animals also have intrinsic interests must be accepted. This principle is commonly expressed as "animal rights." Moore explains, "Unless you have a strong basis philosophically of animal rights, values which confer upon them rights to exist, and to live free of pain, and not to be killed unnecessarily, you will never get a protective regime that will be effective. They'll always be treated as exploitable commodities that can be used for commercial purposes, as long as it makes a buck on the free market."

Some two hundred years ago, the British philosopher and social theorist Jeremy Bentham proposed that, since animals can suffer, they have the *right* not to be made to suffer needlessly.[9] The nineteenth-century historian William Lecky suggested that there was a steadily expanding circle of moral concern, which had grown to embrace other nations and other races. Ultimately it would protect other species as well.[10] Henry Salt, the American social reformer, developed these ideas into a complete doctrine of how our relations with animals might be completely transformed.[11]

Salt's ideas, long a central theme in vegetarian, anti-vivisection and animal-welfare movements, attracted little attention in the wider society until recently. They have been revived in two influential books: *Animals, Men and Morals*, edited by Stanley and Roslind Godlovitch and John Harris, and *Animal Liberation*, by Peter Singer. All four authors are Oxford-trained philosophers.[12] Singer's book, which has had the greatest public impact, is a critique of "speciesism," a term coined by psychologist Richard Ryder, also of Oxford. Like "racism" or "sexism," the term refers to arbitrary discrimination, in this case against members of other species.

These ideas are now being translated into action by groups ranging from the influential Fund For Animals (started by Cleveland Amory to "put cleats in the running shoes of the little old ladies") and Greenpeace International,[13] which coordinates more than a million members through nine national organizations, to hundreds of smaller groups that, according to a study commissioned by Harvard University, often make up for what they lack in money with dedicated volunteer work. Some, like the Society for Animal Rights (SAR) and Attorneys For Animal Rights (AFAR), specialize in low-key, careful legal strategies, while People for the Ethical Treatment of Animals (PETA) organized the infiltration of the Maryland laboratory of Edward J. Taub, which led to the first conviction of a scientist for abuses in handling his research animals.[14] Others have sought more "direct" methods of publicizing their goals, including attacks on fur stores and ranches, research labs and "factory-farms," in Europe and North America, for which a group calling itself the Animal Liberation Front (ALF) has often claimed responsibility.

This radical animal-rights philosophy not only opposes pollution of the environment or depletion of animal species, as does the environmental movement, but rejects the use of animals for any purpose that causes them suffering or death. Therefore, it is opposed to the raising of animals by modern intensive methods and to meat-eating in general, as well as to the use of animals in painful laboratory experiments or product tests. It also opposes hunting, fishing, trapping and fur ranching, as well as rodeos, circuses, zoos and aquariums. No single issue, however, stirred so much controversy as the campaign to end the annual Newfoundland harp-seal hunt, which climaxed in 1983 with the decision of the Council of Ministers of Europe to ban the import of white-coat pelts into the European Economic Community.

A man poses with buffalo skulls and horns at a railroad siding at Saskatoon, Saskatchewan, in August 1890.

A trapper with his dog sled fifty miles from Norway House, Manitoba.

Inuit hunters use their dogs to assist in hunting polar bears near Ross's magnetic pole, 1951.

Trappers load fur bales onto toboggans.

The campaign against the seal hunt developed over twenty years, and by the time the Council of Ministers made its decision, some five million letters had been received by the EEC (whole classrooms of children wrote), most of them calling for the ban. Wildlife conservation had become a high-profile mass movement with considerable political clout.

The anti-sealing campaigns are interesting, not least because they show a blurring of the boundaries that distinguished ecology from animal rights. The first protests against the hunt, beginning about 1964, stressed how the seals were killed; and traditional anti-cruelty groups, like the New Brunswick SPCA and the Ontario Humane Society, took the lead. When the Canadian government took steps to insure that the seals were killed humanely, measures that won the approval of the animal-welfare establishment,[15] Brian Davies broke with the New Brunswick SPCA in 1969 and set up his own International Fund for Animal Welfare (IFAW) to push for total abolition of the hunt.

By contrast, Greenpeace went into the seal campaign in 1976 from an ecological perspective: what was at issue, the group said, was not *how* seals were killed, but that overharvesting threatened the harp seal with extinction.[16] But as the world scientific community came to accept the effectiveness of the Canadian quota-management system, Greenpeace, too, moved to an animal-rights position, that is, that seals shouldn't be hunted at all. Beginning from the two poles of traditional animal welfare and modern ecology, the IFAW and Greenpeace both came to espouse an animal-rights philosophy. "People are just automatically accepting that animals have rights," says Patrick Moore.

The recent political successes of animal-rights groups, however, obscure some serious contradictions. Ecology has been called "the subversive science," because it forms the basis for a critique of the ravages of uncontrolled industrial and economic expansion.[17] The victims of the anti-sealing campaign, however, have not been corporate polluters or land developers, but the people who live closest to the land. Most Newfoundland sealers are independent fishermen for whom sealing is a vital component in a yearly cycle of catching lobster, herring, groundfish . . . and seals. For the Inuit of the Canadian Arctic, sealskins were a principal source of cash to finance the subsistence hunt. For both these groups, the destruction of the market for sealskins has brought considerable hardship and animal-rights groups may succeed in doing what half a century of corporate and government manipulation have as yet failed to accomplish, in wiping out the last vestiges of traditional Inuit culture.

All this is especially tragic in light of two recent scientific reports. Both the 1982 study by the International Council for the Exploration of the Sea (ICES) and the 1983 report of the scientific council of the thirteen-nation Northwest Atlantic Fisheries Organization (NAFO) confirm that Canadian quotas were allowing the seal populations to *rise*. At least since quotas began in 1972, harp seals have not been endangered.

The mounting campaign against fur trapping now threatens to disrupt the lives of some one hundred thousand trappers in Canada. Up to sixty per cent of these trappers are Indians or Metis. For many, fur income is a main source of cash to subsidize the traditional hunting-based economy; this is income that can not be readily replaced in the north. Fur trapping is one of the few activities through which native people have been able to successfully participate on their own terms in the dominant economy. Moreover, trap lines often represent the Indians' single most powerful *de-facto* claim to their land.

Bringing aboriginal trappers off their hunting territories is a crucial step toward "clearing the land" for pipelines, power dams and other high-tech frontier "development" projects, and all the disruption of wildlife habitat they bring with them. For this reason, many wildlife biologists question whether the demands of the animal-rights groups are even really in the interests of wildlife. They argue that without a strong lobby of native groups, trappers, hunters and other wildlife users, habitat can never be protected against the ravages of the real enemies of wildlife: "the dammers, the ditchers, and the developers."

> The law deals harshly with man or woman
> Who steals the goose from off the common,
> But lets the greater felon loose
> Who steals the common from the goose.[18]

And so we arrive at the extraordinary situation in which "ecologists," having adopted the animal-rights philosophy, now unconsciously serve the interests of mining consortiums and hydroelectric developers by undermining the economies of people who still live in direct relation with the land. Is this absurd inversion "accidental," merely an aberration in an otherwise consistent doctrine? Or does it reveal an irreconcilable contradiction at the very heart of the animal-rights philosophy?

A central tenet of that philosophy is that western man has set himself apart from the rest of creation by defining himself as "outside" nature. But by disenfranchising the very people who still have a direct commitment to the land, the animal-rights philosophy facilitates the growing hegemony of the techno-industrial complex, widening rather than healing the rift between man and nature. In other words, animal-rights ideas may be more a symptom of our disease than a cure.

These are serious questions, because animal-rights groups have far-reaching effects. The Mobilization For Animals (MFA), an umbrella group, has organized mass demonstrations this year in Los Angeles, Washington, Chicago and other cities against fur trapping and the use of animals in research laboratories. The MFA's national coordinator, Richard Morgan, has said, "Agitation for animal rights is part of a revolutionary process aimed at restructuring the major institutions of society."[19] Millions of people supported the EEC sealskin ban. They might be ready to ban fur trapping, too. A more intriguing question is whether they are prepared to give up the use of animals in research labs and product-safety tests and to stop eating meat. In *Animal Liberation*, Peter Singer writes, "To protest about bull-fighting in Spain or the slaughter of baby seals in Canada while continuing to eat chickens that have spent their lives crammed into cages, or veal that have been deprived of their mothers, their proper diet, and the freedom to lie down with their legs extended, is like denouncing apartheid in South Africa while asking your neighbours not to sell their houses to blacks."[20]

More to the point, such a double standard means that a grave injustice has been – and continues to be – done against Newfoundland fishermen and native people.

It should be stated at the outset that this discussion has special significance for Canada, a northern country where much of the land is best suited to raising animals or harvesting wildlife and other natural resources. There aren't many parts of Canada where soybeans or grapefruits will grow; not even potatoes grow in Newfoundland. If these fundamental physical and cultural realities are not acknowledged, it is difficult to understand what half a century of debate on the "Canadian identity" has been about. The Inuit say that the philosophy of animal rights is merely the latest outburst of the cultural and economic imperialism they've come to expect from Europe and the South.[21]

Peter Singer has stated that he believes the case for animal liberation is "logically cogent and cannot be refuted." Unfortunately, the public debate invariably jumps from one isolated crisis to the next, with little attempt to make a thorough assessment of the implications of the animal-rights philosophy. Without such an analysis, our actions may have results very different from what we intend. Moreover, public policy will be dictated by public-relations men and slick advertising campaigns.

It is true that by digging into the nitty-gritty – by questioning the assumptions of the animal-rights groups and cross-examining their ideas against their consequences when they are applied in the real world – we may lose some of the "logically cogent" simplicity that characterizes the presentation by Singer and others. It is comforting to believe that vegetarianism or banning sealskins or outlawing fur trapping are simply *right* without having to worry about Newfoundlanders or native people or the expansion of the techno-industrial megalith that whittles away at wildlife habitat. We prefer certainty to doubt. But as Albert Schweitzer said, "When we experience the conflicts ever more deeply, we are living in truth. The quiet conscience is an invention of the devil."[22]

The need to redefine our relationship with nature is one of the most serious challenges of our era. Animal-rights groups have pushed the question brusquely to the forefront. The real discussion, however, has barely begun. Part One of this book sets out some of the *theoretical* foundations of the animal-rights controversy: the animal-rights critique of the western view of nature; the origins of ecology and the animal-rights philosophy; and, by contrast, the Amer-Indian relationship with nature. In Part Two, the major animal-rights campaigns are analyzed. Part Three is an evaluation of the contribution of animal-rights groups and a reassessment of the challenge they pose.

2

The Philosophical Roots of Our Present Ecological Crisis

Animal life, sombre mystery! Immense world of thoughts and dumb sufferings! All nature protests against the barbarity of man, who misapprehends, who humiliates, who tortures his inferior brethren.
  – Michelet (*La Bible de l'humanité*)

The animal-rights movement, as distinguished from traditional animal-welfare or anti-cruelty movements, calls not merely for specific reforms but for a revolution in our fundamental attitudes toward animals and nature. Abuse of the environment and the living beings who inhabit it, it is argued, is the logical result of having defined ourselves as apart from the rest of creation. The split between man and nature is said to stem from peculiarities of our Judeo-Christian cultural heritage and to be aggravated by the rise of our modern scientific outlook.

The separation of man from nature is, however, an ongoing process, probably as old as man himself. Man belongs to a group of mammals called primates, most of which are vegetarians, eating seeds and fruits. Some twenty million years ago, the great forests that had covered much of Africa retreated, leaving vast stretches of open savanna and forcing our forebears to venture out of their shrinking and over-populated groves.[1]

It is tempting to imagine that the biblical story of Adam and Eve sent out of the garden is, in fact, an ancient race memory of this first drastic challenge to man's survival. Like in the Bible story, this change related to man's first knowledge of "good and evil." In open country, our hominid ancestors were suddenly vulnerable. They were also forced to change their eating habits, perhaps at first scavenging for dead meat, then actively working with others to kill as a group.

The emergence of man as a predator gave rise to some distinctively human qualities. Hunting animals that were stronger and faster than man required cooperation, which implied also sharing the fruits of the labor. Hunting also encouraged the development of language and, thus, an enlarged brain, as well as better eyesight, eye-hand coordination, the manufacture of weapons and of tools for removing and dressing skins and the elaboration of planning. An even more radical development was yet to come.

At least ten thousand years ago, men in certain areas began to practise agriculture. Instead of moving on when food became hard to find, they stayed in one place and exploited the land intensively. Long-term residence in one area quickly depleted game animals, so certain animals, primarily herbivores, were domesticated. Wild animals that competed for crops, or predators that preyed on domestic livestock, were classed as "bad," and became fair game for extermination.

But the need to store large stocks of grain from one harvest to the next left agricultural societies vulnerable to attacks from rodents, so certain predators, too, became "good." (Our word "puss," for example, is thought to originate from the name "Pasht," the Egyptian cat deity.)

Agriculture was a major change, because man now controlled his environment rather than merely adapting himself to it. The values of agricultural man are reflected in the biblical injunction, "Be fruitful and multiply, and replenish the earth and subdue it."

> And out of the ground the Lord God formed every beast of the field, and every fowl of the air; and brought them unto Adam to see what he would call them: and whatsoever Adam called every living creature, that *was* the name thereof.

In Genesis 2:19 the special position of man in creation was clearly established as a central theme of western civilization: man was in the world, but not exactly of it. Made in the image of God, he shared something of the Divinity's transcendence.

This notion of man's "otherness" was extended by the Greeks, for whom the body was the prison house of the soul. Pythagoras, like eastern Buddhists, believed that animals, too, had souls, which migrated after death into new bodies; for this reason he criticized meat eating. For Plato and Aristotle, though, it was man's reason that set him apart. Aristotle, in fact, argued that only men, not women, could originate thought. Women might understand, but they couldn't produce new thought. "You have slaves, you have women, and then, glory to be, there's *man*, the great reasoner!"[2]

By the time the Church followed the Roman legions into Europe and consolidated its bureaucratic grip on the medieval world, the Platonic notion of a split between an immortal soul and the prison house of the body was established in Christianity; but much of the Greek love of reason was lost in the transfer. Too great an interest in the natural world was considered not only irrelevant, but likely to impair one's chances of attaining the future life (or even, once the Inquisition got going, of hanging onto an earthly one).

Philosophy was reduced to the handmaiden of theology. The medieval world was a "great chain of being," from God to the angels, to men, and finally down to the lower animals, a strict hierarchy that bore a striking resemblance to medieval social order. According to Thomas Aquinas, the purpose of each link in the chain was to serve those above it. Man, then, could have no duties to animals. (As recently as the mid-nineteenth century, Pope Pius IX cited this doctrine to forbid the establishment of an SPCA in Rome.[3])

As low as animals figured in the medieval vision of creation, the first stirrings of modern science in the seventeenth century did little to improve their lot. French mathematician and philosopher René Descartes said that animals were like "machines," subject to physical laws that could be discovered and understood through careful study. But he was careful to distinguish between matter and the very different stuff of the human soul, for which man's rationality was once again offered as proof:

> For it is a very remarkable thing that there are no men, not even the insane, so dull and stupid that they cannot put words together in a manner to convey their thoughts. On the contrary, there is no other animal, however perfect and fortunately situated it may be, that can do the same. . . .
>
> [This] proves that they are not rational, and that nature makes them behave as they do according to the disposition of their organs; just as a clock, composed only of wheels and weights and springs, can count the hours and measure time more accurately than we can with all our intelligence. . . .
>
> For the rest . . . next to the error of those who deny God, which I think I have sufficiently refuted, there is none which is so apt to make weak characters stray from the path of virtue as the idea that the souls of animals are of the same nature as our own, and that in consequence we have no more to fear or to hope for after this life than have the flies and the ants.[4]

Despite his earnest professions of faith, Descartes and his contemporaries were opening the doors of a new science that would sweep away the authority of the church. By showing that living matter obeyed natural laws, he was asserting the right of reason to broaden its field of investigation. His vivid clockwork metaphor, unfortunately, was to cause animals no end of trouble. Anatomy was one of the tools of the new science, and Descartes begins his metaphor by suggesting that readers "take the trouble to have the heart of some large animal cut open before them."

To study phenomena such as the circulation of blood through the body, scientists dissected living animals. This explains the appeal of a theory that seemed to imply that the yelps of these "animal machines" need not be taken more seriously than sounds produced by some cleverly constructed automaton. In our own time, Pope Pius XII could advise that when animals are killed in an abattoir or scientific laboratory, "Their cries should not arouse unreasonable compassion, any more than do red-hot metals undergoing the blow of the hammer, seeds spoiling underground, branches crackling when they're pruned, grain that's surrendered to the harvester, or wheat being ground by the milling machine."[5]

With Descartes, it is argued, the western lust to dominate nature reached its fullest expression. The world and the animals in it had been reduced to tools with which to further man's own ambitions. New lands beckoned, and explorers reported indescribable riches that might easily be exploited. Gold from the Americas, brought back by the Spaniards, sparked massive inflation; the wealth seemed limitless. Trade, and the economic activity it nourished, combined with the growing practical science to launch the industrial revolution, which, in turn, made possible further exploration and conquest. Even Darwin's discoveries did little to dampen western man's boundless confidence: perhaps we were related to the animals, but we were comfortably at the top of the heap, well above the beasts, if no longer just below the angels. With God dethroned, man was arguably higher than ever, the sum of countless eons of progressive evolution.

It is only in our own time, in the second half of the twentieth century, that the dream has gone sour: depletion of natural resources; pollution of land, air and water; the menace of doomsday weapons, leaking reactors and the time bomb of growing toxic wastes; the extinction of animal and plant species at an accelerating rate. Just when we were most confident that we could control nature like one of our machines, we've been stricken with a terrible doubt.

DESCARTES AND THE ANIMAL MACHINE

Animal-rights writers blame two concepts for our predicament: an exploitive attitude toward nature, which they believe to be inherent to our Judeo-Christian heritage; and the cold, utilitarian "rationalism" of modern science, which began with Descartes. The historian Lynn White, Jr. has collapsed these two causes into one, arguing that the growth of modern science and technology is an outgrowth of the peculiarities of the Judeo-Christian world view.[6]

Descartes comes in for especially harsh criticism from Peter Singer and other modern animal-rights authors, who "expose" his supposed claim that "animals were just machines."[7] The "animal machine" is a popular trigger word in animal-rights discussions, probably because the word is so evocative, combining two apparently contradictory images in a single unforgettable package (a trick frequently used by surrealist painters and contemporary advertisers). The notion that animals are machines is so obviously absurd that it is offered as convincing proof of the fallacy of the scientific world view.

Singer, Carson, the two Godlovitches and others who have popularized this critique recently echo the American anti-vivisectionist Henry Salt. Salt, in his book *Animals' Rights*, condemned Cartesian mechanism as "a theory which carried the 'religious' notion a step farther, and deprived animals not only of their claim to a life hereafter, but of anything that could, without mockery, be called a life in the present, since mere 'animated machines', as they were thus affirmed to be, could in no sense be said to *live* at all!"[8]

Descartes, in fact, never says that animals *are* machines. In the fifth part of his *Discourse on Method*, he writes that "nature makes them behave . . . according to the disposition of their organs," just as a clock or machine functions according to the design and arrangement of its parts. Descartes' point has been so generally accepted today that it's difficult for us to understand what he was going on about. His argument, published in 1637, was directed against the straitjacket of ossified church dogma, which insisted that, as God was the cause of all phenomena, there was no need to study anything but theology. Knowledge that might threaten the authority of the church was not merely frowned upon but vigorously resisted.

Giordano Bruno, an Italian philosopher, was burned by the Inquisition in 1600 for speculating too freely about the relationship between spirit and matter in the Godhead. Galileo, another of Descartes' contemporaries, was obliged to repudiate the Copernican theory of the revolution of the planets in the solar system. Descartes refers to

Galileo in a carefully worded paragraph at the beginning of the sixth part of his Discourse, which immediately follows his disputed "machine" theory:

> I learned that people to whom I defer, and whose authority over my actions is hardly less than that of my own reason over my thoughts, had disapproved of a hypothesis in the field of physics that had been published somewhat earlier by another person [Galileo]. I do not want to say that I had accepted that hypothesis, but at least before their censure I could not imagine that it was prejudicial to religion or to the state, and therefore could see no ground for not professing it if reason convinced me of its truth. This circumstance made me fear that there might be other opinions of mine in which I was misled, despite the great care I had always taken not to accept any new ones which were not very certainly demonstrated, and to write of not that might prove disadvantageous to anyone.[9]

In this climate of very real repression, it is hardly surprising that Descartes follows his argument for the right to investigate freely the workings of the natural world with an affirmation of the authority of the church over the destiny of the human soul. This is why he was at such pains to separate "the machine" from the realm of "spirit." To do a hatchet job on Descartes because he yielded to church dogma on such questions, whatever his personal persuasion, makes about as much sense as criticizing a scientist working in the Soviet Union today for failing to denounce the Marxist state.

In the Middle Ages, the world was seen as a moral battlefield, where good and evil struggled for the salvation or damnation of the human soul. Scores of animals were summoned to law courts, charged with crimes and as often as not found guilty, because it was feared that demons and sorcerers could enter animal bodies to work their mischief.[10] In this context, Descartes' bold move to liberate a tremendous field of inquiry from church control was a considerable accomplishment.

Recent developments have made Descartes' insights, if anything, more appropriate than ever. One could cite the cybernetic theory of Norbert Wiener[11] or the prediction that computers will soon use living bacteria or other small organisms for their programmable, self-reproducing chips. In 1980, the United States Supreme Court ruled that new life forms may be patented by pharmaceutical laboratories.[12] The lines between machines and animals are blurring.

Some of the most interesting versions of the machine analogy, however, are being advanced by animal-rights advocates themselves as alternatives to using animals in research. Plastic models simulate living bodies for crash tests; heart and circulatory functions are mimicked by hydraulic apparatus; digital computers model interactions within the cells. Yet none of this would be possible if living beings were not "machines" obeying similar physical laws. Terence Hegarty describes the possibilities for sophisticated new electrochemical neural models, which could save the lives of thousands of animals now used for research:

> Workers many years ago noted the similarity between the basic "signalling" phenomenon of nerve impulse transmission in men and animals, and the waves of activity which can easily be generated or observed to flow over the surface of an iron wire which has been submerged in nitric acid. . . . This is likely to be relevant to a variety of problems in physiology and medicine which involve electrical phenomena and the cellular tissues of the body. Examples are epilepsy, anaesthesia, electrical coupling between neurons, learning, cancer, heart action, brain rhythms, the physiology of sleep, and the healing of wounds. . . .[13]

Perhaps animal-rights advocates owe Descartes an apology. Descartes himself, however, with remarkable prescience, wrote only a few pages after his much maligned "clockwork" passage:

> I should like to take advantage of this occasion to request posterity never to believe that any ideas are mine unless I have divulged them myself. I am not at all surprised at the extravagances attributed to the ancient philosophers whose writings we do not possess, nor do I judge in consequence that their ideas were unreasonable. They were the wisest men of their time, so I presume their ideas have been badly reported.[14]

JUDAISM

Descartes' "crime" of separating mind from body is seen by animal-rights activists as an extension of the man-nature split, which, they claim, underlies the Judeo-Christian tradition. Mostly they echo Henry Salt, who, in turn, quotes Schopenhauer: "The unpardonable forgetfulness in which the lower animals have hitherto been left by the moralists of Europe is well known. It is pretended that the beasts have no rights . . . a doctrine revolting, gross, and barbaric, peculiar to the west, and having its root in Judaism."[15]

It has become an established part of the animal-rights liturgy to condemn the Judeo-Christian tradition as "anti-nature," while praising eastern religions, which are said to show more sensitivity in this regard. Singer cites animal research in Indian medical labs as the triumph of western attitudes over "the ancient tradition of Hinduism which has more respect for animals than the Judeo-Christian tradition."[16] Lynn White, Jr. believes that "beatniks" show sound instincts when they embrace Zen Buddhism, "which conceives of the man-nature relationship as very nearly the mirror-image of the Christian view."[17] And in Salt's book, *Animals' Rights*, we read that Judaism, "with its hatred of the Gods of Nature," opened a breach between us and the rest of creation, while eastern philosophy "knits men and beasts together ... and unites the whole of Nature in one sacred and mysterious bond."[18]

In support of this simplistic caricature, Genesis is usually quoted. Man is told to subdue the earth and have dominion over the animals. (In an age when few can claim to be Bible scholars, these verses have the advantage of being printed on the first page of the Old Testament.) They have little meaning, however, outside the context of the central thrust of Judaism, "that the earth, being the creation of God, belongs to the Creator and not to man."[19]

The earth is the Lord's and the fulness thereof,
The world and those who dwell therein;
for he has founded it upon the seas,
and established it upon the rivers.
(Psalms 24:1-2)

These verses (which were recited by the Levites in the Holy Temple at the start of each week) assert that man has been granted only temporary tenancy or "stewardship" over the land, not outright title. For this reason, the Jew was required to recite a benediction before enjoying any fruit of the land: "Man is forbidden to enjoy anything without pronouncing a benediction, and whoever enjoys anything in this world without a benediction commits a trespass against sacred things" (the Talmud).

The requirement to rest agricultural land every seventh (Sabbatical) year was interpreted by the sages to be not only of ecological value, but a recognition that man enjoyed the land only as a gift. The laws of the Jubilee year, under which, every fiftieth year, land reverted to its original owners and slaves were freed, were interpreted by the Jewish philosopher Philo as recognition of the precept that man cannot acquire permanent possession of anything:

Do not pay the price of complete ownership, but only for a fixed number of years and a lower limit than fifty. For the sale should represent not real property, but fruits ... [because] the whole country is called God's property, and it is against piety to have anything that is God's property registered under any other masters.[20]

33

This interpretation was based on the biblical injunction, "And the land is not to be sold in perpetuity, for all land is Mine, because you are strangers and sojourners before Me" (Leviticus 25:23). Jews were forbidden even to grieve excessively the death of loved ones, for this would imply they considered them their own possessions, and thereby were setting themselves up as gods. Tithes, the dedication of the first fruits to God, the obligation to give charity, these and other regulations all affirmed that even the products of one's own labors must be "redeemed": "The Holy One, blessed be He, said: I have commanded you to honor Me, but not from your own. Give me what is already Mine, honor the Lord from the substance with which He graced you" (Leviticus 22:27).

From this central principle that man was not the "owner" of the earth followed naturally the precept *"bal tashit,"* "Do not destroy," found in Deuteronomy 20:19-20:

> When you besiege a city many days to bring it under your power by making war against it, you shall not destroy the trees thereof by swinging an axe against them; for from them you may eat, but do not destroy them, for the tree of the field is man's life.

Talmudic scholars expanded this injunction into a broad prohibition against waste of all kind: fruit trees may not be cut for lumber when there are timber trees available; the wood of the olive, the vine, the date palm and the fig may not be burned, even on the Temple altar (presumably to protect these trees, although some authors have suggested it was also because the olive and the vine gave off excessive smoke and were air pollutants); household items may not be discarded if still usable; and, generally, one must never consume more than one needs. The Talmud even stipulates that a naphtha lamp should not be burned too high, because that would waste a valuable resource.[21]

Animals were also to be respected, and the Old Testament includes many laws to protect them. One is obliged to assist a suffering animal, or one too heavily burdened, even if it belongs to one's enemy (Exodus 23:5); in other words, for the animal's sake, not for the owner's. The ox and the ass may not be yoked together, to spare the weaker animal. And "you shall not muzzle the ox when he treads out the corn" (Deuteronomy 25:4). The oral law interprets this rule to mean that any animal may eat undisturbed of the fruits of the land while it is working to help bring in the harvest, threshing or carrying burdens. This again recognizes that neither the animal nor the fruits actually "belong" to man.

One may break the laws of Sabbath to help sick animals as well as sick humans; and animals may not be excessively burdened, mistreated or made to work without adequate rest and food.[22] There is even a passage in the *Talmud* that warns: "Thou thinkest that flies, fleas, and mosquitos are superfluous, but they have their purpose in creation as means of a final outcome."[23] In fact, anyone who still believes that the Old Testament granted man absolute dominion over creation would do well to read the rebuke Job received out of the whirlwind (Job 39-49):

> Knowest thou the time when the wild goats of the rock bring forth? or canst thou mark when the hinds do calve? . . . Who hast sent out the wild ass free? . . . Will the unicorn be willing to serve thee, or abide by thy crib? . . . Gavest thou the goodly wings unto the peacocks? or wings and feathers unto the ostrich? . . . Hast thou given the horse strength? has thou clothed his neck with thunder? . . . Doth the hawk fly by thy wisdom, and stretch her wings toward the south? . . . Doth the eagle mount at thy command, and make her nest on high? Behold now Behemoth, which I made with you. . . . He is the chief of the ways of God: he that made him can make his sword to approach unto him. . . .

Although animals could be used for food, this too was not an absolute right, but severely circumscribed by rules and obligations. Apart from the well-known restrictions about which animals might be eaten (which imply limits and restraint, without which no ecological balance is possible), the actual method of killing is closely regulated. Knives must be carefully sharpened, and the animal must be killed with a single stroke. The ritual slaughterer, who kills for the entire community, was another institution that insured expertise, and therefore more humane killing. Care in the handling of animals was also encouraged, as damaged animals were considered "unclean," and thus unfit for consumption. In all, a host of rules and interpretations added up to a code of humane treatment of animals that is impressive even today. The twelfth-century theologian Maimonides wrote:

> It is prohibited to kill an animal and its young on the same day (Leviticus 22:28) in order that people be prevented from killing the two together in such a way that the young are slain in sight of their mothers; for the pain of animals under such circumstances is great. There is no difference in this case between the pain of man and the pain of other living things.

Historian W.E. Lecky, who cites Maimonides, says the theologian believed animals might have some kind of future life, to compensate for the suffering they endured on earth.[24] Lecky is often quoted in animal-rights writings for his detailed descriptions of abuses to animals through history (especially in the Roman circus) and for his conviction that the circle of human sympathy would gradually enlarge to include the animal kingdom. Such writers choose, however, to ignore Lecky's praise of "that tenderness to animals which is one of the most beautiful features in the Old Testament writings. ..."[25] Noting that there had never been any wild-animal combats staged among the Jews, Lecky comments that, in general, "the rabbinical writers have been remarkable for the great emphasis with which they have inculcated the duty of kindness to animals."[26]

CHRISTIANITY

As Lecky observes regretfully, the Catholic scheme of redemption isolated man as never before from the rest of creation, and the idea of duties to animals had no place in the teachings of the early Christian fathers. The best Lecky can do is to observe that while animals had little official status in the church, the stories of the saints, many of whom lived alone as hermits, encouraged a general feeling of sympathy for animals. To mention a few examples from Lecky's fascinating list: an Egyptian hermit would sit under palm trees in the desert, while a lion ate from his hand; another lion warmed Saint Poemen through cold winter nights, and lions buried Saint Paul the Hermit and Saint Mary of Egypt. (Cree Indians also tell stories of hunters being buried by bears, burial being a real problem for people who travel alone in the wild.)

Saint Helenus and Saint Pachomius crossed the Nile on the backs of crocodiles. Stags often accompanied hermits and carried their packs, and in the legends of Saint Eustachius and Saint Hubert, Christ is said to have taken the form of a hunted stag, "which turned on its pursuer with a crucifix glittering on its brow, and addressing him with a human voice, converted him to Christianity." Saint Bridget kept pigs and Saint Colman lived with a cock, a mouse and a fly: "The cock announced the hour of devotion, the mouse bit the ear of the drowsy saint till he got up, and if in the course of his studies he was ... called away to other business, the fly alighted on the line where he had left off, and kept the place."[27]

Lecky also suggests that the general "softening" power of Christian teaching may have had some indirect influence in lessening cruelty to animals. But Albert Schweitzer noted that it is hardly surprising that early Christian teaching gave little account to animal suffering, since primitive Christians lived in expectation of a speedy end to the world, when the sufferings of all creatures would cease.[28] "For I reckon that the sufferings of this present time are not worthy to be compared with the glory which shall be revealed in us" (Romans 8:18).

36

The end didn't come as quickly as had been expected, but thanks largely to the barbarian invasions that smashed classical culture, the church that had been established to prepare for the Apocalypse spread across Europe. The delay in the Messiah's return was all the more reason to keep oneself in readiness. The physical suffering of animals didn't merit much compassion, but then human pain didn't, either: torture or burning at the stake were considered a small price to pay for the chance to save one's immortal soul.

Despite its otherworldly preoccupations, Christianity did exercise a certain "softening" influence, as Lecky suggests. In addition to the lives of the saints, there were many popular medieval fables in which animals were taken to represent various virtues. Elephants were believed to be especially wise and thought to gather in certain parts of Mauritania to worship the sun and moon. Dolphins, reputed to take good care of their young and to be fond of human children, were a symbol for Christ. These tales helped to narrow the theological gap between humans and animals.

Keith Thomas has documented that humane attitudes toward animals were certainly common in Europe (alongside cruelty) at least by the sixteenth century.[29] More to the point, however, most people, until recently, lived close to the land and had daily contact with all kinds of animals and plants. The judgments on western values by Salt, Singer and others tell us more about their own alienation from nature than about the traditions they purport to describe.

EASTERN PHILOSOPHY

The Christian idea of "compassion" no doubt encouraged the emergence of animal welfare in the west. Ironically, however, the animal-rights writers claim that their new philosophy developed in the west out of need, as there was no tradition of respect for animal life like that found in eastern thought. It's an attractive idea that one can import guidelines for a new relationship with nature as easily as importing fuel-efficient automobiles, but it doesn't stand up to close examination.

One of the most impressive ethical principles in Indian religions is the doctrine of "Ahimsa," "the refusal to kill or harm any life." This doctrine was stated as early as the third or fourth century BC, in Jain texts:

All the saints and lords in the past, in the present, and in the future speak thus, teach thus, announce thus, and explain thus: One may not kill, mistreat, insult, torment, or persecute any form of life, any kind of creature, anything with a soul, any kind of being. This is the pure, eternal, enduring commandment of religion which has been proclaimed by the wise ones who understand the world.[30]

In obedience to this principle, Jains have no blood sacrifices or animal combats, and they don't hunt or eat meat. Jain monks sweep the ground before them as they walk and wear a cloth across their faces to avoid accidentally crushing or swallowing small insects. For the same reason, they don't practise agriculture. Most Jains are merchants, which indicates how impractical it is to try to universalize such an extreme interpretation of *Ahimsa*.

But not only is Jain practice impractical for most people, it is not based on compassion, as we understand it. Eastern philosophy, not unlike early Christianity, considers suffering to be the necessary companion of physical existence. The object of Jainism was to perfect the practitioner, to reduce as completely as possible his "attachments" to the physical world. Violence is seen as the greatest of attachments; non-violence was based not on compassion for the suffering of other creatures, but on the principle of non-activity, which Albert Schweitzer has defined as world- or life-denying.[31]

Jains enunciated, perhaps for the first time, the idea that ethics couldn't be restricted to humans alone; but because they were primarily interested in perfection of the self through non-activity, "the Jains pass right by the great problem as if it didn't exist."[32]

The "great problem" for Schweitzer is that there can be no rational excuse for excluding animals from our ethical sphere, but he is forced to acknowledge that it is impossible to live on this earth without harming other creatures. Man, he says, "is under the law of necessity which forces him to kill or injure, with or without his knowledge."[33] As a doctor, Schweitzer is thankful when a new drug allows him to cure sleeping sickness; but he feels obliged to recognize that by doing so, he is committing "genocide" on whole populations of bacteria. When he chooses to rescue an orphaned kingfisher, he accepts the need to kill fish every day to feed it. When a wild boar he has raised begins to ravage villagers' chickens, Schweitzer stoically cans it and serves it for dinner.

It is impossible to codify "boundless" morality (that is, morality not limited to humans) into absolute rules, Schweitzer argues, and he criticizes Indian philosophy because "in incomprehensible fashion it clings to the illusion that not to kill or harm is completely possible."[34] The practitioner of *Ahimsa* is satisfied to avoid harming others, but feels no obligation to actively help; yet if an animal is sick or injured, it may be more merciful to kill it. Strict adherence to *Ahimsa* allows animals to multiply until they starve, rather than cull them to levels that could be adequately nourished. We are continually obliged to make choices, Schweitzer insists, to sacrifice one creature to save another. Non-killing should never be allowed to become an end in itself: "A true reverence for ethics is shown in the fact that man recognizes the difficulties inherent in it."[35]

The Buddha did expound a doctrine of compassion, but it remained limited because Buddhism, too, is ultimately world-denying: there is little to gain from eliminating specific abuses, for suffering is believed to result from the will to live, and can be ended only by not "striving." Compassion, says Schweitzer, even in Mahayana Buddhism, remains contemplative and intellectual. Tibetan Buddhists, for example, would smother their cattle to remain faithful to the commandment forbidding "bloody sacrifice."

Hindu ethics look good on paper, but according to Gandhi:

I hardly think the fate of animals is so sad in any other country in the world as it is in our own India. We cannot make the British responsible for this; nor can we excuse ourselves by pleading our poverty. Criminal neglect is the only cause of the deplorable condition of our cattle.[36]

Gandhi is praised by Schweitzer for facing up to the contradictions within the Hindu ethic toward animals: Gandhi killed a calf that was mortally ill and in pain, much to the horror of his Hindu followers, and advised farmers to kill poisonous snakes and monkeys that threatened their crops.

In China, Lieh-tse (of the school of Lao-tse) proposed that the minds and souls of animals were like those of humans; and the *Kan-Ying P'ien* (the "Book of Rewards and Punishments") of the Sung dynasty (960-1227 AD) set down in great detail the obligations to be merciful to animals and warned against destroying even a flower without reason. But all too early, Chinese ethics froze into scholasticism and failed to have much influence on the public treatment of animals.[37]

Schweitzer concludes that eastern philosophy fails to come to grips with the questions it purports to solve:

The difficult problem, whether man can avoid killing and harming, is neither propounded nor dealt with. Men are allowed to cherish the illusion that they can avoid killing and harming living creatures and really fulfill the *Ahimsa* commandment. Indian ethics neglect to teach men to feel the whole weighty burden of their responsibility towards animal creation.[38]

And so we come back to the start. The western Judeo-Christian tradition is not so "anti-nature," nor is eastern philosophy quite so harmonious, as animal-rights writers would have us believe. We are still left to account for our present ecological crisis.

Lynn White, Jr. argues that it was Christianity's separateness from nature that encouraged westerners to exploit the earth ruthlessly.[39] Europe's technological superiority was established even before the scientific revolution: by 1000 AD, water power was used for industrial purposes; in the twelfth century, wind power was harnessed; and the weight-driven mechanical clock (the model for Descartes' animal-machine) was introduced early in the fourteenth century.

But White himself admits that even animals affect their environments, sometimes radically (as in the case of coral), and man has certainly done so for a very long time. The banks of the lower Nile have been "man-made" for at least six thousand years. Some believe that it was prehistoric man's fire-drive hunting that first cleared forests and created the great grasslands, eliminating the early "monster" mammals, obviously well before Christianity or Judaism.[40] Moreover, it is only since about 1850 that an extraordinary marriage between science and technology launched the greatest revolution in human culture since the development of agriculture. The meeting between science, which had been the philosophical preserve of the aristocracy, and the technology of the working classes was facilitated, White suggests, by a wave of democratization that swept Europe at the end of the eighteenth century. Christianity, however, was at best only an indirect influence on the emergence of democracy.

The particularly rapid ecological disruption of the United States can also be related to democracy.[41] In Europe, after the dissolution of the Roman Empire, land was held ultimately by church or monarch; the notion of private property developed only slowly through the Middle Ages. From the start, however, the United States was primarily a nation of small independent landowners. The one thing the new nation didn't seem to lack was land and natural resources, and for small, often isolated homesteaders, habitat and wildlife were likely to be seen as obstacles rather than limited resources in need of protection. With few traditional constraints, industrial innovations were quickly adopted in the "new land."

Western civilization, says Lewis Moncrief in a critique of White, threatens the environment because it has been successful. It is wealthy societies that consume most resources, and when wealth is concentrated in dense urban conditions, waste quickly overwhelms the "flushing" capacity of the ecosystem.

Moncrief identifies democracy, technology, urbanization, increasing individual wealth and an aggressive attitude toward nature as contributing to the present ecological dilemma. The Judeo-Christian tradition may have influenced each of these somewhat, but religion cannot be singled out as a main cause. If eastern cultures have yet to produce such obvious ecological havoc, it is probably because they are still relatively poor:

It might be bad in China with 700 million poor people, but 700 million rich Chinese would wreck China in no time. . . . It's the rich who wreck the environment . . . occupy more space, consume more of each natural resource, disturb ecology more, litter the landscape . . . and create more pollution.[42]

The root of our ecological crisis lies in technology, urbanism and wealth. Animal-rights groups, however, have to date attacked those who live closest to the land, who are poorest and who have remained relatively aloof from mass technological society: sealers, fur trappers and native peoples. Before we consider this extraordinary contradiction more closely, we must trace the origins of the modern ecology and animal-rights movements.

3

The Origins of Ecology and Animal Rights

... this great continent could not have been kept as nothing but a game preserve for squalid savages.
  – Theodore Roosevelt (*The Winning of the West,* 1889)

CONSERVATION

The Europeans who first came to North America came to exploit it. In search of a western route to the Orient, they found instead a vast continent teeming with fish, lumber and furs. They would have preferred the spice routes of the Portuguese or the gold and silver that the Spanish found in Mexico and South America; but they settled down and did their best to make the venture pay.

In New France, always a state-run venture, manufacturing was banned to keep the colony dependent, and to ensure the supply of manpower for fur trading. So successful was the venture that beaver in the vicinity of the St. Lawrence settlements were quickly exhausted and both traders and Indian middlemen were obliged to penetrate ever deeper into the hinterland.

The British colonies along the Atlantic coast had an equally dramatic impact on wildlife: hundreds of thousands of deer and beaver pelts were exported; wolves, cougars, wild pigeons, parakeets, trumpeter swans and many other species were decimated.[1] Unlike the Indians, who had a sense of respect and interdependence with animals, the new invaders seemed intent to wipe the animals out: "They wanted to have power over all life ... to destroy or mutilate life at its very quick, lusting in their dark powers to annihilate all living impulses ... a deep lust for vindictive power over the life-issue."[2]

With little knowledge of or commitment to the land, they acted as if the bounty was limitless, an illusion that persisted as long as the

42

frontier was expanding westward. The opening frontier and a rising population gave America a dizzying sense of freedom and limitless progress.

By the end of the nineteenth century, however, the last frontier had been reached. From barely four million in 1790, the population of the United States swelled to seventy-six million; they lived in three million square miles.[3] The extension of the railway west permitted furs and wild meat to be shipped back to the eastern markets, and a growing "army of destruction" of commercial hunters destroyed the buffalo herds and supplies of fur bearers. Many hunters crossed into less-populated Canadian territory.

The first laws to protect wildlife were often ineffective, or came too late.[4] In 1874 President Ulysses S. Grant refused to sign a bill passed by Congress that would have protected the remnants of the bison herds that had once numbered sixty million head. Grant calculated that the extermination of the buffalo would undermine the independence of the Sioux, whose land was coveted by settlers.

Curiously enough, it was wealthy white game hunters who pushed successfully for a system of effective controls. Fearing that the loss of the frontier would weaken the spirit of self-reliance and resourcefulness that, he believed, had built the new nation, president and big-game hunter Theodore Roosevelt, with naturalist G. Bird Grinnel, founded the Boone and Crockett Club "to promote manly sport with the rifle." "Hunting big game," they affirmed, was "a sport for a vigorous and masterful people."[5]

The Boone and Crockett Club, and the American Game Protection and Propagation Association (organized and financed by large corporations such as Remington, Winchester, Marlin, duPont and other arms and ammunition manufacturers) pressured Congress to enact conservation measures: the Lacey Act of 1900, prohibiting interstate traffic in birds or mammals killed contrary to state laws; the federal Migratory Bird Law of 1913; and the Migratory Bird Treaty signed with Canada in 1918.

Significantly, the international treaty disregarded the needs and legal rights of native hunters, who were never involved in the negotiations. G. Gordon Hewitt, chief negotiator for the Canadian delegation, declared that wildlife needed protection from "lawbreakers everywhere, both white and Indian."[6] He justified his position by arguing that Indians had been "corrupted" by their contact with white traders and their weapons, and that without strict conservation measures, traditional hunting rights would soon be rendered meaningless.[7]

The disregard for Indian rights in this period is clearly summed up by Arthur Meighan, Canadian minister of the interior in 1918: "We

Stanley Post trappers.

An Inuit woman hanging up a sealskin to dry. Repulse Bay, Northwest Territories, 1966.

Preparing a meal at a trapper's camp.

Horace Flett sews up fur bales. Caribou Post, 1947.

still leave them enough to trap on, but even if we did not, thirty bushels of wheat to the acre is a lot better than a few squirrels caught by the Indian."[8] Crude as it may sound to our ears today, the statement is very close to what animal-rights writers now advocate.

From the start, conservation philosophy in the United States was split between the "no-use," transcendental "cult of the wilderness," as expressed by naturalist John Muir, and the "wise-use" utilitarian principles of resource managers, arms manufacturers and white big-game hunters. The "wise-use" philosophy came to dominate policy and achieved some success in certain areas. In 1903, the first United States wildlife reserve was set up; and in 1910 the sale of wild meat was prohibited in New York State (it was later prohibited elsewhere), allowing the recovery of white-tail-deer, caribou and pronghorn-antelope populations. Alaska fur seals, which numbered about two million in 1870, had been hunted nearly to extinction; but an international treaty in 1911, signed by the United States, Great Britain, Canada and Japan, and a careful strategy of harvesting only "bachelor" bulls (only one in twenty of which ever breeds) rebuilt the herd to about one and a half million, the optimal size for available fish supplies. Beaver, which were exterminated in many areas, have more recently been reintroduced and protected by trap-line and quota systems, and are now plentiful throughout their traditional range.

However, human population grew too, and by the 1940s naturalists were warning that the problem with a "wise-use," self-interest-oriented philosophy was that most species are of no apparent use to men at all.[9] Only by accepting that nature was a unified whole, they argued, could the value of predators, for instance, be appreciated.

The detonation of the first A bombs at the end of World War Two and tests on the Bikini Islands in the early 1950s highlighted dramatically that burgeoning technological power made urgent the need to reevaluate the impact of our society on the environment; but through the period of rapid economic and industrial growth in America in the 1950s and 1960s, little account was taken of ecological damage. Only at the end of the 1960s was some attempt made to assess the costs. The turning point was signaled by the publication in 1962 of Rachel Carson's *Silent Spring*; DDT made the interdependence of all the elements of an ecosystem unmistakably clear.

A flurry of interest in ecology peaked as the decade ended. Protests about the Newfoundland seal hunt, which had grown from 1964, resulted in the creation of Brian Davies' IFAW in the fall of 1969. That same year, the United States Congress passed the Endangered Species Act, to stop the importation of spotted cats, which had been publicized by Cleveland Amory's Fund For Animals and by Alice Herrington's Friends of Animals. Greenpeace was founded in Vancouver in 1971, and in 1972 the United States Protection of Marine Mammals Act banned the import of nursing mammals younger than eight months old. In 1973, the Washington Treaty was signed, which led to the Convention on International Trade in Endangered Species of Wild Flora and Fauna (CITES), to which more than eighty countries are now signatories.

Increased public awareness about the importance of conservation made the work of wildlife managers easier. When Kenya went to the World Bank some time ago for funds, they were instructed to eliminate poaching in their national parks; the poaching was stopped. But when concern for conservation becomes a rejection of killing of any kind, the strategy can have unexpected results. There have been conflicts in Africa in the national parks where elephants were over-populating:

> The manager said you'd better kill off 3,000 or 6,000 elephants, or they will kill off your park. The park people said, this is a national park, we cannot kill, we'll let nature take its course. While the argument was taking its course, 3,000 elephants died during a drought, and then two years later another 3,000. And so the end result was the same, except the park was blighted – all the trees were knocked down and everything else. Looking back, I think it would have been better to have killed the 3,000 elephants, utilized the meat and the ivory for a developing nation, and spared the park the destruction that ultimately took place from the over-population of elephants.[10]

In Canada, controversy over the Atlantic seal hunt led the government to introduce strict regulations about how seals were killed and carefully monitored quotas on how many were harvested. Recent scientific studies have confirmed that these measures were effective, yet the international protest against sealing actually *gained* momentum after 1972, climaxing with the EEC ban on white-coat seals in 1983.[11]

To understand this shift in the ecology movement, this resurgence of a "no-use" philosophy, just as the public was beginning to understand the principles of "wise-use," we must trace the origins of the animal-rights movement.

ANIMAL RIGHTS

After biblical times, the first glimmers of concern for animals appear in the work of certain Greek and Roman writers, who questioned the central role of man in creation. Lecky credits Plutarch (46-120 AD) as the first to propose kindness to animals purely from benevolence: "A good man will take care of his horses and dogs, not only when they are young, but when they are old and past service. We ought certainly not treat living beings like shoes and household goods, which when worn with use, we throw away."[12]

Henry Salt quotes Porphyry, from the third century AD: "For he who loves all animated nature, will not hate any one tribe of innocent beings."[13]

However, the classical world never developed a concern for animals into a coherent system, and with the barbarian invasions, the collapse of the Empire and the problems of setting up a multinational ecclesiastical bureaucracy to take its place, other issues took higher priority.

Repeated waves of barbarians conquered and were absorbed, the year 1000 came and went and the Apocalypse didn't come. Europe began the second millennium with a series of crusades, which accomplished very little. In 1212, fifty thousand children marched from France and Germany, to be mowed down by Moslem soldiers before reaching the Holy Land. Saint Francis, who considered animals and even inanimate things his brothers and sisters, although he ate meat, died in 1226. This was a period when the writings of the classical world were being rediscovered. Preserved by Islamic scholars, the works were translated from Arabic into Hebrew by European Jews, and then into Latin. Thomas Aquinas used Aristotle's philosophy to give a rational structure to Christian theology, much as Maimonides (1135-1204) had done for Judaism.

More important, the rediscovery of classical geography and astronomy provided the basis for a new science of navigation. The Christian countries had been bottled in for centuries by Moslem control of the Mediterranean and the eastern frontier (Constantinople itself fell to the Turks in 1453), but by the end of the fifteenth century the Moslems were pushed from Portugal and Spain. The development of navigation, ship-building and, not least, firearms enabled Portugal to venture down the coast of Africa and around the Horn to the spice ports of the Indian Ocean, bypassing the Turkish monopoly on the overland route.[14]

The age of discovery and exploration followed, bringing a flood of new wealth, inflation, the whittling away of the power of landowners and others who depended on fixed rents, and the rise of the bourgeoisie. All this was part of restructuring a feudal society into an industrial one, a transformation that created unprecedented wealth. And hardship. In the seventeenth century, the populations of the cities of Europe swelled with impoverished workers and beggars who had been displaced from the land; workhouses and "hospitals" were constructed to confine them.[15] The restrictions of medieval feudalism had been broken, but so had the network of mutual obligations and security.

It was out of this turmoil that the notion of natural rights was developed, as expressed by François Voltaire and Jean-Jacques Rousseau in the mid-eighteenth century. (Rousseau's *Social Contract* was published in 1762.) A model for this notion of "rights" was America, where the frontier provided ample room for expansion, creating a sensation of liberty and boundless potential for progress:

> The new territories not only had free fertile land and other riches, but an invigorating climate – air free from kaisers, czars, kings, secret police, inquisitions, a situation unprecedented in human history. Here a novel doctrine was born: "All men are endowed by their Creator with certain inalienable rights – life, liberty, and the pursuit of happiness."[16]

A firm relationship developed between America and France during this period. Having lost New France to the British in 1759, the French were not adverse to helping the thirteen colonies in their bid for independence. And when the French Ancien Régime was brought down in 1789, the key to the Bastille was sent as a gift to the president of the young republic that had shown the way. (The key hangs to this day in the Mount Vernon estate of George Washington.) Thomas Paine, the British political theorist who called for America's independence in his *Common Sense* (1776) and was named secretary of the United States Committee for Foreign Affairs in 1778, associated himself with the French Revolution and was elected a member of the National Convention in 1792.

A hundred years later, Henry Salt, in his book *Animals' Rights*, cites Paine's *Rights of Man* (1791) and Mary Wollstonecraft's *Vindication of the Rights of Women* (1788) as landmarks in the development of a general theory of rights that he believed would eventually expand to embrace non-humans as well. He notes that in 1792 a spoof on the works of Paine and Wollstonecraft appeared anonymously (but was later attributed to Thomas Taylor, a Platonist), entitled "A Vindication of the Rights of Brutes." "A notable instance," Salt comments good-humoredly, "of how the mockery of one generation may become the reality of the next."[17]

The animal-rights philosophy was modelled on the rights of humans as expressed by Paine and others. But if these ideas reflect the sense of freedom and progress stimulated by the expanding American frontier, we have the strange irony that, philosophically, the idea of animal rights is rooted in the unprecedented destruction of nature, wildlife and the Indian cultures.

Ortega y Gasset has observed that another source of the sensation of freedom and progress that swept Europe was the industrial revolution, which, by rapidly expanding production, created "an illusion of limitless abundance and ease."[18] Industrialization, as we know, has brought us to our present ecological crisis – so again we have the strange contradiction that the philosophical roots of the animal-rights movement in fact derive from a process that is fundamentally at odds with the protection of natural habitat and wildlife. As we shall see later, this fatal contradiction is, if anything, even more in evidence today.

This is a good moment to comment on another basic animal-rights argument. Peter Singer, in his book *Animal Liberation*, often compares animal rights to other liberation movements.[19] However rhetorically useful, his comparison of the animal-rights movement to the campaign to end black slavery has a forced quality to it, until we realize that Singer took his argument straight from Salt's *Animals' Rights*, which was published barely thirty years after the United States had fought a bitter war over slavery.[20] Salt, moreover, borrowed the core of his argument from Jeremy Bentham, who was writing in 1780, when slavery had just been banned by the French, but was still practised in the British dominions: "The French have already discovered that the blackness of the skin is no reason why a human being should be abandoned, without redress, to the caprice of a tormentor. It may come one day to be recognized that the number of legs, the villosity of the skin, or the termination of the os sacrum, are reasons equally insufficient for abandoning a sensitive being to the same fate."[21]

It was the bourgeoisie, of course, whose rights were affirmed by the French revolution. The industrial revolution was in full swing; and in the nineteenth century came the nostalgic protest of the Romantics, poets like Shelley and Keats, who were reacting against the increasing separation of man from nature through growing cities and machine technology. Shelley's wife, Mary Wollstonecraft Shelley, wrote the most memorable warning against the dangers of the new scientific and technological order in her first novel, *Frankenstein* (1818).[22] (Mary was the daughter of anarchist theorist William Godwin and feminist Mary Wollstonecraft.)[23]

The Romantics' nostalgia for nature contributed to the sympathy for animals in England that resulted in 1822 in the enactment by parliament of the first animal-protection legislation ever passed, a bill "to prevent the cruel and improper treatment of cattle." Shelley's protest against the abuses imposed on farm animals was quoted by Salt: "The bull must be degraded into the ox, and the ram into the wether by an unnatural and inhuman operation, that the flaccid fibre may offer fainter resistance to rebellious nature."[24]

Two years later, in 1824, an Anglican priest, the Reverend Arthur

Brome, started the organization that in 1840 would receive royal patronage and become the RSPCA. In 1835, this group helped pass legislation that regulated the treatment of animals in slaughter-houses, and outlawed bull baiting.

In 1859, Darwin's *Origin of Species* was published, stating clearly that humans had no scientific basis for setting themselves completely apart from the animals. Ironically, Darwin's work would, over time, be used to support both sides of the argument about animal rights. Some would claim that man's dominion was naturally ordained, mere "survival of the fittest;" others countered that there could be no moral justification for exploiting creatures to whom we were related. The concept of "evolution," moreover, suggested an evolution of sensi-bilities, which had grown to include other nations, other races, women and children and must finally embrace animals as well.

In 1867, Karl Marx published his *Das Kapital*, advocating still another interpretation of social evolution. Marx asked Darwin if he might dedicate his work to him. The development in the second half of the nineteenth century of the labor movement also had its influence on animal-rights philosophy, and Salt (writing just ten years after Marx's death and four years after the anarchist Prince Kropotkin's *Mutual Aid Among Animals*) pointed out that animals were not merely our fellow creatures, but also our "fellow workers," and deserved consideration for this, if for no other reason. Like Marx (and unlike the Romantics) Salt believed that the industrialization of modern society offered great possibilities for liberation:

> The use of machinery is often condemned, on aesthetic grounds, because of the ugliness it has introduced into so many features of modern life. On the other hand, it should not be forgotten that it has immensely relieved the huge mass of animal labour, and that when electricity is generally used for purposes of traction, one of the foulest blots on our social humanity is likely to disappear. Scientific and mechanical invention, so far from being necessarily antagonistic to a true beauty of life, may be found to be of utmost service to it, when they are employed for humane, and not merely commercial, purposes.[25]

Through the first half of the nineteenth century, people concerned with animal welfare were concerned primarily with improving the treatment of domestic cattle and beasts of burden, and with the elimination of blood sports like bull baiting and cock fights. In mid-century, however, vivisection, cruel experiments on living animals that until then had been practised only occasionally, was brought into the mainstream of scientific endeavor (and public protest) by the gruesome demonstrations of Doctors François Magendie, Claude Bernard, Paul Bert and others of what became known as the Paris School.[26]

In 1864, the RSPCA offered a prize of fifty pounds for the best essay against vivisection and when Eugene Magnum, a student of François Magendie's, performed experiments on live animals at the Congress of the British Medical Association in 1854, he was prosecuted by the RSPCA under provisions of the Martin Act of 1822. Magnum fled back to France and the prosecution failed, but controversy over the affair led Queen Victoria to donate money to the RSPCA and to express her personal concern about how animals were treated in science. In 1875, a Royal Commission was set up to investigate vivisection. As a result of that inquiry, the Cruelty to Animals Act was passed in 1876, requiring special permits from the Home Office for any experiment likely to cause pain to animal subjects. (Of course opponents charged that by licensing vivisectionists, the bill did more to protect scientists than animals.)

One of the many notables to write against vivisection at this time was the Oxford mathematician Charles Dodgson, known today as Lewis Carroll. By 1882, Oxford had become the centre of an anti-vivisection confrontation when Doctor Burdon-Sanderson, a vivisectionist who had testified before the 1875 Royal Commission, was appointed to work at the university. (One of the strongest supporters of Burdon-Sanderson was Dean Liddell, whose daughter Alice had so fascinated Carroll.) In the tumult that ensued, John Ruskin, the noted art critic, resigned his chair in protest. (Godlovitch, Godlovitch, Singer, Ryder and other modern Oxford animal-rights advocates are working in an Oxford tradition that goes back at least a hundred years.)

A second Royal Commission was established in 1906, in response to the increase in the numbers of animals used in research after the establishment of the first commercial laboratories in 1901. Two major anti-vivisection conventions were held in England in 1909, and at least four of the leaders of the World League Against Vivisection became cabinet ministers in the Labour government that came to power in 1929. But to the bitter disappointment of anti-vivisectionists, that government did nothing to control experiments; in fact, as a result of the 1925 Therapeutic Substances Act (to regulate the quality of new vaccines and serums that were being produced) more animals than before were used. By 1939, a million animals a year were used in experiments in Great Britain.

After World War Two, Air Chief-Marshal Lord Dowding, hero of the Battle of Britain, led the campaign in parliament to publicize the plight of laboratory animals, and in 1963, after years of continued pressure, the government named the Littlewood Committee to study the whole question. That committee reported back in 1965, the same year the Bramwell Committee issued its much-publicized report on the conditions of animals raised in intensive "factory farms." Powerful agrobusiness, pharmaceutical and medical lobbies ensured that virtually no legislative action was taken on either of these reports; but public interest was aroused, and needed only an issue to focus its concern. Anti-sealing campaigners would find a well-prepared environment when they came to Europe. The "cultural revolutions" of the 1960s flared and then as quickly subsided, but the animal-rights movement steadily gained momentum. In 1971, climaxing a decade in which a number of animal-welfare books were published in England,[27] the Godlovitches' *Animals, Men and Morals* appeared, providing animal-rights activists with a comprehensive ideological framework.

While animal-rights campaigns tended to focus on individual problems, *Animals, Men and Morals* brought them all together. Most significantly, several essays in the book aimed at presenting a comprehensive moral argument for animal rights.[28]

Until the book's publication, it was argued, there had been only vague expressions of sympathy for animals, but benevolence can be a flighty sentiment.[29] As Oliver Goldsmith observed in the eighteenth century, "they pity, and then they eat the objects of their compassion."[30] Montaigne (1533-1592) is often cited as one of the earliest moderns to consider animals; like Pythagoras and da Vinci, he would often set captured animals free. But even he admitted unabashedly that despite the "squealing of the hare in my hounds' jaws . . . hunting is a very great pleasure to me."[31] Bentham justified eating animals for "their pains do not equal our enjoyments."[32] And Schopenhauer concluded when his own supper was at stake: "Man deprived of all flesh-food, especially in the north, would suffer more than the animal suffers in a swift and unforeseen death; still we ought to mitigate it with the help of chloroform."[33]

Man's benevolence, the new animal-rights philosophers conclude, is too whimsical to protect animals. Therefore they set out to establish a comprehensive system, which is "logically cogent and cannot be refuted. . . ." "Once the full force of moral assessment has been made explicit there can be no rational excuse left for killing animals, be they killed for food, science, or sheer personal indulgence."[34]

Their goal is not to provide "yet another manual on how to make brutalities less brutal." Compromise on this central point, they say, is "simple unthinking weakness." Roslind Godlovitch argues that the logical conclusion of caring about suffering without refusing to kill should lead us to simply exterminate all animals, once and for all.[35]

Traditional animal-welfare groups, it is charged, have protected their "nonpolitical" tax-exempt status by steering away from the difficult problems of farming and lab animals, and sticking with "safe" activities like collecting stray dogs and cats.[36] Many, in fact, through state-pound seizure laws, supply animals to laboratories. Roslind Godlovitch points out the irony that "progress in animal welfare has come to mean more painless methods of slaughtering animals [so that] it is not considered absurd that the RSPCA spends considerable time and effort killing unwanted but perfectly healthy cats and dogs 'to prevent cruelty." Peter Singer claims that some groups, like the Animal Welfare Institute (which has published books against fur trapping), have close links with organizations that promote the use of animals in experimentation.[37] Others have been shown to have extensive investments in pharmaceutical and cosmetic companies, which are among the biggest users of laboratory animals.[38] In 1982, Eleanor Seiling (UAA) charged that board members of the Humane Society of the United States (HSUS) were affiliated with laboratory animal-lobby groups.[39]

Animal-rights groups also differ from traditional welfare groups, in theory at least, by not restricting their moral umbrella to "cute" animals. Singer claims to oppose the use of rats and mice in labs as strenuously as he opposes the use of dogs, cats and primates. He also holds that one cannot logically oppose hunting without rejecting factory farming and meat eating. "Why, for instance, is the hunter who shoots wild ducks for his supper subject to more criticism than the person who buys a chicken at the supermarket? Overall, it is probably the intensively reared bird who suffered more."[40]

Experimentation on animals and raising them for food "cause more suffering to a greater number of animals than anything else that humans do," says Singer. Two hundred million animals are used in research labs and for product testing, and in the United States alone, hundreds of millions of cows, pigs and sheep and about three billion poultry are slaughtered each year.[41] Moreover, these are activities in which almost everyone participates, both by eating meat and because taxes and money spent on drugs and other products pay for experimentation on animals. Singer concentrates on farming and laboratories, and undertakes no discussion of hunting, fur trapping or other activities that exploit animals. For he believes that these evils would quickly disappear if the two main "officially promoted and almost universally accepted forms of speciesism [factory farming and laboratory experimentation] can be abolished. . . ."[42]

About 186,000 seals were being killed annually off the coast of Newfoundland before the EEC ban; that number of cows, sheep and pigs die each hour in the United States alone, along with one million chickens. It was only the killing of seals, however, that provoked a flood of letters to the EEC Council of Ministers. Why did the campaign against killing seals reach such large international proportions? And why have several governments chosen to go along with this campaign?

Despite the surge of interest during the past twenty years in ecology and animal issues, there are serious contradictions within the animal-rights movement. There is a split between traditional animal-welfare groups and animal-rights groups; and even within animal-rights groups there are sharp divisions over strategy and tactics.[43] One issue that sparked great public response was the exposé in 1973 of the United States Air Force's plans to test poison gas on beagles.[44] Yet many objecting to the use of dogs for such tests would have little sympathy for rats or mice, for example. A 1974 survey showed that three-quarters of the British population opposed testing cosmetics or weapons on animals, but far fewer rejected animals being used for drug or medical research. Many anti-trapping groups do not oppose the use of animals in laboratories. And certainly few of the five million people who wrote letters to the EEC were contemplating vegetarianism.

The seal campaign cut across most of the lines that fragment the animal-rights movement. For the politicians, seals became a convenient "safety valve." Under tremendous pressure from anti-vivisectionists and critics of factory farming[45] (but prevented by powerful lobbies from acting in these areas), the politicians thought a ban on Canadian sealskins was a way to placate a troublesome public outburst without sacrificing any major European interest. Of course, far from being "placated," animal-rights activists have only grown more militant. (In Part Three, the major animal-rights campaigns are examined in detail.)

Animal-rights groups claim that to bring animals within our moral sphere of concern, we must stop using them for our own needs. But this is not the only way of perceiving a moral bond between man and animals. For some cultures, using animals and respecting them have never been mutually exclusive.

4

The World of the Cree Hunter

I'm going to sing a song of the inlanders
The people from the east . . .
They saw a pack of deer come swimming across the lake towards them,
They didn't use guns to kill the deer
They didn't use guns, they used something else . . .
  – Cree hunting song

Environmentalists argue that until we recognize that the entire ecosystem is an interdependent whole in which we participate, there is no hope of avoiding ecological apocalypse. The indigenous Indian population of North America developed a holistic vision of their place in nature; the notion that native people may suggest a way out of our present dilemma is a common undercurrent in the ecology movement. For example, Greenpeace named its protest ship the *Rainbow Warrior*, fulfilling the Cree myth that after the white man despoiled the country, people of every race and color would band together to defend the earth as the Warriors of the Rainbow.[1] But how do you translate a vague sympathy for native people into a practical ecological perspective on nature?

The traditional ways of North America's aboriginal people have been seriously disrupted by the often violent spread of European settlement. In some areas, however, especially on land that was too cold or too rugged to support agriculture, the old ways have continued. One such region is the vast boreal forest of northern Quebec, homeland of several Indian nations, including the Cree. Their life is still largely based on hunting animals, and their vision of man's place in nature is very different from that of the European inheritance.

Animals are considered to be "persons" by the Cree, as are a whole range of living and nonliving things. The appropriate relationship among persons is one of reciprocity:

> When we think about reciprocity we might think about economic or military reciprocity. But for the Cree, reciprocity is a very much bigger idea than that, and it really gets into their relationships, not just with other people, but with animals. From within that view of things, if you mistreat animals in the same way that you mistreat people, or if you disrespect animals in various ways, you're bound to provoke some kind of reaction which will not be in your own interests. So the notion of reciprocity in some ways unites the cultural and the natural domains – the human and the animal.[2]

Indian hunters, says Doctor Colin Scott, who has lived and hunted with the Cree of northern Quebec, have a profound respect and love for the animals they hunt; and they believe that the animals also love them: by "giving" themselves to hunters, they make possible the continuation of human life. Having acknowledged animals as persons, however, how does one justify killing them? A number of Cree myths address this dilemma.

Chischihp, a mythical creature who never eats and regards all animals as his "pets," desires human women and takes two as his wives. Having entered into human society, he discovers he has obligations: the women are hungry and want him to kill animals. At first he refuses, but when the women threaten to leave, he jumps over the side of the canoe and swims underwater, in his characteristic manner of hunting. He comes up under a moose that is browsing in the shallows and kills it with his spear. Having killed, he goes on to taste meat, although at first he is shy about this, and runs off into the bushes crying that it was a dog that stole the strip of meat. He returns with thorns in his fingers, which became sewing needles (the female counterpart to the man's spear) when his wives remove them. With these needles, they will sew him clothes, another symbol of his continuing integration into society.[3]

But Chischihp fails to respect the obligations and limitations on human society that arise from killing: he instructs his wives to make his clothes not from the hide, but from fatty membranes and other parts of the moose considered to be the best food of the animal. This ostentatious display, wasting the animal's gift of food, shows that Chischihp has failed to reciprocate, to respect the moose that gave itself to man. His downfall is inevitable.

Dressed in his immodest costume, Chischihp dances himself into a frenzy, a sign of his lack of self-control; his clothing is torn from him

A Wemindji Cree hunter, Matthew Hughboy, retrieves a Canada goose at a spring hunting pond.

Canada geese suspended and spinning on cords around the fire in a Cree spring lodge.

A summer fishing camp.

Demaris Stewart cleans a catch of whitefish and speckled trout. Traditional tipi frames, covered with canvas and floored with evergreen boughs, are the most practical dwellings for spring, summer, and fall hunting and fishing.

and he dances on naked. Later that night, he is roused from his sleep by pain. He thinks his wives are pinching him, but finds instead two rotten logs, symbols of corruption, full of biting ants. In a fit of jealousy he kills his two best "buddies," men "with whom he eats," people with whom he shares the closest bonds of reciprocity.

Chischihp's attempt at socialization is a failure. He flees in his canoe, and breaks a sack of blood from the moose he had killed into the water, so the villagers will think he is dead and also to return the moose's gift. But later that evening, Chischihp's singing alerts the villagers that he is still alive. Two herons are instructed to drink the water of the lake, so that the diving Chischihp may be captured; but he bursts the herons with his spear and the lake fills up again.

He calls that if they will send his wives, he will go away. The wives are sent, he tips their canoe and drowns them, severing his last link with human society, and is transformed into a diving bird. After giving up his mythical non-eating existence, but failing to respect the limits by which human life is defined, Chischihp has finally found a form in which he can satisfy the requirements of reciprocity. An edible diving bird called Chischihp still lives in Cree territory.

The myth of Chischihp expresses the fundamental existential problem that human life is impossible without killing, and resolves it by affirming the limitations that must order and restrain such killing. Chischihp failed to respect the moose that had given itself and ended by violating his closest human relationships, killing his buddies and his wives. The similarities between human and animal relationships is made very clear, and of course the relationship between animals and people is a matter of survival for hunting peoples.

The close relationship between the hunter and his game is expressed on the popular level in Cree society by the common use of sexual metaphors to describe the chase and hunting metaphors to describe relations between men and women. The same word in Cree, for example, may be used for "penis" or "gun," "shot" or "sperm":

> There's of course a humorous side to these kinds of metaphors, and people get great mileage out of them in terms of informal joking and so on. But there's a serious side to these relationships too, because the kind of love that men and women feel for each other is something that is an appropriate symbol for talking about the intimacy of the relationship between hunters and game. And conversely, because hunters have a very real love for the animals and feel that that love is reciprocal, it's a nice way and a powerful way of talking about genuine affection between men and women in human society. [4]

Nevertheless, animals are eaten, people are not. This distinction is underlined by many stories of cannibals. In one, a father and son capture a woman, have intercourse with her and then eat her. When they return to the woods, they become weak and die. By failing to distinguish the appropriate relation with women (reproduction) from that with animals (food), the cannibals have "consumed their own reproductive powers," which results in death.

To most Europeans, used to thinking of death as a violent event, something that opposes our will, it is difficult to imagine how a hunter could describe the relationship with his prey as love. What is the reciprocity the Cree share with their game? What do the animals get?

Cree are perfectly aware that animals will avoid their traps or flee if they detect the hunter's presence; they know that individual animals don't necessarily "give" themselves. Reciprocity is worked out at a species level. Aboriginal hunters have territories within which "tally-men," older respected hunters, keep track of the game populations and control how much is taken each year. Hugh Brody describes how, on a hunting trip with Beaver Indians in Northeastern British Columbia, the men watch animal tracks and marks on the bark of trees where beaver have chewed. They are collecting data about the condition of the land. "He was checking his fields, counting stock, reviewing assets. . . ." Upon entering a region they had not hunted for several years, the leader decided that beaver colonies were still not sufficiently replenished; they left them and rode on to another territory that had been rested even longer.[5]

Animal populations that grow too dense may become diseased, and Indians see hunting as a way of protecting them. But taking too many animals is also disrespectful and, of course, if you overharvest, the animals won't be there later. "I think the animals need the Cree hunter to harvest them; I think the hunter needs the animal to survive . . . these two make the world turn," says Thomas Coon who, as a teenager, supported his family by hunting and trapping. Coon is now director of traditional pursuits for the Cree Regional Authority.[6]

Hunters are united with their animals through the mystery of death:

> Killing animals reminds you not only of animal death but of your own death, and forces you to confront the fact of your own death. In Cree religion, our waking lives are not all reality. The realm of dreams and of life beyond death are equally a part of our reality and experience, and the reciprocity between hunters and animals occurs across that threshold of death.[7]

Dreams are one way in which the living may communicate with the realm of death, and often a hunter or someone in his household will have a dream that foretells an important kill, a moose or a bear.

(Indians will say an animal is "preparing to give itself.") The animal may not appear in its own form in such a dream but as a human who is wounded or dying. A human is given on the "other side" in exchange for the animal given to the hunter in the waking world.

This relationship between human and animal lives is expressed in myths like the story of the boy who lived with a black bear. When the boy's human father comes to claim him the bear, who is called the boy's "grandfather" (animals are often considered to be the "ancestors" of humans), gives himself to the hunter, with the reminder that whatever the hunter does to animals he does to himself. The bear "takes off his jacket" (his body) and passes it out of his cave to the hunter, who puts it on (a hunter will carry a bear carcass on his own shoulders back to camp). Symbolically, the hunter has become the bear, or the bear the hunter.[8]

Adrian Tanner recounts a myth from Labrador about a boy who marries a caribou girl. The boy takes on the perspective of the animals, while the beautiful girl is seen by the other hunters as an ordinary female caribou. He marries her and joins the caribou, which appear to him to be Indians. When human beings shoot a caribou, the boy sees a running person throw off a white cape, which the hunters pick up as the carcass.[9]

The reciprocity between animals and hunters, between waking world and world beyond, is completed upon the death of the hunter: a human has been given on "this side." Often an animal will appear to take his place. "People will notice a goose which behaves oddly and flies down low over a village close to the time of a funeral, for example, and they will say that is the person who died. So the reciprocity is fulfilled, finally."[10]

There are other ways in which Cree may cross the line that normally separates men from animals, life from death, the apparent from the veiled. Adrian Tanner has observed the importance of the symbol of a membrane that both separates and communicates between two worlds. The ritual drum, a large tambourinelike instrument, is one example. Another is "scapulimancy," hunting divination for which the thin membranelike shoulder blade of a small animal such as a rabbit or a porcupine is burned until a pattern appears that can be interpreted.[11] A third is the "shaking-tent" ceremony, described by Thomas Coon:

> Communication between the animal and the Indian hunter or trapper is usually done by a very elderly person. And that's what people used to call the shaking tent. This tent is structured in a certain way. It's almost formed like a beaver lodge, but it's very slim and taller than a beaver lodge. The elder will go in there and sometimes they will use the traditional drum. They will sing traditional songs of hunters ... and what this tent does, it shakes at such a

speed and such a harmony that you can hear the canvas almost beating with the harmony. The hunter is right there in the middle of the tent, and what you can hear in there . . . is voices – strange voices. He's communicating with an animal. It's the spirit, the spirit of an animal, and the hunter communicating together. That is respecting animals. Some people sing for black bear, some people sing for a moose or beaver. . . . This was one of our gifts we had, I guess, from the good Lord, that we are able to communicate with the animal.

Rather than justifying killing as the Europeans do, by lowering animals, by denying their intelligence or that they have a soul, the Cree recognizes animals as "persons" with whom the proper relationship is one of reciprocity and equal exchange. In part, this attitude is a simple acknowledgment that human survival is dependent upon, or interdependent with, the survival of animals: institutions such as hunting territories and tallymen ensure that game is not overharvested. In religious terms, overharvest is considered a form of disrespect, which will cause the animals to leave an area.[12] Conversely, a shortage of game is a sign that proper respect has not been shown, and hunters are called upon to review past behavior and to make special efforts to regain the animals' favor. In practice, respect is shown through rites and customs.

A basic principle is that animal gifts must not be wasted. George Gladman, a Hudson's Bay Company trader, accompanied two Indian families in the James Bay region on July 28, 1818. He noted in the Eastmain House post journal:

Near Great Whale River, saw a white bear, and soon after, a she bear and two cubs. One of the latter my people shot, but the old one, though wounded, could not be driven from it. The Indians were unwilling to kill the old one, not having carriage in this canoe, and therefore we left the dead cub in the Dam's protection, and they actually deprived themselves of this delicacy rather than destroy what they could not carry away.[13]

In the Chischihp myth, disrespect was shown in wasting food by using it for clothing. In general, every part of an animal is used, and special care is taken that meat is not allowed to spoil. Hunting with the Cree in our own time, Colin Scott was able to affirm that this principle continues. Allowing meat to spoil (perhaps by failing to clean a carcass quickly enough), especially in the case of important animals like beaver or bear, is likely to result in some misfortune or even death overtaking the guilty hunter. The offended animal may withhold his gifts, which is serious not only for the hunter, but for the community that depends on his skills. When every possible part of the animal has been consumed or used the bones remain; these are generally returned to the element from which they came. Beaver bones are returned to the water, from which more beaver will emerge.

Among Pacific Coast Indians, salmon are considered to be a race of supernatural beings, who live in a great house under the sea. They "dress" in clothes of salmon flesh when it comes time for a run, to sacrifice themselves for the benefit of humans. "Since the salmon people's migration is considered to be voluntarily undertaken, it follows that it behooves human beings to take pains not to offend their benefactors."[14] Returning salmon bones to the water ensures that they are allowed to return to their underwater house, from which they reappear the next season. If bones are carelessly lost on land, salmon people may be reborn missing parts of their anatomy, and the annual visit may not be renewed.

The Beaver Indians of northeastern British Columbia take care to arrange neatly and cover with branches any inedible parts of an animal left behind at the scene of a kill. When a moose they were butchering was found to carry an unborn calf, that, too, was carefully handled:

First, they prepared a thick bed of partially digested browse which they poured from the animal's stomach. Then, painstakingly, they began to remove the foetus. Each part of the surrounding reproductive system was disconnected from the womb and set aside. Then the womb itself was placed on the bed of the cow's stomach contents and sliced open. As the amniotic fluids flowed from it, Atsin very carefully guarded against their running onto the snow. . . . "You've got to be careful," he shouted. "If the water goes on the snow, then right away the weather will go hard and cold. And pretty soon we'll all be frozen to death!"[15]

Among the Cree of northern Quebec, the skulls of animals such as beaver or bear are often hung in trees, as a sign of respect, and to prevent dogs and other animals from gnawing them. The hard cartilage from the trachea of Canada geese may be tied in bundles in the branches of trees, where the wind may blow through them "to call other geese."[16]

There are many ways in which respect for geese is shown: the first geese of the season are formally greeted, and when the last birds leave, the hunter expresses the wish that he too may live another season "to enter again into this transaction with the geese." A Cree hunter will spend a great deal of time searching for a downed bird, even after an exhausting day of hunting. While white hunters spread out over as wide a territory as possible, Cree form a circle in one spot and avoid hunting the same area two days in a row, to give the geese time to rest and feed. Such courtesy, of course, has the advantage of encouraging the birds to stay longer in the hunters' territory, as do Cree prohibitions against hunting at night (when the flash from rifles can be seen) or on calm days (when a shot will be heard over a wider area and startle more birds).

A wide range of apparently mystical or religious traditions reveal the ecological wisdom of the Cree. Killing many more geese than usual, for instance, may be interpreted as meaning that the hunter has little hunting time left in his life. On a societal level, it serves as a reminder that if too many geese are killed, the people are ultimately endangered; on a personal level, such ideas act as internalized constraints against killing more than is needed. Similarly, certain birds, although edible, are considered "unlucky" or may be shot only if it is done perfectly, so that the bird dies instantly and falls within sight of the hunter. Such taboos and restrictions serve to keep the hunter constantly aware of the need for restraint, and of the importance of striving for "impeccability" in his hunting activities.

As a result, hunters are constantly watching the animals, monitoring their activities and seeking to interpret their needs, to adapt their own behavior to that of the animals. The Beaver Indians of British Columbia:

> ... wait, watch, consider. Above all they are still and receptive, prepared for whatever insight or realization may come to them, and ready for whatever stimulus to action might arise. This state of attentive waiting is perhaps as close as people can come to the falcon's suspended flights, when the bird, seemingly motionless, is ready to plummet in decisive action.[17]

Feasts are held to mark the first kills of important game animals each season, and there are elaborate rituals for preparing and cooking the food for such feasts: animals are usually cooked in as close to their natural form as possible, and cut up only upon serving. A strict order may be observed for serving, and a small plate of each type of food served will be prepared and thrown into the fire as an offering to the animal spirits.[18] Most important, feasts express the central role of sharing in Indian culture. As the animals have shared their gifts with humans, so people must share with each other.

Feasts are models of hunting society. Food gifts from the animals are shared among the community, consumed and handled respectfully, so that further gifts will ensue. Certain parts of animals are traditionally distributed to particular elements of society (the head of larger animals for elders or respected hunters, fore parts for men, hind parts for women) to emphasize that the hunter acts only as a medium to distribute gifts that are already designated for their recipients. Often it is the elders, not the hunters, who distribute meat at a feast, for the elders have a longer relationship with the animal benefactors.

It is believed that animals will give themselves more willingly if the people share the gifts generously. A hunter who kills a large moose distributes the meat throughout the community, knowing that by doing so the animals will come to him more easily in the future.

So we find that reciprocity in the human community is intimately linked to an attitude of reciprocity between people and nature, and maybe there's a lesson in that for modern society in which we seem to have terrible environmental problems. We seem to have a lack of respect or understanding about nature, leading us into various kinds of problems. And perhaps those problems would be less severe if the relationships between people in our society were better and less exploitative, and more in a spirit of reciprocity. Perhaps that's one of the things that traditional hunting societies have to teach us.[19]

This chain of relationships among the hunter, the hunted and the community is the opposite attitude of agricultural or industrial man, who begins by making a plan and then sets out to force nature to conform to it. It is this enormous difference of outlook that has made it next to impossible for Europeans to understand the wisdom of hunting cultures. The inability or refusal to appreciate the sophistication of Indian society and its subtle relationship with its environment has played a crucial role in rationalizing the cultural (and often physical) genocide that has accompanied the ongoing occupation of Indian land in North America by Europeans.[20]

Two great civilizations, which had developed very different ways of being in the world, met when Europeans first came to America. It was a moment in history that could have enriched both cultures. Instead, the newcomers, set in their mad rush of colonization and blinded by presumptions of absolute truth and manifest destiny, swept aside Indian culture without bothering to find out what it was. As European expansion disrupted the land and undermined the foundations of Indian society, it became increasingly easy for the Europeans to pretend that there had been nothing there of value in the first place.

Now that we are faced with the ecological price of our technological "Great Leap Forward," we can more readily appreciate the sophistication of the philosophy and way of life that permitted Indians to participate in nature and to use animals without losing respect and even love for them. Today it is native groups who are fighting the hardest to defend the land from further devastation by hydroelectric dams, gas and oil pipelines, mines and their inevitable camp followers of roads, boom-and-bust towns, all-terrain vehicles and a population with little commitment to the land. As Alan Cooke has pointed out, the wealth of animal and plant resources, in the long run, outvalues any oil field or mine.[21]

Many in the ecology movement express admiration for the holistic spirit of the Indian view of nature, and it seemed for a time that the environmental movement might give us one last chance to profit from the ecological wisdom of Indian society: maybe North America could become the setting for a fruitful marriage of European and Indian traditions. Ironically, recent events have seen leading elements of the environmental and animal-rights movements pitted against native people over two issues that strike at the heart of the aboriginal way of life: the campaign to stop the seal hunt and the call for a ban against trapping fur-bearing animals.

These are important issues, not only because they call into question the rights of native people to continue their traditional ways of life, but because they reveal a fundamental contradiction within the ecology and animal-rights movements themselves. European society may, as animal-rights critics claim, have cut itself off from the natural world. Indian society, however, is inseparable from native beliefs in the close relationship between human and animal worlds. One would expect ecology and animal-rights advocates to be the native groups' strongest allies in their fight against the encroachment of industrial technology into the remote wildernesses of Canada. Instead, animal-rights campaigns now pose a grave threat to the very survival of the last remaining North American hunting cultures. How has this incredible, and potentially tragic, inversion of values come to be?

PART TWO

PRACTICE

The twenty-year campaign against sealing dramatically traces the movement from the two poles of traditional animal welfare and modern ecology to a radical animal-rights position that has little relationship to either. The "seal wars" comprise: (1) the first wave of protest, from the 1964 Artek film to the founding of the International Fund for Animal Welfare in 1969; (2) the second wave in 1976 and 1977, marked by the involvement of Greenpeace and the visit to Newfoundland of Brigitte Bardot; (3) the 1983 EEC ban on whitecoats, and the 1984 IFAW fish boycott.

The mounting campaign against fur trapping is following many of the same patterns as did that against the seal hunt: as government moves to minimize cruelty and the danger of overexploitation, the animal-rights stance comes increasingly to the fore. There are strong indications that animal-rights groups will make fur trapping the central issue for the rest of the 1980s. The campaign against trapping may have severe repercussions on native groups and others who still live close to the land, and work to the detriment of the interests even of the wildlife it claims to be protecting.

Animal-rights advocates say that factory farming and laboratory-animal science cause by far the most suffering to animals, but because they strike deep into every sector of the society, they are unlikely soon to become popular campaigns. Instead, they serve to bolster the animal-rights attack against native trappers and others who still retain a close relationship to nature.

5

Sealing:
The Twenty-Year War

"To face, who could, an old dog hood
But a plucky Newfoundlander?"
  – Newfoundland folk song

Sealing was worth $13 million to Atlantic Canada in 1981. About $7 million went to the more than three thousand fishermen and two thousand Arctic Inuit who hunted the seal.[1] After the European Economic Committee banned the import of white-coat seal pelts, and the collapse of the market for sealskins as a result of the protest movement, the value of sealing was slashed to less than $3 million; income to sealers fell to $1.3 million. In more personal terms, fishermen who had earned an average of $2,000 – often one-third of their annual cash income – for four to six weeks of work saw that slip to less than $400.[2] Inuit average income from sealskins (usually from Ring seals) fell from $450 to $100; in many parts of the Arctic they haven't been able to sell any sealskins for more than a year now. This is despite the facts that Inuit don't hunt "baby" seals at all, and that the EEC explicitly exempted native products from their ban. For the Inuit, seal money was often the main source of cash to finance the rest of the subsistence-hunting activities. But the market for sealskin was gone.

Ironically, the income of the *anti*-sealing groups is now more than the total earnings of the seal industry in its best years. Brian Davies' International Fund for Animal Welfare (IFAW) brings in more than $6 million a year in donations. With a staff of only thirty people worldwide, the IFAW makes as much money as three thousand Atlantic sealers shared before the IFAW-sponsored EEC ban smashed the market for sealskins, and six times what the sealers made in 1983. (Greenpeace USA takes in another $5 million.)[3]

Born in a South Wales mining village in 1938, Brian Davies emigrated to Canada, where he enlisted in the army and was stationed at Camp Gagetown, New Brunswick. He began working for the New Brunswick SPCA as a field secretary in 1961, and became interested in the seal hunt in 1964.[4] In 1969 he broke with the SPCA to form his own IFAW, which today has some eight hundred thousand members worldwide. Davies' salary is now reported to be about eighty thousand dollars.[5]

After the EEC ban, only 64,500 seals were taken in 1983, down from 153,500 in 1982, and more than 190,000 in 1981. In fall 1983, after a massive campaign organized by Greenpeace, Rieber Incorporated, in Norway, the main buyer and processor of sealskins, announced they would buy no white-coat pelts in 1984.[6] The IFAW, however, was not satisfied, arguing that "ragged-jackets" and "beaters" were also "babies" in need of protection. The IFAW unleashed an eight-million-letters campaign calling for a boycott of Canadian fish products in Great Britain and the United States, attacking a $1.6 billion export industry, and exerting tremendous pressure on the Canadian government, fish-packing companies and of course the fishermen themselves. The save-the-seals movement proved that wildlife conservation could attract wide public support.

Ironically, studies by two important international scientific bodies – the International Council for the Exploration of the Sea (ICES) and the Northwest Atlantic Fisheries Organization (NAFO) – have recently established that the Canadian quota-management system, imposed in 1972, is functioning effectively in terms of conservation: the harp-seal population is rising, after a period of apparent overexploitation in the 1950s and 1960s.[7] This conclusion was confirmed in April 1983, when the eighty-one-nation CITES (the Convention of International Trade in Endangered Species) voted down a West German proposal to list harp and hooded seals on the Convention's Appendix II (a provision of the Convention to monitor trade in animals that resemble, and might be mistaken for, endangered species).

Harp seals are not endangered and, according to international animal-welfare agencies, the carefully regulated hunt is now at least as humanely conducted as any slaughterhouse operation.[8]

Nonetheless, groups like IFAW and Greenpeace continued to mount ever larger and more aggressive campaigns, and no less prestigious a body than the EEC Council of Ministers went ahead with their ban of March 28, 1983. All of which has caused Arctic Inuit to comment that the European tradition of ignorance and insensitivity toward other cultures has remained remarkably unchanged during the centuries.[9]

Animal-rights advocates claim that the "success" of the anti-sealing lobby reflects a significant shift in the public attitude toward wildlife and animal life in general. On closer examination, however, it is not at all clear that this is so.

PROLOGUE AND ACT ONE OF THE GREAT BABY-SEAL CAMPAIGNS: CULTURES IN COLLISION

Sealing was begun by native Indians in Canada, and it is deeply rooted in Newfoundland tradition. The increasing commercial importance of the hunt in the late eighteenth century encouraged many Devonshire fishermen to settle permanently in the small and isolated coves of the island. [10] (Previously, they had come only for the summer cod fishery and returned home each winter.)

Hunting seals on the spring ice was hard and dangerous work, especially in the days of wooden ships. Calvin Coish lists eleven ships that went to the bottom in seven seasons at the start of the twentieth century. [11] All 173 crew members went down in the icy waters with the *Southern Cross* in 1914, and 78 others were lost on the floes when a storm separated them from their ship, the *Newfoundland*.

The "disasters of 1914" and pressure from William Coaker's Fishermen's Party, which won eight seats in the previous election, finally prompted the Newfoundland government to inspect sealing ships (only three of the "wooden walls" passed), and to impose better conditions for the sealers. For the first time the sealer's basic diet of hard tack and black tea would be supplemented with hot meals, such as pea soup, twice a week, causing one tough old sealing master, Captain Abram Kean, to lament, "Too much luxury, that's what! Why I can remember when we never even had stoves aboard, 'cause the owners thought the men would stay and warm themselves 'stead of going on the ice. . . . Now sealing's pure luxury, with engines to do the work and bunks and hot food . . . it's not a man's game anymore." [12]

This is the same Captain Kean who had ordered the men of the *Newfoundland* out on the ice, despite signs that a storm was brewing. Kean was the only captain to bring in more than a million seals before he retired in 1934, and he eventually became Newfoundland's minister of fisheries (the first fisherman to reach such power) and was awarded the Order of the British Empire by King George V.

It was another sealing captain, Arthur "Viking" Jackman, who piloted Admiral Peary's first Arctic expedition in 1886. Another sealer, Captain Bob Bartlett, piloted the 1898 voyage and all Peary's polar expeditions after that. And it was a sealing vessel, the *Terra Nova*, that carried Scott to the Antarctic on his ill-fated mission to the South Pole in 1911.

By World War One "wireless" was routinely used on the sealing ships, to help locate the herd and to warn about bad weather. In 1922, the first airplane was used to find the seals, raising fears that men would have too great an advantage: developments in technology were upsetting the traditional balance between hunter and prey.

In the late 1930s, overexploitation of the White Sea harp-seal herds brought Norwegians to the Newfoundland "Front," with sophisticated new steel-hulled ice breakers. The threat of submarines kept sealers away from the region during World War Two, but thereafter the Norwegians returned as did Canadian ships equipped with refrigeration units, which permitted hunters to stay longer at the Front, without damaging the pelts. This was especially important after 1952, when, for the first time, pelts became more valuable than seal oil, for which substitutes had been developed.[13]

In 1949, Newfoundland joined Canada and the Canadian Fisheries Research Board began a full-scale study of the seal populations. They concluded in 1956 that the seals were probably being exploited at too high a level, and advised that a quota be placed on the number of seals hunted. But by then Norway, Denmark, France and the United States were stepping up their interest in the hunt, and Canada's three-mile limit did not extend to the Front.[14]

The first rumblings of protest came during the mid-1950s, when Doctors Joseph Cunningham and Harry Lillie filmed scenes at the hunt. Back in England, Lillie published a book and Cunningham declared sealing to be "utterly degrading and cruel."[15]

In 1961, twenty-eight ships took part in the hunt, aided by radar, scout planes and government icebreakers: sealing had entered a new era. Canada proposed that the hunt be controlled by the Northwest Atlantic Fisheries Organization (NAFO), but the European members could not agree on a formula.

In 1962, helicopters were first used to bring men to the seals and to ferry back pelts, and charges flew that "helicopter hijackers" were swooping down to steal pelts panned by the ships' crews.[16] Even the Russians got into the act that year, arriving with a seven-thousand-ton ice-breaking sealing vessel, and two giant helicopters to carry their men into the herds.

The climax came in 1964. One hundred fifty planes and helicopters took part in the hunt that year, in a "gold-rush" atmosphere that saw the arrival of many inexperienced hunters. There was great waste – more seals were killed than could be carried away – and the Canadian Audubon Society appealed to the Canadian minister of fisheries to control the hunt. It was estimated that by 1964, the herd numbered about 1.5 million, down by 200,000 from 1950, and from perhaps 3 million in the mid-nineteenth century.

The most important event of the 1964 season, however, was carried out not by sealers, but by a film crew. Artek Films of Montreal had been commissioned by the Quebec government to produce a series of nature films about fishing and hunting around the province. Sealing was to have been just one of the series, but on their arrival at the end of the hunt, the crew claimed to be shocked by what they saw. Scenes of a "sealer" poking and tormenting a live seal, rejected by the Quebec government, were used to make an independent film called *Les Phoques* ("The Seals").[17] A wave of outrage erupted in Quebec when the film was shown on the French-language network of CBC television, Radio-Canada.

Suspicions would later be cast upon this film. Doctor Douglas Pimlott, a University of Toronto zoologist and representative of the Canadian Audubon Society, identified three of the people in the film: two of the "sealers," including one shown shooting at seals with a modern rifle with telescopic sights, were members of the film crew.[18] The third man later swore an affidavit that the scenes that sent shock waves around the world had actually been staged:

I, the undersigned, Gustave A. Poirier, of the Magdalen Islands, declare having been employed by a group of photographers, one of which had a beard, around March 4, 1964, to skin a large seal for a film. I solemnly swear before witnesses that I was asked to torment the said seal and not to use a stick, but just to use a knife to carry out this operation, where in normal practice a stick is used to first kill the seals before skinning them.[19]

The Federal Standing Committee on Fisheries and Forests conducted hearings in April 1968 and concluded that "grossly misleading information had been purveyed by the Artek film" and that "irresponsibility had been shown by the producers of the film and by the CBC for not enquiring into its accuracy before screening."[20] But the film had its effect.

In response to the chaos that had marred the 1964 hunt, the Canadian government (after consultation with sealers and humane associations, including the New Brunswick SPCA representative, Brian Davies), introduced new regulations that shortened the sealing season, issued licences to keep track of who went on the ice, limited aircraft to "spotting" the herd, set standards for the club used for killing, legislated that seals be dead before skinning began and set a quota of fifty thousand whitecoats for the ship-based Gulf hunt. (The Front was still beyond Canadian jurisdiction.) These measures, however, were lost in the storm of international protest raised by the Artek film, thanks in great part to a Montreal journalist, Peter Lust.

Editor of the Montreal-based German-language weekly *Nachrichten*, Lust had fled Germany with the rise of Nazism in 1933. He returned with the American army in 1945, witnessed the horror of the death camps of Dachau and Buchenwald and swore then that if ever again he saw such evil he would fight against it with all his force. After seeing *Les Phoques*, Lust wrote a series of passionate articles, including "Murder Island" (referring to the Magdalens), which were picked up by the German *Hamburger Morgenpost*, and then reprinted in more than three hundred newspapers throughout Europe. (Germany, as we shall see, has played a central role throughout the seal campaigns.)

In 1966, Brian Davies headed the New Brunswick SPCA's new "save-the-seal" fund; he wrote articles for the Canadian *Weekend Magazine*, which brought in a rush of letters and donations, including a check for eight hundred dollars from Doctor Bernhard Grzimek, known in Europe as the "high priest of conservation." Grzimek showed *Les Phoques* on his German television nature show later that year. He also brought Davies to England, to the *Observer* Wildlife Exhibition in London. Diplomatic intervention by the Canadian High Commission prevented the exhibition from screening *Les Phoques*, so they showed the black-and-white film Harry Lillie had shot at the 1955 hunt.

Grzimek and Davies were plugging into an environment that had been well-primed to hear about seals: in 1965, two British government commissions, the Littlewood Committee and the Bramwell Committee, had reported abuses against animals in laboratories and on factory farms, stirring considerable public concern. Powerful pharmaceutical and agrobusiness interests insured that little government action was taken to implement the recommendations of the Bramwell or Littlewood reports, but the save-the-seals campaign blossomed.

In 1967, Peter Lust published *The Last Seal Pup*, an emotional outcry against the hunt; the influential German humane organization Tiershutz called for personal boycotts of sealskins, and in 1968 the London *Daily Mirror* (circulation fifteen million) sent a team to cover the hunt.[21] What went largely unheard was the verdict of veterinarians and humane societies who also witnessed the 1968 hunt: that the new Canadian regulations appeared to have curbed abuses.

Doctor E.A. Costello, a veterinarian with the Canadian department of agriculture, wrote: "At no time did I witness an act of cruelty." Doctor R.A. Jones, of the Royal School of Veterinary Medicine, gave similar testimony.[22] Perhaps most telling, Doctor Lars Karstad, who went to the hunt on behalf of Brian Davies' "save-the-seals" fund, examined, with Doctor H.C. Lolinger of West Germany, the carcasses of 361 seals, determined that for only twelve seals (about three per cent) did he not detect lesions that proved absolutely they had been at least unconscious and probably dead, when skinning began. Moreover, these twelve, too, had probably been killed humanely. "I did not see any instance of intentional contravention or disregard for the sealing regulations," Karstad wrote in his report, a conclusion he stuck by even when Brian Davies requested that he modify it.[23]

Doctor Douglas Pimlott, who observed the hunt in 1967, concluded that the clubs used that year also conformed to government regulations and had been properly used. Pimlott added that, in the course of working in Newfoundland, he himself had gained

> ... a profound respect for the simple, dignified, uncomplicated people who go to the sea as fishermen and sealers. ... Their entire way of life has been centered around the killing of animals, fish, seals, seabirds, moose or caribou. They are, however, decent, ordinary people, not sadists. They simply do not perpetrate inhumane crimes such as the ones described by Peter Lust [in] The Last Pup.[24]

As early as 1967, the Canadian Audubon Society became alarmed that the furor about sadistic killing was obscuring the very real question of whether seals were being overhunted. The Society made representations to the International Union for Conservation of Nature (IUCN) in Geneva (now the research and administrative arm of CITES) that a harvesting quota on harp seals be imposed.

The increased concern about the conservation of wildlife species resulted by 1969 in the United States Congress passing the Endangered Species Act, which was strengthened in 1970 by New York State's Mason Act. In 1971, Canada and Norway set up a Joint Commission on Sealing, and for the 1972 hunt, finally, a quota was imposed on the number of seals harvested. Most important overall, in 1973, the Washington Treaty was signed, establishing the Convention on International Trade in Endangered Species (CITES). Slowly, the upper levels of public administration began to come to grips with the conservation issues that had been so forcefully raised by the new ecology movement.

Meanwhile, a fundamental change was occurring in the ecology and animal-rights movement. Brian Davies, no longer dependent upon the opinions of veterinarians and conservationists, was playing now to a larger house. In the fall of 1968 he returned to Europe, where the influential *Paris Match* ran a series of articles on Davies and the seal hunt, illustrated with photographs taken by Davies. Letters of support were received (and printed) from such notables as Princess Paola of Belgium and Princess Grace, and more than thirteen thousand dollars were donated to the "Save the Seals Fund."

In 1969, *Paris Match* sent a reporting team with Davies to the ice, and the *Daily Mirror* ran photographs of Davies and his children with seal pups. Demonstrations took place at Canadian embassies from New York to Brussels, and *Life* magazine ran a story called "Canada's Bloody Business." Just as the humane societies were coming to believe that Canadian regulations had stemmed the worst abuses of the hunt, and as the seal hunt began to be a secondary concern, Brian Davies was only beginning. At the end of 1969, he broke with the New Brunswick SPCA to set up his own International Fund for Animal Welfare (IFAW).

Until he joined the SPCA in 1961, Brian Davies considered himself a career soldier: "Even today I love war films and tape them," he says. "My favorite reading is World War Two military history. There's a sense of glory about war."[25]

When asked by an interviewer if he didn't see a contradiction between saving animals and his fascination with warfare, Davies admitted: "There is a contradiction, but I never considered it."[26]

In fact, Davies likes to think of the IFAW as a "commando group." When gathering evidence for a campaign against the consumption of dogs and cats in the Philippines, he hired three British paratroopers, ex-Special Air Services men – "mercenaries for animals," he called them.[27]

Despite some 800,000 members worldwide and more than $6 million in donations, the IFAW issues no membership cards, no thank-you letters and has no use for grassroots decision-making: "I'm afraid if you want to save animals in a fast-moving world, there's no time for democracy," Davies says bluntly.[28]

In the spring of 1970, Brian Davies brought to the hunt Alice Herrington, president of the New-Jersey-based Friends of Animals, a radical animal-rights group that researched and publicized abuses to animals in laboratory science and fur trapping. In 1970, Davies' *Savage Luxury: The Slaughter of the Baby Seals* was published; in 1971, a militant call for acceptance of animal-rights philosophy was issued from England, with the publication of *Animals, Men, and Morals*, edited by John Harris, Stanley Godlovitch and Roslind Godlovitch.[29]

The first hint that the new animal-rights philosophy might make its mark on public policy came in 1972, when the United States Congress passed the Marine Mammal Protection Act, banning the import into the United States of products from nursing animals younger than eight months old, a bill aimed squarely at the Canadian white-coat hunt. Suddenly conservation was no longer the central focus.

From a conservation perspective, it is preferable to hunt "baby" seals, a large percentage of which will perish before reaching maturity in any case. Scientists say, as a rough rule of thumb, that one breeding adult has the same ecological value as four white-coat seals, and one of the reasons the Canadian Fisheries Research Board gave for the decline in the harp-seal herds after World War Two was that too high a proportion of adults was being harvested.

In the age of television and color-picture magazines, however, a photograph of a fluffy white-coat seal outweighs many lines of careful ecological reasoning. Brian Davies understood that and, in 1974, hired the advertising firm McCann-Erickson to launch a hundred-thousand-dollar campaign to "Stop the Seal Hunt." It was an election year in Canada, and the IFAW sponsored billboards stating: "90,000 baby seals will be clubbed to death again this year. Unless you speak up. Demand a commitment from your candidate." A Gallup poll revealed that 52% of Canadians opposed the hunt, and 11% said they'd vote against a candidate who didn't. The figures set Davies dreaming: "Imagine what that 11% could do if it were a united front."[30]

Ex-career soldier Davies is fond of quoting the classic military theorist Karl von Clausewitz, who counselled pitting one's greatest force against the enemy's weakest point. Davies has summed up his theory of political action succinctly: "You save animals by sticking it up the backsides of politicians at election time. And that takes money."[31]

To get that money, in 1975 the IFAW commissioned Roberts Ketchum International to make two half-hour films, which were distributed to the television networks. Media interests had died down since 1968, but Davies' persistence through the lean years of the early 1970s was about to pay off. In 1976 reinforcements arrived from the west coast of Canada to help rocket the seal campaign back into the headlines.

ACT TWO OF THE GREAT BABY-SEAL CAMPAIGNS: GREENPEACE AND SEX APPEAL

"As we headed out in the final run toward the fleets, it seemed to me that we were like a seagoing gang of ecological bikers, bikers who had adopted the Satyagraha philosophy of Mahatma Gandhi, but who rode high-powered roaring machines across the waves and whose collective aggressive energy was more in tune at times with the mood of pillagers descending on a helpless village than 1960s hippies coming to tuck flowers into the rifles of National Guardsmen. If there was any other basic sense of it, it was the dreamlike sensations that we were reincarnated Indian warriors whooping and hollering as we surged down out of the hills towards the wagon train."

–Robert Hunter, describing Greenpeace attempt to intercept Russian whaling fleets (1975). *Warriors of the Rainbow.*

Greenpeace was founded in 1970 by Canadian activists who sought to protect the environment and protest the development of nuclear weapons. Nuclear holocaust, they argued, would be a catastrophe not only in human terms, but for the whole biosphere.[32] The group's first action was to sail an old fishing boat, the *Phyllis Cormack*, to the atomic-test range at Amchitka Island to try to force the American military into a double-bind situation: they could call off their test or blow innocent people out of the water in full public view. As it turned out, the stormy Bering Sea prevented the *Phyllis Cormack* from ever reaching Amchitka; but the protest made its point and, perhaps more important, Greenpeace proved that the media would respond to their swash-buckling style.

It was four years later, in 1974, with the start of the save-the-whales campaign, that the Greenpeace image began to emerge. As Robert Hunter has written in his history of Greenpeace:

> There hadn't been much to celebrate so long as we were opposing bombs. It was a very negative game. But now, instead of fighting death, we were embracing life. It was not just that we wanted to save the whales; we wanted to meet them, to engage them, touch them. For the first time there was a transcendent element lying at the center of the undertaking. There was a Holy Grail.[33]

Drawing on the philosophy and tactics developed by the Yippies during the Vietnam War protests, Greenpeace pulled the levers of the mass media to gain worldwide coverage for their actions in the whale campaign. With remarkable frankness, Robert Hunter recalls how he organized his press releases as another of the group's boats, *Greenpeace V*, steamed out to intercept the Russian whaling fleet:

> All I had to do was make sure never to quote myself. Instead I invented quotes, placed them in the mouths of agreeable crew members, then reported to the outside world what they had said. As a journalist, I was a traitor to my profession. As news manager for the expedition, I could control the shaping of our public image. And when things got slack, I could arrange for events to be staged that could then be reported as news. Instead of reporting the news, I was in fact in the position of inventing the news, then reporting it.[34]

Greenpeace's exposure of a Russian whaling fleet close to the California coast helped stir political pressure for a two-hundred-mile limit to replace the outdated twelve-mile jurisdiction. In 1975, Greenpeace successfully lobbied for a ban on the capture of orcas ("killer whales") in British Columbia; a year later, Washington State followed suit.

It was at the end of 1975 that Greenpeace's Paul Watson and Walrus Oakenbough first came up with the idea of spraying harp-seal pups with green dye, to ruin the market value of their fur. In fact, most "white-coat" seal pelts are bleached and dyed prior to marketing, but the scheme had media appeal. (Interestingly enough, the plan was at first opposed by Paul Spong, who had spearheaded the Greenpeace whale campaigns: Spong's beloved orca whales ate seals.)

A more serious problem, Robert Hunter recalls, was that the seal campaign would involve walking a tightrope between the ecological argument Greenpeace was supposedly committed to and an idea with irresistible media value: "the depths of emotion that the killing of 'babies' generated in the breasts of millions of urban people, who otherwise, with their cars and swimming pools and electric gadgets were the worst environmental destroyers of all."[35]

Not least worrisome for Greenpeace was their class consciousness: it "was going to be a bad situation if we had to go into Newfoundland and face off against men who were the bottom rung of the working class, because then the contrast between the 'elitism' of the environmental movement and the agony of the workers could achieve such a high profile that more would be lost than gained."[36]

In fact, in the spring of 1976, Greenpeace did face off against the sealers. Confronted with an angry crowd in St. Anthony, Newfoundland, Greenpeace backpedaled furiously. At a meeting on March 10, 1976, in the St. Anthony high-school auditorium, Patrick Moore (then vice-president for policy) declared:

> We don't want to interfere with your livelihood. We want to stop the Norwegians from killing the seals. Join with us in stopping the Norwegians so there'll be more seals for you in the future.[37]

When the sealers objected that spraying the seals with green dye was no way to help them, Greenpeace president Robert Hunter announced that, as a gesture of good faith, the dye would be handed over to the people of St. Anthony. Moreover, Paul Watson revealed that the IFAW had loaned Greenpeace $7,000 for their cross-country trek, but that when Greenpeace learned that Davies' objective was to end the hunt completely, the money was returned.

That night in St. Anthony, Greenpeace argued that the important issue was conservation, not that the white coats were attractive. Bob Hunter declared, "After all everyone's a cute little pup at one time."[38] The confrontation ended with Greenpeace and the Newfoundland fishermen's union issuing a joint call to the Canadian government to establish a two-hundred-mile limit to protect the seal herds. The Greenpeacers distributed membership cards to the jubilant fishermen and their families and were allowed to roar away in their shiny red-and-white Bell Jet Ranger II helicopters for the sealing grounds.

Having lost their green dye, the Greenpeacers contented themselves with covering white-coat seals with their bodies, while French photographer Jean-Claude Francolon shot off rolls of film. The media coup came when Bob Hunter and Paul Watson took their "existential leap" (as Hunter called it), standing in the path of the giant icebreaker *Arctic Endeavour*. The ship stopped for only a few minutes, but it was long enough for the cameras to catch the spectacle of the huge steel ship towering over two stubborn protesters. The medium, as another Canadian had taught, would determine the message that millions of television watchers would receive.

Not least important, Greenpeace had brought a woman onto the ice. In Robert Hunter's record of the scene, Eileen Cheevers became a prop in a carefully staged morality play:

> She was the first of her sex to come to this place where, for centuries, Newfoundland males had entered their manhood by steeling themselves to kill the most beautiful infant creatures they'd ever seen. . . . A man was crunching across the ice [after a pup], not even having to run, yet coming up on it swiftly, and the pup's mother was bobbing up and down in a nearby blowhole, powerless to answer the desperate wailing of the infant that was not long ago safe inside her. . . .
>
> [The pup] had turned around and was snapping at its destroyer, even though it could not hope to reach with its small teeth any higher than the man's boots. In that instant, it was no longer a seal, but a small deviant boy with fantastic courage. . . .
>
> The next seal hunter found himself blocked by a furious young woman, breathing harshly and gasping at him: "No! No! No!" He elbowed her aside and her light body could not resist the rocky muscles of his arm. . . . Not far away, Jean-Claude Francolon was there to capture the moment he had been waiting for, when a woman from the twentieth century would rise between a man armed with primitive killing tools and an animal that died in its infancy to service equally primitive female vanity, a new age in collision with darkest antiquity. [39]

A few days later, Brian Davies arrived on the ice with seven stewardesses, who would carry the seal story around the world, he said. But Davies was too late. He had been upstaged on his own battlefield.

The media circus peaked in 1977. To feed the "media goat," Brian Davies brought photogenic starlet Yvette Mimieux with him to St. Anthony. She was afraid "there'll be no animals left for my grandchildren to see," she told reporters. Greenpeace decided to avoid a repeat encounter with the Newfoundlanders, and shifted their base camp to the quieter shores of Blanc Sablon, Quebec. Carefully keeping their image distinct from that of the IFAW, Greenpeace stressed the ecological problem: "[The] east coast harp seal hunt is not an issue of what is a humane or inhumane way of killing. The real issue is that at the present rate of extermination, the harp seal will be extinct in five years."[40]

Paul Watson, who, according to Hunter, "had a bit of a militaristic streak in him, and delighted in giving each crew member a specific title,"[41] again set his machismo on the line against the sealers. This time he handcuffed himself to the "whip" (a chain used to haul seals aboard) of the *Martin Karlsen*, and got dunked into the cold Atlantic for his trouble.

The media coup of the 1977 season, however, went to a new player: Swiss "philanthropist" Franz Weber had sworn to bring six hundred international reporters to the ice. He offered to collect $400,000 in Europe to compensate the "150 sealers" if they'd stay home (referring presumably to the ship-based sealers, and conveniently overlooking thousands of landsmen and native hunters).

Weber also dreamed up a much-publicized scheme to establish a synthetic-fur factory in Newfoundland, and a plant to make toy "harp-seal" dolls. ("We're sealers and fishermen and we're not going to work in any factory," was the Newfoundlanders' angry response.)[42] Weber's plan showed an ignorance of population conditions in Newfoundland. He didn't seem to notice that fishermen are scattered in hundreds of isolated coves and harbors, not conveniently gathered in towns just waiting for a factory to be built.

Weber arrived at Blanc Sablon in March 1977 with sixty, not six hundred reporters, and without either money or jobs for the Maritimes, but he did bring Brigitte Bardot. The photograph of Bardot hugging a seal pup that appeared in Europe after that visit had perhaps more impact than any single action to rally Europeans for the import ban on white-coat hunting in 1983. What is less well-known is that bad weather prevented BB from making use of the Greenpeace helicopter that was supposed to carry her to the ice fields. In fact, a number of observers have argued that the white-coat pup she embraced was stuffed.[43]

But in a world governed by instant communications and public-opinion polls, the medium is indeed the message. As Robert Hunter wrote: "Until her arrival, the seal hunt story was all blood and death. But now it was blood and death and sex. No more potent combination could be put together."[44]

In the wake of the extensive media coverage of the 1977 hunt, seal prices fell dramatically. But the anti-sealing campaigners also felt the tension of so many headliners fighting for the center of the same stage. There were disputes among the different protest groups about the use of helicopters, which were in short supply, and after Paul Watson was dunked into the Atlantic, Brian Davies commented testily: "People who don't know what they're doing shouldn't be allowed out there."[45] Greenpeace criticized Weber and Davies for stressing humanitarian concerns instead of conservation.

Within Greenpeace, hostility flared between Paul Watson and Patrick Moore.[46] There were criticisms that Watson's wild behavior on the ice called into question Greenpeace's reputation as a serious ecology group. Watson, for his part, charged that Greenpeace had made a profit on the 1977 campaign and announced that he would set up his own organization, which he wanted to call the "International Wildlife Survival Foundation."[47] Moore countered that Watson had overspent his sealing-campaign budget by $25,000.[48] By September, Watson had decided his foundation would be called the "Earthforce Environmental Society," and that in 1978 he would spray-paint baby seals with green dye.[49]

Some attempt was made to rally support for the hunt. Tom Hughes, of the Ontario Humane Society, complained on national television that while "aging film actresses" had no trouble getting their message to the public, no one wanted to listen to "a rather dull humane society." It was time to challenge how money collected by groups like IFAW was being "raised, used and spent," Hughes said.[50] Newfoundland Premier Frank Moores travelled to England to complain about the large sums IFAW was raising to end the hunt.[51]

The counteroffensive appeared to have little effect. Members of Greenpeace were back on the ice in 1978, bringing with them two United States congressmen. One, Leo Ryan of California, had in March 1977 introduced a resolution into the United States House of Representatives condemning the Canadian hunt.[52] In London, Greenpeace supporters carried placards reading: "Help us stop this filthy, inhumane slaughter." In Washington, a demonstration was organized by the Animal Protection Institute of America, which also launched a campaign to send one million postcards of protest to the Canadian prime minister.[53]

More significantly, at the Hague, Brian Davies, the student of von Clausewitz, had found the enemy's weakest point. He announced that his group would now concentrate on "damaging the market for sealskins" in Europe.

ACT THREE OF THE GREAT BABY-SEAL CAMPAIGNS: THE EEC

After receiving some five million letters and cards opposing the seal hunt, in March 1982 the EEC Parliament instructed the commission (the administrative organ) of the Common Market to draft a resolution for banning the entry of seal products into the European Economic Community. In October 1982, the commission presented its resolution to the Council of Ministers (the EEC's authoritative body). The "special advisor on seals" who assisted the commission in the preparation of the resolution was Brian Davies.

Canadian official complaints that the material on which the commission based its work was incomplete and one-sided were supported by a report submitted in November 1982 by the eighteen-nation International Council for the Exploration of the Sea (ICES).[54] This report indicated that the seal hunt was well-regulated according to scientific standards, and that the Canadian quota-management system was effective: the harp-seal population was steadily increasing, not declining as protesters maintained. The report concluded that the northwest Atlantic herd had grown from a range of about 1.2 to 1.6 million in the late 1960s, to 1.5 to 2.0 million in the late 1970s.

As a result of these conclusions, the Council of Ministers delayed official action of the commission's resolution until further study could be completed by the scientific council of the Northwest Atlantic Fisheries Organization (NAFO). Its conclusions wouldn't be complete until June 1983. In the interim, some EEC members undertook a "voluntary ban" on the import of white-coat skins and effectively wiped out the 1983 hunt.

The NAFO committee on harp and hooded seals, which met June 13 to 17, 1983, at the Bedford Institute of Oceanography, in Dartmouth, Nova Scotia, included scientists from Canada, Norway and the EEC. Their report confirmed the ICES study, but concluded that the harp-seal population was probably rising faster than had been previously estimated. Pup production for 1978 to 1980 was estimated to be in the range of 350,000 to 600,000 per year. (Canadian quotas for 1982 and 1983 were 186,000. However, because of the EEC ban, only about 75,000 seals were taken in 1983, including those taken by Arctic Inuit, who are not restricted by quotas.) If 200,000 seals were taken in 1984, the NAFO study concluded, the herd would continue to grow at a moderate rate; if hunting continued at only the 1983 level, the population increase would be rapid.[55] In fact, because of poor markets and bad ice conditions, less than 30,000 seals were taken in 1984.

Despite these clear guidelines, the EEC commission chose to report to the council of ministers that "the *possibility* that the population has decreased since 1967 cannot be ruled out."[56]

The NAFO scientists admitted they could not absolutely prove that the herd had increased, given the tremendous difficulty of "counting" millions of seals over a thousand square miles of marine wilderness, but their mathematical models did show that such an increase was overwhelmingly likely. The commission's report to the Council of Ministers so obscured the results of the ICES and NAFO studies that the Canadian government felt obliged to submit a report (called the Commentary) stating that Canada was "deeply concerned about the serious misrepresentations and inaccuracies," and protesting especially the "biased interpretation of the recent NAFO Scientific Council's advice."[57] The Commentary concluded:

> The Commission's report uses the 1983 NAFO advice to conclude that cautious management of harp seals is necessary. It is the Canadian position that the NAFO advice confirms that the management of harp seals by Canada has indeed been cautious.[58]

The EEC commission was charged by the council of ministers to undertake bilateral discussions with Canada and Norway, in order to attempt to make the proposed ban unnecessary. The commission reported that Canada accepted "to undertake new measures in relation to the management, killing methods, and conservation of harp and hooded seals if there was scientific proof showing the necessity, in exchange for a commitment from the Commission to base its report and recommendations to the Council exclusively on scientific considerations. . . ."

The Commentary retorted that:

> No "exchange" was contemplated or suggested. On the contrary, Canada's policy with regard to the management, harvesting, and conservation of marine species has been based consistently on scientific considerations, regardless of whether or not the Commission takes a scientifically based approach to the relevant issues.

The commission's report also took Canada to task for reducing the quota on hooded seals by only twenty per cent in 1983, in spite of concern expressed by ICES scientists about these seals.[59]

What the commission omitted to state, the Canadians protested, was that Canada unilaterally lowered these quotas in reponse to the ICES recommendations, while the EEC failed to lower at all the hooded-seal harvest in its own, completely unregulated Greenland hunt.

> Given the apparent unwillingness of the EEC to regulate the hunting of hooded seals in Greenland, the Canadian authorities are somewhat perplexed at the intent of this statement, and question whether this recommendation . . . is intended to apply to all catches of hooded seals in the Northwest Atlantic, or simply to Canadian catches.[60]

The commission's report expressed "hope" that the directive (to ban the import of white-coat skins into Europe) would reduce the negative impact of low prices for native Inuit-produced pelts. In response, the Commentary pointed out that the anti-sealing protests had already damaged the market for all seal products, including those produced by Inuit; and there was no reason to believe the EEC ban would do anything but make things worse.

In response to the commission's complaint that "no action was taken by Canada and Norway to meet the objections against the killing of newborn seals,"[61] the Canadians replied that Canada's action had been to "explain both in private and public fora the irrationality of these objections, and to propose an international organization to explore these issues further."[62]

The Commentary concluded:

> The Canadian authorities are disappointed that the Commission's report to the European Council contains so many obvious errors and misleading conclusions drawn from objective scientific evidence. It is difficult, of course, to produce an objective and factual report when the issues have been prejudged from the outset, when the conclusion is irrational in terms of science and logic, *and when the aim is to satisfy the demands of powerful pressure groups.* The Commission may, at some time in the future, wish to proceed on a rational, objective and conservation-oriented basis to develop a reasonable international approach to seal management problems. Canada remains prepared to co-operate with the EEC and Norway on this basis.[63] (italics mine)

The Canadians hadn't been completely surprised by the commission report. During meetings on January 31 and February 1, 1983 in Ottawa among representatives of Norway, Canada and the EEC to try to avoid the confrontation, Canadian fisheries officials presented all the relevant statistics about the hunt. The EEC commission representatives informed them bluntly: "We didn't come here to negotiate . . . we're here to see if you will stop killing those baby seals, or else we'll go ahead with the ban."[64]

Despite Canadian objections and the evidence of the ICES and NAFO studies, the EEC directive of March 28, 1983, was passed into law in October. Disturbed by the objections levelled at the commission report, however, the council of EEC ambassadors (called COREPER) asked the commission for further reports every six months.

In private conversations with Canadian officials, the Europeans "excused" going ahead with their ban in the face of all available scientific data by admitting that it was politically necessary, and claimed that they were imposing the minimum ban possible.[65] Their reasoning went as follows: harp-seal pups molt their fluffy white coats for the mottled-gray "ragged jacket" at about two weeks old, at which time their mothers stop nursing them, and they are on their own. Legally, therefore, the hunters had only to delay the hunt about a week, and the pelts would be eligible for entry into the EEC.

Such fine theoretical distinctions, however laudable in diplomacy, served only to further muddy already troubled waters. Animal-rights groups used the EEC directive as "proof" that their cause had been right all along, while the legal loopholes kept the protest fires burning and money flowing into the war chests of the protest groups. The temerity of the EEC decision to ban white-coat pelts allowed the protest campaign to reach more intense levels in 1984 than ever before.

CITES 1983: BOTSWANA

Meanwhile, the European community's vendetta against sealing received a rebuff from an unexpected quarter. At the end of April 1983, a general meeting of the eighty-one-member (eighty-six members as of June 1984) Convention on International Trade in Endangered Species (CITES) met in Gabarone, Botswana, in southern Africa at the edge of the Kalahari Desert. There was no meeting room in Gabarone large enough for such a gathering, so a blue-nylon tent was erected on the lawn of the local Holiday Inn.

Canada had a special interest in the ten days of intense lobbying that preceded the three-day plenary session, because West Germany (president, at the time, of the EEC) had proposed listing all *Phocid* (earless) seals, which include harp and hooded seals, on Appendix II of the Convention. This appendix lists species that, although not endangered, resemble species that are endangered. (The seals would be listed because they resemble monk seals, which are endangered.)[66] In the screening committee, where resolutions are prepared for plenary, Petra Dimer, the German journalist who had drafted the proposal, tried to prove her point with a dramatic gesture. She arrived in the committee room carrying a large sealskin that had been specially dressed and dyed in bands of six colours. She turned to Arthur Frayling, chairman of the International Fur Trade Federation, and challenged him: "You are supposed to be a knowledgeable furrier. Can you guess what this pelt is?"

Her question was absurd – pelts do not often come into a country dyed six different colors – but Dimer was trying to prove that even experts couldn't tell one sealskin from another. Frayling, a tall, distinguished-looking Scot of the old British-Empire mold, who sports a dashing RAF moustache, didn't hesitate a moment.

"I do not have to guess, madame," he retorted. "I know for a fact that this is the pelt of a Ukrainian horse."

There was a moment's silence – after all, Arthur Frayling was for many years the head of the London Hudson's Bay Auctions, and knows as much as anyone about furs – then the committee room rocked with laughter. The tension had been broken, and many felt that the German resolution lost much of its power from that moment.

Listing on Appendix II does not actually limit trade, but in the context of the recent EEC import ban against white-coat skins, it was widely believed that listing on any CITES Appendix would serve to further deteriorate markets and would be seized upon by protest groups as encouragement.

Resolutions to list seals were originally proposed by three countries: Uruguay, Gambia and West Germany. Gambia, a tiny country on the west coast of Africa that was once a British colony, has no direct interest in seals, but the chief conservation officer of that country, a Briton named Eddie Brewer, is known to have strong sympathies for the IFAW and other animal-rights groups. (Gambia was also the sponsor of a resolution at the 1983 CITES meeting to outlaw trade in furs caught with leghold traps, which had serious implications for Canada.) But when the Canadian ambassador to Senegal approached the Gambian president to ask why his country was backing the resolution on seals, the president admitted that he could not give an answer.[67] Gambia subsequently withdrew its proposal. Uruguay also withdrew from the resolution, after diplomatic contacts by Canada.

In the intense lobbying that preceded the vote, representatives of Canadian Inuit and Indian communities, as well as the newly formed Canadian Sealers' Association, were very active. (There were some 120 non-governmental organizations [NGOs] from many countries represented at the CITES meetings, outnumbering the official delegations.)

It was soon clear that few delegates had heard anything but the anti-sealing side of the story. Many were surprised to learn that the native people still trapped and hunted in Canada. Few small countries can afford thorough research or even to send delegates to the hundreds of conferences that now determine international policy on a host of issues including conservation and wildlife management. Animal-rights groups have seized this opportunity to provide such countries with "research materials" and position papers.[68]

At times, emotions rose to the surface. One non-official Canadian delegate commented aloud on the irony of Canadians being accused of "inhumanity" by the Germans: "In 1939, some people in Germany were saying that certain other people had no right to live," commented the Second World War flyer in a voice loud enough to carry to a table of Germans across the room. "Seems to me this resolution boils down to about the same thing."[69]

When the plenary sessions finally got under way, the large blue tent was hot and stuffy, crowded with some 350 people. A few small desktop fans labored vainly to stir the air near the speakers' platform. As the meeting started, electricians were still laying down wires for the translation service. The head of the American delegation lazily swatted flies with a long-handled swatter.

The Botswanian chairman was unprepared to handle such a large meeting (a copy of *Robert's Rules of Order* was flown in from UNEP, in Nairobi). Doctor Sidney Holt, the representative for the Seychelles Islands, was the first to take the microphone to speak on the seals resolution; he spoke for fifty-nine minutes of the two-and-a-half hour debate. Doctor Holt is in fact British, not from the Seychelles. He has, however, received grants from the IFAW for their "seals project."[70]

A number of other delegates spoke for and against the resolution, but when Peter Ernerk of the Inuit Tapirisat rose to speak, the chairman, visibly rattled by the growing intensity of the debate, for the first and only time imposed closure – there was a two-minute limit for all unofficial delegations – cutting off the Inuit representative after he had spoken for only three minutes.

One of the most dramatic incidents of the meeting then took place, a moment that, most agree, turned the balance of the debate. Peter Ittinuar, an Inuit member of the Canadian parliament and special advisor to the Canadian delegation, had been sitting with the Inuit NGO delegation. He stood up holding the text of Peter Ernerk's speech, walked slowly around the front of the gathering, behind the chairman's dais, to the Canadian delegation on the other side of the Big Top, and read the speech aloud. Ittinuar was able to say what no other government official could have put so bluntly: that the German resolution was pure politics, and had no relevance to either science or ecology.

The Canadian position was helped when the delegate from St. Lucia asked if the German resolution wouldn't unfairly advantage Greenland sealers, whose products would enter the EEC directly through Denmark. The German delegate defended the right of free trade within the EEC for ten minutes, without answering the question; this added to the impression of European deviousness. It was left to the delegate from the EEC to admit that the Greenland sealers' products would enter Europe freely without CITES permits; as part of Denmark, Greenland was considered to be already within the EEC.

A two-thirds majority was needed to pass the German resolution. It was defeated twenty-seven to twenty-three, with six abstentions, in a secret ballot.[71] The vote was an impressive rebuke to the Europeans, who had lobbied hard, seeking international support for their decision to ban the import of white-coat pelts. One is unable to ignore the paternalism of Europe's attitude throughout the seal confrontation: from Britishers who pop up as representatives of distant South Seas islands or as wildlife commissioners for tiny African states, to the total disregard for the livelihoods and cultures of native hunters in Canada, and Canadians in general.

The presence of Canadian sealers and native groups was credited with turning the tide on an issue the Germans had been certain they'd win.[72]

The IFAW had lobbied hard, too. Ian McPhail, coordinator of the British wing of the IFAW, was in Botswana. A portly figure who sports a monocle and a full white beard, McPhail boosted his morale between sessions by playing a tape of Wagner's "Ride of the Valkyries" at top volume in his hotel room; but not even the vision of Norse warrior maidens in glinting armor, riding fiery steeds, was enough to carry the day for the IFAW in Botswana.

Another "Great White Father" of the animal-rights movement was also in attendance. Stanley Johnson had come to Gabarone not for the seals resolution, but to win support for a separate EEC proposal that would allow the European community to be represented by a single delegate to CITES. Potbellied and dynamic, Johnson is a British member of the European Parliament, a colorful individual who is said to like to write two or three novels during a vacation. Another of his hobbies has been the EEC ban on whitecoat skins, and it was largely thanks to his good offices that Brian Davies was well-received by the EEC commission.[73]

Because of a shortage of meeting rooms in the Holiday Inn, it was common to see little groups of delegates huddled together on the lawn, their garden chairs pulled into tight defensive circles, like wagon trains awaiting an Indian attack. A central attraction during the meetings was the Holiday Inn swimming pool. (During the conference, Botswana was in the throes of the worst drought in two hundred years. To accommodate the invasion of swimming, bath-filling and toilet-flushing visitors, water in Gabarone was rationed when the conference ended.) Beside the pool, relaxing after a hectic day's sessions, Stanley Johnson confided to a Canadian delegate that he'd "carried the seal business about as far as possible for now." Johnson's new project was to take a hand in tightening up management of wildlife in the Kalahari. Botswana's only exports are diamonds and beef. The threat to ban Botswana's beef imports into the EEC, Johnson calculated, might be an effective lever.

WHAT REALLY HAPPENED...

In May 1983, in keeping with its ecology-minded image, Greenpeace published a two-volume *Guide to the Scientific Literature on Harp and Hooded Seals*, including an extensive annotated bibliography.[74] Thanks to twenty years of protest, harp and hooded seals are now probably the most thoroughly studied wild-animal population on earth. Significantly, the findings of the 1982 ICES report are not summarized in the lengthy bibliography, although a critique of the report by Sidney Holt, as vice-chairman of the IUCN Species Survival Commission, is included as an appendix. (The NAFO report was released after Greenpeace published the guide.)

The trick used in the guide, to obscure scientific support for the Canadian quota-management system is to state that "despite these measures [Canadian quotas implemented in 1972] pup production has declined from about 645,000 in 1951, to about 352,000 in 1979."[75] Apart from the fact that only the most pessimistic figures have been used (for example, ICES estimated pup production in 1979 was in the 350,000 to 600,000 range),[76] nowhere in the Greenpeace publication are these figures broken down to show the more important picture: from 1951 to 1971 (when it is generally agreed populations did fall), and from 1972 to the present (when quota management allowed the herd to rise at about three per cent per year, even before the EEC ban and the destruction of the seal market).

Patrick Moore, director of Greenpeace, now denies that the debate had ever been about numbers:

And that's why the seal hunt was such a special issue. It's not the same as the conservation of whales or the preservation of an endangered species of tiger, or something. It's a completely different issue. What the seal hunt represented was the paramount focus for public attention on the need to change our basic attitude and relationship to nature and to the species that make it up. . . .

It wasn't primarily a question of wildlife management or economics or politics or science, or any of the other things they tried to argue their way around. It fundamentally came down to a question of morality. And in the end, all the animal-welfare organizations in the world recognized that and rallied around it at that level. And in fact, the imposition of the ban by the European community on the importation of seal-pup skins into Europe was based on the right of any nation to stop the importation of things from other countries, whether it be pornographic tapes or literature which was degrading to children, or whatever it happened to be. Sealskins were placed in that category ... and that reinforced the fact that all along it had actually been a moral or ethical issue, rather than a scientific one.[77]

Moore is saying that the seal hunt became an animal-rights issue. But is it true, as Moore now argues, that the discussion had never been a scientific one? Greenpeace carefully distinguished itself from the IFAW in 1976, criticizing the accent Davies put on cruelty; in Newfoundland, Moore, Robert Hunter and Paul Watson promised the people of St. Anthony that they wanted only to stop the big Norwegian ships. In 1977, Greenpeace spokesmen warned that unless quotas were reduced, the seals would be extinct in five years. Greenpeace continues to call itself an ecology group; and its recent publication, however biased, would suggest that it did still accord some importance to science.

More to the point, how many people who sent in their dollars to build a lobby powerful enough to sway the European parliament were aware – or are aware even today – that the seals were not in danger of extinction, and that the Canadian quota-management system had been turning the tide of previous overexploitation since 1972, four years before Greenpeace went out on the ice? The question of whether the seals were really endangered is important. For, if they were not, it is difficult to understand how the seal hunt was less morally justifiable than any other slaughterhouse operation. Peter Singer and others condemn all slaughter, even for food, and even of domestic animals. Patrick Moore and Paul Watson are also vegetarians, and cannot be accused of inconsistency. Brian Davies, however, who has been by far the most important driving force in the seal campaigns, is not a vegetarian: "I just haven't been able to kick the habit of eating meat," Davies says bluntly.[78]

Does the international support the seal campaigns have attracted represent politicians responding to the awakening of a "new attitude" toward nature, as Patrick Moore suggests? American politicians were prepared to make political hay when it wasn't inconvenient. The 1972 Marine Mammal Protection Act and the 1977 resolution of the United States House of Representatives, unanimously condemning the Canadian hunt, were both politically useful, but illogical. For, since 1911, the United States government itself had administered the controlled harvest of the Pribilof fur-seal herds, a project that has proved the viability of managing wild-seal populations even after they had been hunted perilously close to extinction. (Administration of the harvest was passed to the Pribilof Islands Aleut community in October 1983.) But as Doctor Richard Van Gelder, curator for mammals of the

American Museum of Natural History in New York, has pointed out, white-coat seals were of little economic importance in the United States economy:

> So it was a very nice political throwaway for all our legislatures to get together and say, we're not going to let any of these products into the United States. . . . It didn't cause anyone in the US to suffer from the loss of trade,and it sounded good. . . . God and Mother-hood.[79]

The anti-sealing protests have been especially popular in Germany, where Harald Traue is a clinical psychologist. Doctor Traue believes that there are deep psychological motivations behind the striking mass appeal of the call to "save baby seals":

> There is a common law in human beings, and in animal beings too, that is called in German, *Kindkinschema*. That's a scientific term: "child form." This is a term from the biology of animal behavior and it means that when animals, and humans too, are very young, they have a little body and a very large head with large eyes, and all the forms are rounded. And if you see such a form, an animal or a human being, you feel very good toward it. You feel like a mother. And that's a biological law.[80]

According to Doctor Traue, biological instincts combined in the baby-seal campaigns with some old-fashioned political considerations. Showing the killing of baby animals is a sure way to stir angry feelings, but the animal "children" were far away from Germany – an ideal political football.

During elections for the German Bundestag, the foreign minister, Hans-Dietrich Genscher, leader of the FDP (Federal Democratic Party), declared in an interview with *Bild am Sonntag*, "The seal slaughter is cruel and cannot be justified, even on economic grounds. I feel solidarity with the many citizens of our country who object to the killing of seals."[81] The German magazine *Der Spiegel* observed wryly: "It is still a moot question whether the FDP faction in the Bundestag did more for the survival of the seals, or the seals did more for the survival of the FDP."[82]

In Germany, moreover, Doctor Traue explains, there were additional considerations. Germany is living through a trying period, socially and culturally. Nazis didn't simply disappear from Germany after the war; many retained positions of prestige and power. While this Nazi presence remained there could be little real discussion within Germany of what had taken place there during the 1930s and 1940s. It is only now, forty years later, after most of these men have died or are old enough to have lost their power, that the unspeakable is beginning to be spoken. A society under this kind of stress, says Traue, welcomed an issue on which to vent pent-up emotions.[83]

Germany has played a special role throughout the "seal wars." It was Peter Lust, a witness to the horror of the concentration camps in 1945, who first fired Europe's outrage against the seal hunt with his article "Murder Island." One of the first Europeans to respond to the call of Lust's articles was Doctor Bernhard Grzimek, "the high priest of Conservation," who showed the Artek film on his German television show. Grzimek in fact admitted, "It is always a weak platform to fight cruelty to animals in other parts of the world from a country which had allowed 6 million Jews to be killed most cruelly and had invaded Eastern countries where another 20 million people have been destroyed."[84]

Incidentally, Grzimek sent an inspector to Newfoundland after the Canadian quotas and regulations were initiated in 1972 and announced: "We have no more complaints, everything was all right."[85] Grzimek now says that the seals are not endangered, and he has distanced himself from the anti-sealing movement he helped to launch. His recent pronouncements, however, have been noticeably less well publicized than the earlier ones.

In the campaign for the EEC ban on white-coat pelts Germany was the leader, and threatened to act unilaterally if the EEC failed to reach agreement. This was a powerful threat, as Germany was the main market for sealskins.[86]

There is another reason to divert German attention and emotions to "safe" issues, according to Doctor Traue. Germans today feel themselves to be very much on the firing line in the nuclear buildup between east and west. This, too, explains the strong appeal of a movement to "end the suffering." A decade ago German students were concerned politically, protesting American involvement in Vietnam or increasing militarism in the world; today young Germans prefer to worry about baby seals.

Other factors affecting the German protest movement are general to western society: increasing urbanization and reduced contact with nature, although here, too, West Germany is an extreme case of the compartmentalization of life functions. Babies are born in one wing of a hospital; old people die in another. People no longer see life begin or end, says Doctor Traue. Old people are hidden away in special homes, the handicapped in others. Only certain parts of the life cycle are acceptable and, therefore, made visible. As a result, when death (or birth, for that matter) is shown on television, it is shocking to people brought up in a sterilized, homogenized, climate-controlled environment. Only one or two generations ago most people were brought up on farms or had relatives who were. Today we are seeing the first generations to have had no contact with the land, with animals, with raising and harvesting their own food. While part of this generation has felt this to be a loss and tries to go "back to the land," most have chosen to lash out instead at those who still live close to nature: "Possessed, as it were, by some archetypal rage at his own exclusion from the Garden of Paradise, by some torturing remembrance of that disgrace, we have scoured the earth for vestiges of Eden and laid them waste wherever we have found them."[87]

Finally, perhaps it is not entirely coincidental that a vast movement has sprung up against killing baby seals (which, as Doctor Traue has explained, with their round bodies, short limbs and large, predominant eyes, are virtually an archetype for the infant) precisely at a time when abortion has become such a widespread dilemma in our society.[88] Even those who support the right to abort often feel obliged to justify this by arguing that the fetus is "not really alive" or "not really human," rather than acknowledging that we can choose, at times, to take life. It is not impossible that a certain feeling of guilt about widespread abortion (and even contraception) has played some part in the campaigns to "save the baby seals."[89]

And, since much has been made of the "grief" of the mother seals (and the maternal feelings of human females who have supported the protests), it should be noted in passing that although harp seals live about thirty-five years (about as long as humans did until rather recently in their development) mother seals nurse their pups for only ten days to two weeks. A few days later, if the hunters arrive or not, the female harp seals mate (although actual conception will take place only when they are again out at sea, a remarkable adaptation to ensure that the new pups will not be born too early). The females slip into the water and don't concern themselves with their offspring again. This relationship can hardly be compared to the bonding – of twenty or more years – that takes place between humans and their young.

THE PEOPLE: NEWFOUNDLAND FISHERMEN AND INUIT HUNTERS

Newfoundland

For politicians in Europe and America the seal hunt was at times little more than a game of media management and opinion polls, but the decisions that resulted had very real effects on the people who live in

Newfoundland and the Canadian Arctic. Sealing goes back some four hundred years in Newfoundland, but only recently have modern methods and higher world prices allowed fishermen to look forward to a standard of living approaching that of the rest of the western world.

Many invested their profits from sealing as down payments on better, safer fishing boats – long liners that cost anywhere from $300,000 to $500,000. Some of those boats have been repossessed by the banks, as a result of sealing-industry losses after the EEC ban on whitecoats. Only 60,000 pelts were sold in 1983, down from 186,000 the year before, but fishermen had spent anywhere from $40,000 to $50,000 to reinforce their vessels for ice conditions.

The anti-sealing groups like to pretend that the seal industry had little economic importance, as most sealers made relatively small amounts of money. But Mark Small, a fisherman and a landsman sealer and president of the newly formed Canadian Sealers' Association, doesn't agree:

> Because thousands of small-boat people go out and kill seals every year, and whether it's a thousand dollars or two thousand, it means a lot to people that only make five or six thousand in a year. So if you make a thousand on seals, it means a lot. To a man probably who makes fifty or sixty thousand a year that doesn't mean much, but to me and to other fishermen, it means a lot.[90]

Traditionally, sealing and fishing have been complementary in Newfoundland. In bad years, one compensates for the other to some extent. Seal money would come after a long winter without fishing. The money was used to pay off debts or fit out fishing boats for the new season, and the fresh meat was a benefit. Often merchants would advance supplies and gear needed to ready the boats against money from sealskins in the spring. Now, without a market for sealskins, credit has been cut off.

To make things worse, after a spring without money from sealskins, 1983 was one of the worst summer fishing seasons Mark Small can remember. All along the rugged northeast coast of Newfoundland, the packing plants were closed because there was simply not enough fish. Some blamed the big foreign fishing trawlers. Some claimed the seal populations were getting too large:

> Scientists tell us that the cod stocks are coming back, but the fishermen don't see it that way because every year it's harder for us to get any cod. And turbot was a big thing here, and that's just about gone, the turbot fishery. And I've been out and seen seals come up with the turbot in the winter time, and we took eleven turbot out of one seal. . . .

This summer I went up to Labrador because there was just no fish on this part of the coast. . . . And we went so far that there was a lot of seals around. And they were competing with me for the codfish . . . so what has happened, if the seals are not culled and if they're allowed to increase like they've been increasing this past four or five years, then they'll be competing with me for the fishery . . . so I think somewhere down the road, the seals are going to have to be culled out.[91]

Scientists believe that, by 1983, seals were eating as much fish as the total catch by fishermen of all nations in the northwest Atlantic. With the reduced hunts in 1983 and 1984, the seal herds are increasing rapidly and their consumption will increase.

But is it possible that Newfoundland people have become insensitive to the animals they exploit, as the animal-rights advocates argue? That they can no longer be trusted to look out for the survival of the seals? For the protest groups, sealers epitomize the most barbaric and cruel tendencies of mankind. According to Bernhard Grzimek's *Animal Life Encyclopedia*, published in 1972, harp seals are "skinned alive" and "literally tortured," and their babies "slain in a gruesome manner," by "generally inexperienced, unemployed people who are recruited for a few days for the hunting season."[92] It is true that fishermen are "unemployed" through the winter, which is why the sealing season is so welcome. They are, however, hardly "inexperienced." In pronouncements such as this, it is the protesters who show appalling insensitivity.

But have the sealers lost their feeling for nature? Is it true they have no regard for the animals they hunt?

No, no, no. No, you won't find that. I mean, I've been sealing now for ten or fifteen years, and we go out sealing and there's hundreds of birds, sea birds around all the time, but we never take up our gun and shoot a bird. And we kill seals because we feel it's part of our livelihood, we've done it for years, and I would be the first one to say no, you know – let's not kill the seals – if I knew they were endangered. But from my experience, the seals are not endangered, and the population is increasing. You go out sealing, and you travel for miles some days, and there's only herds of seals on the ice, you know. So if I knew that they were on the decrease, I would be one of the first to say, okay, let's call a halt to it until the population gets up again, because I need the seals, and my boys are going to need them if they go to the fishing boats, so it would be pretty foolish to go out and endanger the species.[93]

A party of hunters patiently waits for seals.

A nitsiaviniik (baby ringed seal) taken by Inuit hunters—one of only forty or fifty taken in 1978—near Clyde River, Northwest Territories.

butchering a beluga whale.

A bearded seal being skinned for "rope" at Lake Harbour, Baffin Island. The meat is also used for food.

An Inuit woman and her child at a summer camp surrounded by an array of food.

The remains of a seal carcass inside an Inuit tent.

LYNN WHIDDEN

Children play in the recently relocated Cree community of Chisasibi, Quebec, 1982.

Preparing ringed sealskins.

GEORGE WENZEL, McGILL CENTRE FOR NORTHERN STUDIES AND RESEARCH

The Arctic Inuit

It is common, in the ecology movement, to compare the ideal attitude toward nature being proposed to the reverence with which native people in North America traditionally regarded their environment. So it's not surprising that the effect that the destruction of the sealskin market has had on the Inuit people of the Arctic is something animal-rights advocates prefer not to be reminded of. Greenpeace and others try to get around this dilemma by claiming that it is the international commercial fur markets they're after, not subsistence hunters – native people. But can a line be drawn between the two?

George Wenzel is an anthropologist and research associate at the Centre for Northern Studies at McGill University; he has hunted with Arctic Inuit for the past twelve years. He objects to the decision by animal-rights groups to attack groups who are "about as low as you can go on the socioeconomic scale in Canada, groups who have virtually no power to resist this type of international movement."[94] Newfoundland fishermen and Inuit hunters are being forced to give up a vital component of their local resource system:

> Some complaints by people in the south come from the fact that Inuit no longer engage in hunting for subsistence alone, but also for commercial purposes by the selling of sealskins . . . [but] subsistence has to encompass cash. Money has become as much a resource as any living animal in the north, and to be deprived of that in a time when all your equipment requires money – the capitalization of a hunter runs roughly ten thousand dollars a year – and to be deprived of local access to money means that . . . they have to trade hunting time to earn money away from the community, away from their families, and so forth, in order to come back and squeeze as much hunting as they need to do into much less time. Time has become a currency that was not there before, and it's being imposed directly from the outside. The whole idea of choice – do I want to work in a mine, do I want to work on an oil rig, do I want to be an office worker, do I want to be a full-time hunter – is being lost, because that hunter option, for instance, is no longer there . . . or will not be there in the near future.[95]

Ironically, it was higher prices for sealskins, in the early 1960s, that allowed many Inuit to modernize their hunting techniques, investing profits in better rifles, snowmobiles and power boats. These made life easier, but the hunter was suddenly dependent for his maintenance on much higher levels of cash income. Ringed sealskins, the main Inuit harvest, sold for $1.50 in Baffin Island in 1955. By 1963 the price rose to $12.25, as a result of better processing techniques and therefore increased use of seals to make garments. Young ringed-seal pelts rose from $4.00 to $17.50 during the same period.

By the spring of 1967, after the Artek film and Peter Lust's book, the sealskin market in Switzerland was down to five per cent of its former level, and sales in West Germany were off fifty per cent. Ironically, it was the adult ringed seals hunted by native Inuit that suffered the most drastic decline, because white-coat pelts were often dyed before marketing and were not easily identifiable to the public as seal. By the summer of 1967, most buyers refused to purchase ringed-seal skins at any price, although the Hudson's Bay Company artificially stabilized the market at $2.50 a pelt ($2.00 to $4.00 below cost) because of the hardship the collapse of the market would bring to northern areas. Higher levels of mechanization meant that, by 1967, the cost of harvesting a sealskin had risen from $4.50 to $6.00 per skin (for gasoline, motor maintenance, ammunition and so on).[96]

Prices for sealskins rose somewhat after 1969, but following the rowdy 1976 and 1977 protest campaigns, the bottom again fell out of the market for Inuit furs. Ringed-seal pelts sold for $14 at Clyde River in 1974; by August 1977 they fetched $10, by November 1977, about $1. Costs of equipment and supplies had risen fifty per cent from 1972 levels, and Inuit hunters were again caught in a situation that was very serious, as it was sealskin money that paid the expenses for other subsistence-hunting activities.

Hunting has an obvious economic value to people who still take more than seventy per cent of their food from the land. But anthropologist George Wenzel believes it has still more profound importance in a society where virtually all men, and some women, hunt at least part of the time, and in which the people identify themselves as hunters. Hunting defines the relationship of the Inuit to their environment, and is the vehicle of communication between the generations. A boy knows what to do when he faces his first polar bear because he's learned from older people, as George Wenzel explains:

> There is a constant flow of information about animals and the land, moving through the society, from older generations to younger generations. ... The idea that man and animal share the same environment means that you look at an animal the way you would approach a human being – as an entity that deserves respect, and has to be treated in certain ways, and is not open to misuse – and this means that you have to be in constant contact with an animal or with a species.

This touches on the central contradiction of the animal-rights groups' position. Inuit and other hunting people study and respect animals because their lives literally depend on them. It is when we are no longer dependent on our environment, or think we're not, that contact is lost and, with it, respect for other life. George Wenzel points out that, in a culture that identifies itself as part of the natural world, the problem of morally justifying killing animals takes on a very different perspective than in the cities down south:

It's not seen as a problem at all; it's seen as a natural relationship. They all occupy the same landscape, whether on the sea or the sea ice or the land. They were all put there to interact. In fact, the animals give themselves to people. To not take an animal when you need it would be in a sense a misuse of that animal. The Inuit talk about this in regard to certain game-management policies. The problem of only hunting a certain number of animals . . . means that the surplus of animals that's been created by the game managers will leave an area, because they're not being used . . . at least, this is the way people see the problem, Inuit people.

The Inuit understanding of not wasting animal "gifts" has received some scientific support. Findings indicate that wildlife populations respond to higher levels of predation by producing a greater number of offspring or by better caring for those that they have. The NAFO study of harp seals, for example, observed that as a result of overexploitation of the herds through the 1950s, fertility rates appeared to have risen. By contrast, if too few animals are hunted, overcrowding or difficulty in finding food will cause higher mortality rates, and the animals whose gifts have been refused will indeed "leave." The more scientists learn about hunting people, the more it is known how sophisticated their interactions with their prey and with their environment actually are. George Wenzel explains how the sealing protests, with their disastrous effect on the sealskin market, have broken this relationship:

It certainly has had an economic impact, in the sense that seals were what one might call a bread-and-butter species, that is, the animal that you can go out in an evening and hunt and perhaps get $16 for the skin as well as the food. That's your gas money to go hunt another species that may not produce money. That certainly has had an impact. I think a more important impact is the idea of disrupting this interdependence that Inuit see existing between themselves and the animals who are occupying the north.

And even beyond that is the whole idea of the rights of native people, a major question here in Canada, one in which outsiders have criticized the Canadian government for treating Inuit and other native peoples in a colonial fashion. And now Inuits see certain individuals and groups from outside Canada, as well as in some cases inside, essentially taking away any meaning to these rights. If they can't hunt – and this is how they define their self-image – then what's the point of all this talk about native rights, of aboriginal rights and title?

The destruction of the sealskin market has brought hardship to the Arctic. Many people had too little stove oil through the winter; without gasoline for motorboats and snowmobiles there is less fresh meat, more dependence on government assistance, and the malnutrition that store-bought food brings to native peoples. As Hugh Brody has observed, "poverty," as long as there is plenty of meat on the table, is not poverty at all.

For the Inuit, the wrecking of the sealskin market means more than just economic distress. Ironically, the animal-rights movement may succeed in doing what more than thirty years of government and corporate manipulation had as yet failed to do: destroy the last vestiges of the traditional aboriginal way of life in the north. Animal-rights advocates may justify the dislocations their actions cause to the lives of others by claiming to act in the name of a revolutionary new world view. But from the Inuit point of view, George Wenzel says, it looks a lot like something they've seen before:

> As one Greenlander put it very nicely, what Canadian and Greenland Inuit are being faced with is a new form of imperialism from Europe. In the eighteenth and nineteenth centuries, a highly colonial, certainly mercantile, type of imperialism was imposed on all native people in North America, and particularly Inuit. From the Inuk's point of view today, there's this reversal: don't do what we wanted you to do, don't trade furs, don't hunt animals, don't do what you did traditionally and what has become your tradition because of contact with us. Change again. This is, to many Inuit, just a new form of imperialism.

THE 1984 IFAW "FISH BOYCOTT"

"Canadian Fishermen Kill Baby Seals – Don't Buy Canadian Fish!"

In October 1983, the EEC implemented its official ban on the import of white-coat sealskins. The ban gave the protests against sealing an official stamp of approval, which the animal-rights groups lost no time in exploiting. Meanwhile, the confusion over the definition of when a baby seal is a baby seal provided Greenpeace and the IFAW with an opening to charge that "the slaughter continues" and to ask for further contributions from their loyal membership to end the hunt "once and for all."

"KISS THIS BABY GOODBYE!" announced "Save the Seals: The 1983/84 Greenpeace Campaign" newsletter. Unabashed, the letter quotes the Quaker principle of "bearing witness," and declares that the goal of Greenpeace is to "obstruct a wrong without offering personal violence to its perpetrators . . . our greatest strength must be life itself, and the commitment to direct our own lives to protect others."[97]

At the end of 1983, Greenpeace coordinated a massive and successful card-mailing campaign to force Rieber Incorporated of Norway to agree not to buy Newfoundland white-coat pelts in 1984.[98] (Ironically, there may be some long-term positive benefits. Forced by Rieber's decision to search for alternative markets, perhaps in the far east, the newly formed Canadian Sealers' Association may succeed in taking control of its own industry, thereby putting an end to one Greenpeace argument, that the sealers are merely pawns of the big processing companies.)

A few weeks after the EEC confirmed its ban on white-coat imports, the IFAW launched a new campaign. In November 1983, newspaper advertisements appeared in England: "DON'T BUY CANADIAN FISH." The argument was that since fishermen made more money from fish than from seals, they could be pressured into abandoning sealing to save the fishing industry. In fact, the campaign had the effect of driving a wedge between sealers, and the fishermen's unions and fish-packing companies. The $100 million British market for Canadian fish is primarily for tinned salmon, which is fished by west-coast fishermen who don't seal.

At the end of April 1983, Stephen Best, then Canadian coordinator of the IFAW, contacted the Native Brotherhood of British Columbia, an Indian association, many of whose members are salmon fishermen. Best wrote that the IFAW fish boycott was "intended to cause as much serious social and economic hardships on the numerous families dependent on the BC salmon industry as possible . . . that is why economic boycotts are called."

Best warned that once British importers turned to new suppliers, probably Alaskan:

> The BC industry will have great difficulty, if and when the boycott is lifted, renewing their traditional relationships with their UK customers. . . . It is quite possible, and indeed likely, that the BC salmon industry will never again enjoy its present market position in the UK and other EEC countries.
>
> I am sure that the Liberal government and the Canadian Sealers' Association appreciate your rather significant sacrifice in support of their cause and that when you need them they will, as has always been the case, be right there with you – all the way.[99]

Although he felt that the IFAW was justified in launching a campaign against an industry that supported thousands of people living in areas where there was no possibility of alternative employment, Best took offense when his victims protested:

> ... I am deeply angered by your references to the "genocide" of your people by organizations and individuals who are trying to change the policies of the Department of Fisheries and Oceans. They are not only an uncalled for perversion but also a sickeningly demeaning insult to the integrity of your own people. . . .[100]

The executive director of the Native Brotherhood of British Columbia, Jean Rivard, responded in a letter dated May 25, 1983. He condemned the IFAW strategy, which would create "much social and economic havoc on Indian and non-Indian families, whose livelihood depends on the resources of the sea." Rivard observed that Indians had used these resources "since time immemorial," that the sea provided the livelihood of about half of British Columbia Indian families and that the right to continue to do so was at the very center of the Indian fight "for the recognition of Aboriginal rights and title." He pointed out that his group had seen no indication that the east-coast harp seals were endangered, and therefore saw no reason for anyone to deny others the right to continue their traditional lifestyle:

> ... Mr. Best, while you were upset over our remarks about genocide, we ask you, what is the difference in the annihilation of a people's social, economic, and cultural base, as opposed to doing it physically? Doesn't the destruction of a people's way of life, although slower and more painful, obtain the same results? . . . Why do you want to get your organization into the same pork barrel that discriminates against Indian people? . . . Better still, Mr. Best, why do it at all?[101]

From the new IFAW British "save-the-seals" campaign headquarters at Tubwell House in Sussex, England, four and a half million "information packages" went out to British households. In each was an ominous black folder, lettered in white: "CAUTION: The photos enclosed show scenes of Canadian fishermen killing baby seals. You will find them extremely disturbing." Inside were five small color photographs of men killing white-coat seals – not a pretty sight, certainly: a spike at the end of a bat is driven into the head of a fluffy white animal. Splashes of crimson blot the clean white fur and snow. In one photo, a large adult harp seal, with dark and pale markings not unlike those of certain breeds of cattle, stands protectively over a dead pup, showing her teeth.

"These shocking photos," says the text, "were taken by Brian Davies, executive director of IFAW.... IFAW has launched a campaign to boycott Canadian fish products until the torment that seals like these are suffering is ended for ever."

We don't see the faces of the men killing the seals. We don't see their families or their villages. They are dark figures, in one photo only a silhouette, with the outline of the hakapik dark against the white snow.

Of course, scenes from an abattoir would look even more gruesome. Nor would there be the fresh clean backdrop of snow and ice, and the animals wouldn't appear to be so peaceful. For although Brian Davies' photos aren't pretty, they do appear to confirm that the animals are killed quickly, a task made easier by the young seals' instinctive "deep-dive reflex":

> The officers that were there with me demonstrated that they could walk up to any white coat, put their hand on his forehead, and he would go into the deep-diving reflex. That was something I had never heard of. The reflex that the animal gets just before he hits the water. He expels his breath instead of holding his breath, and his heart slows down to about twelve beats a minute. Well, if he's still on the ice, you touch his head, and he goes into that reflex, you can smash him right there and he won't see it coming.[102]

Janice Henke, who wrote this passage, makes the interesting observation that because the Department of Fisheries is wary of protesters, they have not explained many aspects of the hunt to the public, with the result that most people never learn these important details of seal behavior. Henke points out that in pictures of people posing near baby seals, the animal is actually in its deep-dive reflex:

> A person who didn't know this, however, would say that the pup was smiling, since there seems to be a grin on the animal's face and his eyes are squinted. It looks like a contented thing, but that person has about a minute before the animal will come to and scratch the hell out of them.

Seals also have a physiological "swim reflex," which causes their bodies to wriggle even after they've been killed (much like a decapitated chicken will "run" for a moment). This is probably the source of stories about seals "skinned alive." None of this is explained in the IFAW mail-outs.[103]

The IFAW fish boycott was intended to put the screws to the Canadian fishermen's unions, and especially the packing plants. Canada's fish exports total some $1.6 billion each year, and as the fish boycott gained publicity, some of the packing companies panicked and called on the fisheries minister to cancel the seal hunt.[104] The fisheries minister, Pierre DeBané, finally lost patience with the animal-rights protesters. He vowed that Ottawa would not "cave in" or end the hunt, and he criticized the protesters in strong terms that prompted IFAW to launch a civil suit against him.[105]

Interviewed on British television, Brian Davies sloughed off the fisheries minister's charges: "In fact, when I hear that I feel as Churchill must have felt during the war when Hitler always called him a despicable criminal. When the man who defends the seal hunt is calling people like us despicable criminals, we're doing a job, saving seals."

The fish boycott was "appealing to the British housewife to do something that the rest of the world hadn't been able to do," Davies explained: "British mums can save the baby seals by checking any can or container of fish. If it's got 'Made in Canada' on it, put it back on the shelf."[106]

Two giant British grocery chains, Sainsbury's and Tesco, hoping no doubt to protect sales of stock on hand, announced that they would not reorder Canadian fish until the dispute was settled. One large importer, Findus, also said they would not reorder Canadian fish. (Sainsbury's and Findus both later announced that they disapproved of the boycott and would not allow it to influence their fish orders. Findus published newspaper advertisements stating that only quality determined their buying policies.)

Meanwhile, the IFAW began a computer-organized mailing to launch a similar boycott in the United States, where about eighty per cent of Canada's fish exports are sold. In particular, IFAW announced that they would put pressure on the major users, like McDonald's (the biggest single buyer of Canadian fish) and Burger King. With the letters went the familiar black "warning" pamphlet. Soon, said the letter, the "seal nurseries" on the Atlantic ice would be struck with "a night mare of terror . . . men will be back on the ice. The carnage of the infamous Canadian seal hunt will have started."

Referring to the newly formed Canadian Sealers' Association and its executive director, Kirk Smith, ex-career soldier and war-history aficionado, Davies wrote:

Smith and his gang . . . have the big battalions on their side. "The Canadian government has just agreed to pay a staggering $1 million to keep the baby killers in business. [But] . . . the seals have an even bigger battalion on their side. They have the IFAW (you and me) . . . truth . . . justice . . . and a cause that is right.[107]

Just when the IFAW machine was looking most terrible, however, cracks began to appear in the foundation. In the fall of 1983, after a quarrel with Brian Davies, Canadian coordinator Stephen Best resigned.[108] Meanwhile, the Australian wing disassociated itself from IFAW in July 1983. On Australian radio, on January 26, 1984, the co-ordinator of IFAW Australia, Sue Arnold, charged that Davies had used their photographs and research to put together a newsletter about kangaroo slaughter, which included an ominous black "warning" packet of photographs like that used for the fish boycott:

> Now to the best of our knowledge we believe they raised a sum of $3 million, and we've been unable to get them to account for this money. Not one cent of it has been returned to our office, and we can't get them to account for how they spent it overseas. . . .

Arnold claimed that following criticism by her group Davies circulated a newsletter, in January 1984, "trying to encourage Australian members to donate funds – these are our members – directly to the USA, and he claimed we don't exist. . . . He wants to see Australians send their money overseas for issues. He knows he doesn't have to account for them, and I think it's a scandal that a giant animal-welfare group is taking this action."

Sue Arnold concluded her interview:

> Look, I think the bottom line is that when people give money for charities, they should have receipts, it should have to be accounted for, they should know where it's going.[109]

Meanwhile, as the fish boycott gathered steam in Britain, questions began to be asked there, too. On 17 February, 1984, BBC Radio 4 reported that Tesco, Safeway and Sainsbury's grocery chains had announced they would not reorder Canadian fish until the situation was clarified. Their decision was the result of "tens of thousands" of post-cards. The announcer reported:

> Now, the RSPCA tells us that they're intrigued by this campaign, and that although huge sums of money are clearly involved, they're not certain where it all goes; in fact they've had a lot of calls from people who have had no acknowledgment of their donation. The World Society for the Protection of Animals say that they've also had calls about donations that haven't been acknowledged, and we on "You and Yours" have had queries, too. Now, as we've discovered, it is not easy to find out exactly what the International Fund for Animal Welfare does with its money. It is not registered in this country as a charity, and so doesn't have to file any accounts. It has been reported that the income of the fund is about a million pounds a year in this country, which is a lot of money and a lot of donations, so where does it go?[110]

Brian Davies was asked why IFAW didn't register as a charity in Britain. He replied that it was in order to be free to undertake direct political action:

> ... Whatever it is we want to do, whether it's to save dogs from suffering in South Korea or the Philippines, or to save seals in Canada, it's almost always a government we're dealing with.[111]

Mr. Tim Yeo, a Conservative member of parliament in the United Kingdom, was concerned about the nonaccountability of charities. He stated that charities wishing to undertake political campaigning have only to set up a parallel company through which they conduct their political activities, for which there are plenty of precedents. "And so, the desire to conduct political activities is not a reason for not registering as a charity."[112]

Davies claimed that IFAW's audited books were readily available for public inspection. (The newly formed British section had yet to conduct a full audit, but the United States organization's books were available.)[113]

In his interview on BBC Radio 4, Brian Davies was asked what happened to the one million pounds he said had been raised in Britain. Davies responded that three hundred sixty thousand had been used in a campaign against sealing:

> ... that's a significant part of the one million pounds or so that we would have raised in the United Kingdom. We have a team of people going to the seal hunt this coming March, we have another scientific team doing scientific work there. We have a campaign that will be funded in part from ... contributions made in the United Kingdom to rescue burros (or donkeys as you would call them here) in Death Valley, in the United States, where they are scheduled to be shot; some six thousand of them. We're cooperating with a group called the Fund For Animals and the United States government on that program. We have a researcher right now in the Antarctic – we're doing some work there that we hope will lead to some protection of the Antarctic, and so it goes on.

In the first six months of 1982, in fact, the IFAW had donated $15,000 to the Fund For Animals for the burros project. In total, $33,794 were listed for grants and allocations during that period, including about $4,000 each to Doctors D.M. Lavigne and Sidney Holt and another $1,815 for Doctor Richard Ryder (who published the animal-rights book *Victims of Science*, about abuses to laboratory animals), all for seal research. A total of $705,960 was allocated for "monitoring the harp-seal hunt off the east coast of Canada during March" and "rescuing harp seals and set-up of nurseries for baby seals until of age."[114]

Concerning this last item, the Office of the Canadian Minister of Fisheries and Oceans has commented:

> While we have no way of determining the costs incurred by the IFAW in "monitoring" the seal hunt, it is safe to say that the costs for rescuing harp seals and set-up of nurseries in 1982 was zero dollars. No seals were "rescued" from the ice in 1982, nor were any seal-pup nurseries set up in 1982. There was a small-scale "nursery" set up in 1981, but this was not an IFAW operation, although DFO (the Department of Fisheries and Oceans) officials did "consult" with representatives from the IFAW. . . .[115]

According to a "Seal Rescue Report," written by Davies and mailed to membership of IFAW, the IFAW crew had gone to Prince Edward Island in response to a call from their Atlantic coordinator, Patricia Gray, who said that seals were being washed up on the beaches after a storm at sea:

> Late that night, an IFAW team was back at the Kirkwood Motor Hotel in Charlottetown, which had been our headquarters during the recent and successful protest of the 1981 seal hunt – an IFAW-led action, by the way, which saved some 16,000 seals from the hunters. . . .[116]

Eight seals, Davies writes, had been brought to a local farmhouse, but as caring for them was difficult and secrecy hard to maintain (it was illegal to move live seals from the beaches), a call was made to the fisheries department and a truce declared. Davies records that the fisheries officers, "whom we had considered our bitter enemies," were in fact very cooperative and flew in a veterinarian from Guelph University, Doctor J. Geraci, who was experienced in treating seals. Davies describes how the young seals were carefully tended, then finally, tearfully released: "an emotional moment . . . the fifteenth seal you and the IFAW team saved . . . Goodbye Flipper!"

Doctor Geraci has recorded a somewhat different version:

> . . . Paul Montreuil and I accompanied the fisheries officers to the Clarence Rose farm in Northlake. Thirteen seals were impounded there on a bed of Irish moss. Seven were beyond saving, and I euthanized them. The others were placed into a schedule of rehabilitation . . . any pup not healthy enough to be returned to the wild after a reasonable period of time (two to three weeks) was to have been euthanized by Doctor J. Hyman, a veterinarian associated with the IFAW. The entire program was firmly under the direction of the Department of Fisheries and that fact was accepted by all parties concerned.

On the afternoon of 1 April, I accompanied the fisheries officers to a private game farm where three pitifully starving pups were enclosed within a wire compound. I euthanized them immediately. Two robust, healthy, fully weaned hooded seals, also impounded within a wire enclosure, were released and made their way to the sea with great haste. . . .

The outcome of the rehabilitation program is questionable. Having been involved in seal-stranding programs for ten years, I have come to accept the whole idea of rehabilitation as basically unsound. . . . Many of the seal pups that I examined . . . were emaciated, weak and dehydrated – some had scarcely been nursing for a few days before they came ashore. Under normal circumstances, I would have been inclined to euthanize all but the more robust pups. However, the emotional atmosphere surrounding the event suggested an alternative course of action. . . . By the time the program came to an end in May, twenty-four pups had been euthanized, and twenty-five pups were placed into the nursery program; of the latter, twelve died, and thirteen (nine harp seals and four hooded seals) were ultimately released.

The rehabilitation program was costly in terms of effort. Mr. and Mrs. Rose volunteered their farm, and her inexhaustible energy accommodated the many people involved with the program. (I have just learned that Mrs. Rose suffered a mild heart attack following the episode.) [". . . she loved the whole mission and would gladly do it all again should the seals ever need her," Davies wrote in his "Seal Rescue Report."]

I am principally concerned that the program may not have been in the interest of the seals. . . . Should a similar situation arise, I would recommend that all stranded pups not able to survive without assistance, be euthanized with the greatest possible haste. . . .[117]

A difference of interpretation is hardly unexpected under the circumstances. But are we dealing here merely with personal bias and face-saving on both sides, or with something more calculated? The seal "nursery" came on the heels of the 1981 Prince Edward Island seal-hunt protest, to which Davies refers so glowingly in his "Seal Rescue Report." The hunt became a debacle when weather conditions brought thousands of seals right in to the shores of the island, resulting in uncontrolled slaughter by hundreds of people who were not sealers. Realizing that the government sealing regulations could not be enforced under these conditions, fisheries officials quickly closed the beaches and forbade anyone from killing seals until the ice was carried out to sea again.

Afterwards, fisheries officers Stan Dudka and Jerry Conway walked into a restaurant for breakfast, where by chance they met Brian Davies.

"Well, I guess we won that round," Davies said gaily.

"Now wait a minute, Brian," said Dudka. "You know full well that we were the ones who closed that hunt."

"You know that," responded Davies, "and I know that . . . but the public's not going to know that."[118]

After an impressive start, the IFAW fish boycott appeared to falter. Of the major importers, only Tesco refused to order Canadian fish until the dispute was settled. (It was later learned that they didn't usually reorder in any case before the end of April.) Brian Davies flew back to England in March to bolster the campaign, and it was rumored he would return in time for the hunt with an unnamed member of the royal family. The plan, apparently, was to bring this personage to the ice incognito, involve him or her in an altercation with fishery officers and then dramatically reveal his or her identity.[119] Whether such a royal person was ready to take part in Davies' scheme remains unknown. Before the hunt began, an IFAW helicopter became stranded on the Magdalen Islands. After twenty years of harrassment by the IFAW, the islanders' patience ran out, and with tempers boiling because of the widely publicized fish boycott, a crowd overpowered the RCMP guard and wrecked the aircraft during the night. Police doubted if they would get very far in their investigation. "They're a very tight community here," a local policeman commented.[120]

The loss of the helicopter was a serious blow to the 1984 IFAW seal-hunt campaign. Apart from transporting the mysterious royal personage, there had been plans to use the helicopter to bring United States congressmen onto the ice. In the United States, too, there were indications that the fish boycott was not developing as planned. In March it was decided to picket nine McDonald's outlets in the Boston area to protest that company's refusal to stop buying Canadian fish. Only two outlets were picketed, and Prince Edward Island IFAW members were flown in to bolster the effort.

More significantly, the boycott had opened fissures within the IFAW's inner caucus. Apart from Stephen Best's departure, two other top Canadian IFAW officials were gone by the time the hunt began. One of them was Patricia Gray, coordinator of the Atlantic region, who had often been mentioned in IFAW literature for her brave stand in the midst of the sealers' camp. In September 1983 she quit, unable to accept the plan to attack Canada's fishing industry:

It's particularly unfortunate that the boycott is being launched at the very time when the killing of baby seals has almost come to an end as a result of the Common Market ban . . . we pretty well have it

114

in the bag . . . this is a ridiculous time to launch a boycott. They [the IFAW leadership] don't understand the position in the Maritimes. How can you support an organization that wants to put people out of work?[121]

The other official to resign was Fred Bearisto, a member of the board of directors (there were three directors, including Davies). Mr. Bearisto had been on the board of directors of the New Brunswick SPCA when the "save-the-seals" fund was started in 1964. When Davies set up IFAW Bearisto became founding president, and the Fredericton businessman's practical experience helped guide the fund through its first years. Fred Bearisto still admires the work of IFAW, and he praises Brian Davies for his ceaseless fight against the seal hunt. But the plan to punish third parties, non-sealing and even west-coast fishermen, was too much for the man who had been IFAW's first president.[122]

In the twenty years between the Artek film and the fish boycott, the baby-seal campaign carried animal-rights groups from the concern of a fringe minority to international notoriety. In the process, both traditional animal-welfare groups and ecology groups shifted toward animal-rights positions. Although animal-rights groups are concerned with a wide range of issues, including scientific and medical research, factory farming and meat eating, it is only the baby-seal story that has, to date, attracted such wide public response.

To a great extent, no doubt, this is explained by the media appeal of the fluffy white baby seal. Skilful manipulation of media has allowed groups like IFAW and Greenpeace to carry their message to a large audience. In the end, however, it is highly doubtful if the unprecedented media exposure of the harp-seal hunt in the northwest Atlantic has really contributed to a greater public understanding of the issues. Perhaps the contrary. Whatever the result, animal-rights advocates were preparing to bring the tactics and influence they have gained through the "seal wars" to bear in a new confrontation.[123]

6

Traps and Trapping

Whole species . . . transformed and degraded by the way – boiled down like the beaver into a hat, or like the seal, into a lady's jacket.
   – Henry Salt (*Animals' Rights*)

The organized opposition to fur trapping began in 1925 when American adventurer and spy-turned-diplomat Edward Breck founded the National Anti-Steel Trap League – after an encounter with a trapped bear during a visit to Nova Scotia.[1] The League was established at the peak of the "roaring twenties," when both men and women wore long-hair fur coats: beaver, raccoon and fox. Fur prices, which were high, tempted many to try their hand at trapping. There were virtually no controls or management policies, and between 1919 and 1921, 108 million pelts were auctioned in the United States, including some 23 million tiny moleskins from Europe.[2]

The great depression and World War Two swept away much of the market for long-hair furs, and by the 1950s wild fur accounted for barely twenty-five per cent of North American sales. Most furs were either ranched or farmed: the market had been reduced to more "conservative" furs – mink and "Persian lamb." (Actually these are Karakul lambs, originally from Afghanistan and now extensively raised in southwest Africa.) Ranched mink accounted for two-thirds of retail sales in Canada by 1949. The reduced market for wild furs gave the animal populations a chance to recover, and the decreased importance of fur trapping may explain why, in 1959, the National Anti-Steel Trap League was given the more general name "Defenders of Wildlife."[3]

The value of the fur trade dropped in the postwar years for ranched as well as wild furs: from a total of $521 million retail sales as late as 1943, to just $200 million by 1953, in the United States. To expand beyond the relatively limited market for expensive furs like mink and Persian, the American fur industry made a concerted attempt in the 1960s to stimulate demand for long-hair wild furs again. The furs were reintroduced as "fun furs" and received a fashion boost when Jackie Kennedy bought a leopard-skin coat in 1962. Ironically, this was

116

the same year Rachel Carson's *Silent Spring* appeared, heralding the rise of the new ecology movement.

Through the 1960s there developed a growing awareness of the threat to wildlife, especially in jungle areas, because of the spread of human settlement, which destroyed wildlife habitat. In 1969, the United States Congress passed an Endangered Species Act. This was strengthened a year later by the New York State Mason Act, which banned the sale of thirteen species of animal pelts, including spotted cats, mountain lions, vicunas, polar bears and tigers.[4] Most United States furs are manufactured into garments in New York.

Concern about endangered species in the United States coincided with protests in Canada over the seal hunt, which increased after 1965. In November 1969, when Brian Davies founded the International Fund for the Welfare of Animals, a group called Friends of Animals organized some San Francisco socialites to pledge to wear furs from endangered species no longer. In the spring of 1970 Alice Herrington, president and founder of Friends of Animals, went to observe the seal hunt as the guest of Brian Davies. With them was Jean Le Fevre, of Beauty Without Cruelty, a group founded by Muriel, Lady Dowding, widow of Air-Chief Marshal Lord Dowding, hero of the Battle of Britain and a leader of the British anti-vivisection movement.

Another group to coalesce out of the protest about spotted cats was the Fund For Animals, formed in 1967. Founder Cleveland Amory, in his best-seller *Mankind? Our Incredible War on Wildlife*, recounts that the group's first major campaign was sparked by a visit from an advertising agent representing the E.F. Timme Company, a "fake-fur" manufacturer. Timme was prepared to give two hundred dollars and a fake-fur coat to every "socialite" the fund could find who would publicly denounce the wearing of furs from endangered species. Amory suggested that Timme up the ante to two thousand dollars and proposed the names of five well-known actresses who would decry the wearing of any wild fur. As the actresses were on the fund board of directors, says Amory, they could be counted on to hand over their cash to the fund.[5]

It is curious that Amory, who rarely misses an opportunity to label even scientists as fur-industry "lackies," shows no embarrassment about engaging his own group in the service of the Timme Company. "It's so wrong for a man to think the biggest thing he can do for his wife is buy her a fur coat for Christmas," gushed Doris Day in the advertisements prepared for the campaign. "Buy her a fake fur. They're so beautiful, so lovely, so warm, so pretty to look at. . . ."

Amanda Blake asked women "who know about our vanishing wildlife" yet still want a fur "how *they'd* like to be skinned?"[6] "Killing animals for vanity is a shame," said Amanda.

"Bravo for the women who wear fake furs," said Jane Meadows, giving Timme their two thousand dollars worth. "It's warmer and cheaper and everything else. And you are happy because you don't feel guilty in it. You don't feel like a murderer. . . ."

Mary Tyler Moore sounded less comfortable as a salesperson for Timme: "I have seen so many coats so much more attractive than fur – some fake fur, some fabric. It's in the design, not necessarily the fabric . . . I am aware that there are specific ecological problems, but for me all animals have a right to humane treatment."

Thus the Fund For Animals became the first animal-rights organization to take a page from the advertising world's book and use movie stars as instant authorities on ecology and animal welfare. Media was the message, the media personality's competence in the subject at hand was not.

Cleveland Amory again demonstrated his skilful use of the media in 1972. The Canadian Association for Humane Trapping (CAHT) produced a seven-minute film from footage shot by trapper Ed Cesar and sent a print to the Fund For Animals. The film was called "They Take So Long To Die," a line from an old National Anti-Steel Trap League poem. Amory passed it on to the CBS "Evening News," and on March 21, 1972 an estimated twenty million people across the United States watched animals being trapped by leghold traps.[7] Amory appeared on the program to demonstrate a Conibear trap, arguing that animals deserved at least, in simple decency, a quick death. (The Conibear trap, developed by British Columbia trapper Frank Conibear, was promoted as a humane, quick-kill trap. Subsequent tests have shown that it is not as consistent as was once believed, and groups like the Association for the Protection of Fur-bearing Animals no longer accept the Conibear as a humane trap.)

In his book, Amory gives top marks to the CAHT film for "the startling back-and-forths – on the one hand, an *haute-couture* fashion show with the aloof, nose-in-the-air models parading down the runway to *thé-dansant* music, on the other, pictures of the animals which made those very coats dying in leghold traps, accompanied by screeching music."[8]

Although billed as "filmed on the trapline," it was later revealed that many of the scenes in "They Take So Long To Die" were staged. Animals were trapped live in the wild, released in a compound and caught again in leghold traps where they could be filmed at leisure, sometimes against picturesque backdrops. CAHT made its film to pressure the Canadian government to investigate trapping, and when The Federal-Provincial Committee on Humane Trapping (FPCHT) was set up in September 1973, the film was withdrawn from circulation.

Many of Ed Cesar's scenes, however, were incorporated into

another short film, called "Canada's Shame," produced by the Vancouver-based Association for the Protection of Fur-bearing Animals (APFA). Lloyd Cook, then president of the Ontario Trappers Association, testified before the Canadian Parliamentary Standing Committee on Fisheries and Forestry on 24 February 1977:

The film called "Canada's Shame" does not relate to trapping in Canada today in any way. . . . The way in which leghold traps were used during the filming is ridiculous and an insult to experienced trappers . . . trappers do not trap rabbits, porcupines or mice at any time. . . .

In the first scene, where a muskrat is thrashing in the water, an experienced trapper could see that this animal has been struck directly behind the head in a vital spot which causes quick death. The thrashing that is seen is the same as that of a chicken with its head cut off.

The next scene, where a weasel goes into a cully, its tail goes straight up in the air. This indicates that this animal too died quickly. The scene of a trap being set on a pile of cedar boughs was one of the most ridiculous scenes in the film. No experienced trapper would waste his time making such a set. The weasel is biting at the trap and thrashing around with blood on the snow; it has been my experience when I have cut my hand that blood drops into the snow and never lies on top. I question the amount of blood that is around this trap. Trappers do not set traps in this manner. It is interesting to note that the coyote in the trap, which is a one-spring jump type, is in the trap backwards. When the spring of this trap is depressed, it jumps forward and is considered by trappers to be a trap that can only be used for animals coming one way. Further . . . this is considered to be an otter trap, to catch otter coming out of the water, and is used with a slide lock. . . . There are no traps being manufactured with teeth. . . .[9]

Cook concluded his testimony by denying that trappers were opposed to the development of more humane traps. He pointed out that when the Conibear trap was introduced, trappers across Canada took the trap into the field for testing and worked with the CAHT and the Ministry of Natural Resources of Ontario to suggest modifications that made the trap about thirty per cent more effective.

What is not shown in anti-trapping films is at least as important as what is. A recent film by Arthur Lamothe, for example, about the Montagnais Indians of Quebec, showed probably more blood than the protest films: in one scene, a caribou is killed and gutted. But everything is shown within the context of Montagnais life and culture; the object of the film is to introduce and explain a way of life, not to shock.

PAUL WAGNER, ENVIRONMENT CANADA

An Indian muskrat-trapping camp.

Muskrat taken in a Blake and Lamb trap.

RICHARD STARDOM

Inside an Indian trapper's camp.

Smoking muskrat meat for food near The Pas, Manitoba.

Testing a new muskrat trap.

By contrast, "Canada's Shame" begins with Canadian actor Bruno Gerussi standing before an impressive panorama of snow-covered mountains: "The woods have been tarnished, tainted and shamed," Gerussi intones. "And it makes you angry and ashamed when you are a civilized Canadian." Close-ups of animals in their pristine environment follow. Then a man comes crunching across the snow on snowshoes, cunningly concealing traps as he goes. The rest of the film shows animals from the first scenes being snapped up by traps set in the second.

The trapper is never shown as a complete person (a trick borrowed from advertising photography). His legs stride menacingly across the snow, "invading" the animals' world; his hands push open the treacherous steel jaws of his traps. But his culture – his family, his cabin, the context within which his trapping is situated – is never shown. His relationship to nature is never explained, although of course it is far closer and more intense than that of most urban dwellers who might be shocked by the film.

Equally important, the film never shows these same animals killing or being killed by other animals. Most prize fur bearers are, themselves, predators. Nor does the film show the fierce battles and cannibalism that can occur in a muskrat marsh, for example, when populations rise too high. Critics of trapping often argue that nature will regulate populations effectively without human intervention. Perhaps, but the process isn't necessarily less cruel:

> ... excess or misfit or strange adults may circulate about a marsh, finding and making trouble. They may have gashes around their rumps or tails bitten through. They may have bites into kidneys, bites into livers, intestines, or into any body parts that teeth can reach and penetrate. They may have to walk on elbows after having forelegs hamstrung. . . . A weaned young enters its home lodge and eats the hindquarters off a member of a new-born litter . . . a mother kills a couple of her own weaned young in driving them away before the birth of another litter. A mother may see a young muskrat swimming on the far side of the cleared space surrounding her lodge, swim out to it, and bite it to death with the utmost viciousness. . . . [10]

It may be argued that predators or muskrats in an overcrowded marsh have no choice but to kill. Humans, it is said, do have a choice. All animal populations produce more offspring than are needed to replace their own numbers. The excess must be eliminated one way or another. The central fallacy of the animal-rights groups' opposition to trapping is that they suggest death and suffering would be ended if trapping were banned. Nothing could be more false.

Life is cheap in an overpopulated muskrat marsh, but even noble beasts like tigers and polar bears will kill their own kind if they outgrow their habitat. In areas close to national parks in India tigers have been killing villagers and each other.[11] Polar bears in northern Manitoba are protected; they have also begun to kill each other. Employment for guides and outfitters is desperately needed in northern communities, but the government doesn't dare provoke animal-rights advocates by opening a limited polar-bear hunt, even though, according to wildlife biologists, such a hunt would have no detrimental effect on the bear population.

Suffering caused by hunting and trapping is visible; the alternatives are not. Animals weakened by overpopulation succumb more easily to rabies, sarcoptic mange, leptosprirosis, distemper and tularemia, which often result in long, agonizing deaths – but such death and suffering remain hidden in the woods.[12]

THE OHIO AMENDMENT AND THE MEDIA

In 1977, animal-rights organizers succeeded in adding a proposal to ban trapping to the ballot in the Ohio state elections. It was an important vote, not least because Ohio is the second-largest fur-producing state, after Louisiana. (Ohio produces mostly muskrat, raccoon and fox.) The proposed constitutional amendment read:

> No person shall use in any manner in the trapping of wild birds or quadrupeds any leghold trap in this state. No person shall use any trapping device in a manner which will cause continued, prolonged suffering to a wild bird or wild quadruped in this state.[13]

Defenders of the amendment claimed they were not trying to ban all trapping, but only the use of the leghold trap. Trappers responded that, since more than eighty-five per cent of North American wild furs are taken with leghold traps, the amendment was merely a cleverly worded attack on the whole fur industry. The problem is complex, because no ready alternative to the leghold trap suitable for all species has yet been developed. If quick killing is taken as the criterion for humane trapping, there is the difficulty that some species – coyote and foxes, for instance – simply won't walk into any trap head first. They are more likely to test a new situation with a paw first.[14]

Resistance to the proposed Ohio amendment was led by the Ohio Wildlife Legislative Fund (WLF), a group set up with seed money from the American Fur Industry and from Woodstream Corporation, the major trap manufacturer. Hunters, fishermen and trappers as well as labor unions were recruited into a fundraising and publicity drive.

Proponents of the amendment had been working for almost two years to prepare the public. Two months before the referendum, an opinion poll commissioned by the WLF showed that two-thirds of the electorate would support the ban. Support was strongest among urban, young (less than thirty-five) female voters. With this information in hand, the WLF launched an advertising campaign tailored to this part of the electorate. James Goodrich, campaign manager for the WLF, summed up the approach:

> In any selling campaign, the right messages have to do with benefits for people. We wildlife folks are accustomed to talking about benefits for wildlife. What is good for "the resource" is the vernacular. But raccoons and deer and muskrats don't vote . . . when you are determining the use of a 30-second TV commercial, or the standard 60-second radio spot, or a page of newspaper advertising, considerations other than the perfect balance of each separate message take precedence. You have to grab attention in a sea of hundreds of millions of dollars of other people's messages . . . or you are drowned out.[15]

Goodrich's campaign flooded the media in the final days before the vote, and when the votes were counted on November 8, sixty-three per cent had voted against the ban – a complete turnaround from the earlier poll. Animal-rights organizers were outraged. They quoted what they claimed were highly distorted and misleading WLF advertisements:

> "Your family may face a nightmare. . . . Wild animals, half-crazed with rabies, will attack pets, children, adults. For the sake of your family, vote NO!"

WLF advertisements stressed rats and rabies, animal-rights groups charged, even though most rat traps are killing devices and therefore would not have been banned. According to the Centers for Disease Control in Atlanta, no case of human rabies has ever been known to be caused by a rat bite. The WLF media blitz was timed for the last days of the campaign, so no rebuttal could be made, animal-rights groups charged.[16] Proponents of the ban were especially critical of a television spot produced by WLF in which tame laboratory rats climbed out of a drawer when a mother opened it to get cereal for her children; despite the absurdity of this advertisement, and its irrelevance to the trapping issue, it was apparently effective in swaying the uninformed, urban voters against a ban on traps.[17]

The animal-rights advocates had been beaten at their own game, media management. They claimed they had been "greatly outspent."[18] (James W. Goodrich of the WLF stated that each side spent more than a million dollars.) Brian Davies appealed to his membership to send more money. The IFAW had spent $650,000 in the Ohio campaign against the leghold trap.[19]

Proponents of the Ohio amendment claimed that they were opposed only to the leghold trap. Animal-rights groups have a record, however, of shifting their ground to suit the circumstances.[20] The protest in the 1960s against the use of spotted cats stressed the ecological problems of overexploitation and shrinking habitats. After a series of laws to control the international trade in endangered species, however, the cruelty of the leghold trap again came to the fore.

The Ohio referendum is disturbing because it showed how wildlife issues, far from raising the level of public knowledge about the problems at hand, can deteriorate to a battle of the advertising agencies.[21]

BRINGING THE TRAPPING DEBATE TO EUROPE: A REPEAT OF THE SEAL CAMPAIGN

The Canadian campaign against trapping is led by the Association for the Protection of Fur-bearing Animals (APFA), based in Vancouver, British Columbia. Largely because of AFPA pressure, British Columbia recently became the first Canadian province to partially ban the leghold trap. (However, some say that because wolves, coyotes, foxes and felines are exempted, and because the leghold trap may still be used as a drowning set for aquatic animals, the change is more symbolic than real.)

The executive director of APFA is George Clements, a quiet-spoken ex-school-principal who smiles easily and talks with passion against leghold traps. After the Second World War, he went to teach in a small, primarily Indian northern community. The day he arrived, he went for a walk in the forest and stepped into a trap. The first thought that flashed through his mind was that he'd stepped on a land mine. During the war, soldiers were taught to freeze if they stepped on a mine, to give everyone else time to get clear, for the mines were triggered to explode when you stepped off. ("Then you jumped as far as you could and hoped it would get only part of your leg."[22])

When he realized that he'd been caught by a trap, he was outraged. Like most people, he'd never seen a trap before. He pushed open the jaws and heaved it into the woods. During the next few days,

Clements and his wife, Bunty, found many traps near his school and threw them all into the river. Their crusade against the leghold trap had begun.

George Clements says he's against the leghold trap, not necessarily against all trapping. If more people knew how the leghold trap worked, he says, the outcry would be immediate. He likes to recount his version of how trappers kill the fur bearers they find in their traps: "Move in close and stun it with a stick, but be careful, don't pop the eyes. Then stand on the heart, stomping it to death. . . ."

Clements makes good use of the shock value of describing death to an audience of urban dwellers, who are used to seeing their meat wrapped up in Cellophane. What he fails to point out is that a description of any certified abattoir wouldn't be any prettier.

Pressure from CAHT and APFA led the Canadian government to set up the Federal-Provincial Committee on Humane Trapping (FPCHT) in 1973; but seven years and a million dollars later, nothing useful had come of it, Clements charges. FPCHT recommendations that a humane trap be capable of killing an animal within three minutes means that technically even the traditional leghold trap, which can and often does kill small animals, could be called "humane."

Clements' criticism of the work of the FPCHT is unfair. Before the FPCHT, virtually no attempt had been made anywhere to scientifically evaluate the stress actually suffered by animals in traps. The newly formed Fur Institute of Canada has now been mandated to build on the work of the FPCHT to establish standards for trapping systems for each species to insure that the most humane trapping methods possible will be used. One concrete result that has already come from FPCHT research and guidelines is the publication, in 1984, of a national standard for "Mechanically powered, trigger-activated, humane animal traps," developed by the Canadian General Standards Board (CGSB). This is the world's first standard in this area. One of the founders of CAHT, Neal Jotham, who is also executive director of the Canadian Federation of Humane Societies (CFHS), is a member of the CGSB technical committee that worked on defining the requirements for humane traps. A trap must be capable of "consistently striking and holding its target species between the back of the eyes and the fourth cervical vertebrae with the specified combination of impact momentum and clamping force." The detailed specifications for killing different species quickly and humanely were developed from the findings of FPCHT research. Neal Jotham also heads the Humane Trap Development Committee of the Fur Institute of Canada, which will refine and field-test new trap developments. The irony of the severe criticism to which Canada has been exposed recently over the use of traps, says Neal Jotham, is that Canada was the first country in the world to begin "serious scientific research and development of humane killing-type traps." Some of this research was begun as early as 1968 by the CFHS. And Canada is still the only country where such research is being conducted.[23]

Despite all this, George Clements claims that FPCHT was intended only "to keep the lid on public protest." The newly formed Fur Institute of Canada, he claims, is just more of the same. Frustration with the "slow progress" of the FPCHT, he says, led him to make the short film "Canada's Shame" in 1977. To date, however, he claims, he's been stymied in his efforts to get his message across to the public:

> CBC, for example, has said to us about television, there is no way we will allow your association to purchase any television time to show a thirty-second commercial showing an animal in a leghold trap. So we said to them, well look, we'll back off then, we won't show an animal in a trap, but we want the world to know what a leghold trap looks like. We had a volunteer make a thirty-second commercial, and it showed a trap being set and an individual like a trapper is looking back at it disdainfully. And the CBC has said, no, the subject of the leghold trap has been deemed a controversial issue in Canada, and we cannot allow you to purchase any time whatsoever.[24]

George Clements pleads that his group is too small to lobby effectively. Compared to giants like the IFAW, Fund For Animals and Greenpeace, the APFA claims only seven thousand members. The group has already had more impact, however, than Clements admits. In the spring of 1983, he received a phone call from the Canadian Department of External Affairs asking if he had a film called "Canada's Shame":

> They said, it's being shown tomorrow in Strasbourg, Germany [sic], did you know it? I said no, but we loan it out to various people, and I know we have three or four copies out in Germany. And they said, Well, will you rush down a copy to us? Because we want to know how we're best going to answer some of the charges you make about this cruelty in Canada. Which was quite humorous, from our viewpoint. Well, do you know, they stalled the showing two days, and in that time all the provinces, the federal government and the wildlife service fired off letters saying not to show that film, because the film was specially made to teach trappers how not to trap. And no one contacted us to seek our information. And they were successful. The film was not shown in Europe.[25]

Strasbourg (which has not been German since World War One) has long been famous for producing *pâté de foie gras*, by force-feeding geese until their livers become grossly diseased and distended. Today

Strasbourg is also known as the seat of the European Parliament, and "Canada's Shame" was shown there in the spring of 1983. (It is odd that George Clements was so surprised by his phone call from External Affairs, because the film was introduced at a session of the European Parliament on March 9 by John Ressman, a member of Clements' APFA.)

The Canadian government certainly worried about the screening of "Canada's Shame" in Strasbourg, on the heels of the European ban on white-coat imports. Aboriginal groups were concerned, too: the Native Council of Canada sent letters to all the members of the European Parliament, stressing the importance of trapping to native people.[26]

However, the screening of the APFA films ("Cry From the Wild" was also presented), was a low-key affair. The audience, totalling twelve people, included several journalists and only one member of the EEC parliament, other than the sponsor, Fritz Gautier. Gautier's sponsorship surprised Canadian officials, as he was one of the few German MPs to speak against the ban on white-coat imports and to abstain from the vote. Apparently Gautier made little effort to draw attention to the screening of the APFA films. The only announcement was a pile of photocopied sheets of paper left on a table in the press room, which were later inadvertently covered by the press releases of another MP on another subject. The screening was not listed on the schedule of press conferences and no general invitations were sent to MPs.

Why, then, had Gautier bothered to sponsor the event at all? It could only be surmised that it was to fulfil a commitment made during the recent German elections. Gautier assured Canadian authorities that he was concerned only about cruelty and didn't wish to attack Canada. Nor did he intend to propose a general debate in a full session of the Parliament.[27]

If "Canada's Shame" failed to stir much excitement in Strasbourg, the APFA hadn't been idle in Europe. On January 26, 1983, the *Hannoversche Allgemeine Zeitung* printed an interview with John Ressman, "a member of the executive committee" of APFA, in which capacity he "sacrifices money, health and time in order to influence the Canadian authorities about the evils of the leghold trap."[28] The films ("Canada's Shame" and "Cry from the Wild") Ressman had brought with him, the paper reported, "document the magnitude and cruelty of this type of animal killing." Ressman also came equipped with "data," which, he said, were "based on information published by the [Canadian] government. In each elegant, silky, soft coat made of Canadian mink, there are 3,600 hours of terror of death, says John Ressman."

Ressman could "prove" this statement, said the Hanover paper, with "shocking photographs" of animals that had tried to gnaw off their paws to free themselves, had died of starvation or cold or "were battered to death by the trapper after long days of desperate attempts to free themselves."

Whatever the "shocking photographs" may have proved to the Hanover reporters, Ressman's statement, like most of the article, is nonsensical, as almost all mink coats manufactured in Canada today are made with ranched mink that never saw a trap in their lives. Canada traps about 100,000 mink a year (111,467 in 1977 and 1978), out of a total of from three and a half to four million fur bearers trapped in all, in that country. By contrast, more than one *million* mink were ranched in Canada in 1978, and world ranched mink production was about twenty-four million that year.[29]

Ressman's "data" continued: "At least sixty mink, or forty-five opposums, or else twenty otter or forty-two red foxes must die for a single coat," he said. Unfortunately, little of his report can be borne out. Female mink are smaller than males. About forty to forty-five females, or about twenty-four males, are used to make a fine coat: certainly not "at least sixty." Moreover, the mink used would in almost every case be ranched, not victims of the leghold traps Mr. Ressman claims to be concerned about.[30] (The rest of his data is equally fanciful. Twenty to twenty-five opposums are used for a full-length coat, not forty-five. Eight to ten otters, not twenty. Eighteen to twenty red-fox pelts for a *very* fine coat [where only the dense center backs of the pelts are used], otherwise twelve to fourteen foxes, not forty-two.)

The point is not that the fate of animals is any less important if twelve instead of forty-two foxes are used for a coat. But such blatant disregard for facts that are so easily verifiable casts doubt on the animal-rights groups' contention that they want the public to learn the truth about fur trapping. For they are not well informed, nor, apparently, do they wish to be.

"Approximately three times as many other animals – deer, rabbit, porcupine – walk into the traps, but their skins do not yield profit, and therefore they are killed and discarded," the Hanover interview with Ressman continued. "Trash animals" are a favorite anti-trapping argument. However, trappers are able to control the number of nondesirable animals they catch by how and where they set their traps. A trap set out in the open, for example, may well catch a whiskey jay, as shown in "Canada's Shame," but few traps would be set this way.[31] "Trash" animals obviously mean less income, and a serious trapper will not spend his time in sub-zero weather, with the attendant financial cost, effort and physical danger, just to discard animals.

Trappers consistently report catching very few nontarget animals. How is it then that animal-rights "authorities" cite figures as high as sixty-six to seventy-five per cent?

One of the few writers to reveal a source for her figures is Christine Stevens, one of the authors of *Facts About Furs*, published by the Animal Welfare Institute. Commercial trappers record only the desirable furs they have sold; they have no reason to report any other animals they might catch. To get around this problem, Stevens turned to statistics from the United States government's predator-control programs, where records were kept of every animal captured. The "target" animals in these programs were usually coyotes and bobcats – but over a twenty-year period in one survey, the percentage of "target" animals averaged only twenty-two per cent of the total animals trapped. From this Stevens has concluded that trappers may capture "seventy-eight per cent nontarget animals." She uses this to argue that trappers cannot control which animals they will take in their traps.[32]

Examination of the government report on which Stevens based her analysis, however, reveals that most of the "nontarget" animals were fur bearers – skunks, badgers, raccoons and weasels – none of which would be considered "trash" by a commercial trapper, although they weren't what the predator-control officers were after.[33] Of the remaining "nontarget" animals, almost all were rabbits, which might often be eaten by the trapper, as might porcupines, the next-most-common nonfur animal.[34]

It should be noted as well that native trappers – about sixty per cent of Canadian trappers – also eat lynx, beaver, mink and many other fur bearers. Recent studies have revealed that the economic value of this meat equals or exceeds the money received for the furs.[35]

None of this is explained in the Hanover interview with John Ressman. Instead, it is stated that "in every other country in the world [except Canada] the leghold trap is banned, and in Germany it has been prohibited since 1930."[36] The leghold trap is, in fact, banned in fifty countries (while eighty-six countries are signatories of the CITES agreement). Because the number of countries banning leghold traps is used to add weight to the moral argument that the traps are cruel and should be prohibited everywhere,[37] this figure warrants some analysis.

Of the forty-eight countries listed in *Facts about Furs* as having banned leghold traps by 1980,[38] twenty-three are African (and nineteen of these have banned all trapping): Africa, however, despite the publicity about spotted cats, has never been important in the commercial fur trade. Some African skins do have high values as novelties;

but for obvious reasons fine furs always come from cold climates. Exports of wild fur from Africa to the United States amounted to less than $250,000 in 1978.[39] In that same year, Canada produced about $82 million in wild fur; the United States produced $268 million. Wildlife has, indeed, been severely reduced in Africa during this century, but the main causes have been loss of habitat, sport and trophy hunting, meat hunting and the ivory market.

John Heppes is administrator of the Canadian representation to CITES. He was born in Kenya and brought up in Uganda, and between 1945 and 1962, he worked with the Ugandan Wildlife Service. In much of Africa, Heppes recalls, agricultural plots were often clearings in the bush and were protected only with great difficulty from wild grazers. Farmers were using leghold traps with twelve-inch jaws to protect their plots from wild herbivores, such as bush buck and buffalo. Because their clearings were always close by settlements, the traps posed considerable danger for humans. It was to protect people, not animals, that the British colonial administration in Uganda (as in many other African territories) banned the traps. For hunting, Heppes stresses, Africans relied on pitfall traps (sometimes with cruel sharpened spears at the bottom), or more often, organized spear drives. These at times involved thousands of people forming a great circle, driving all the game into the center, where enough meat could be slaughtered to justify the effort. Otherwise, Africans used logfalls or rifles.[40]

A number of European countries have also banned the leghold trap: Austria, Denmark, Norway, Ireland, Portugal, Switzerland, Sweden, Hungary and the United Kingdom. As the authors of *Facts About Furs* themselves admit, however, "most wild fur bearers have been rare in Europe for centuries." The total European wild-fur harvest in 1978 was just under one and a half million animals: one million were squirrels; three hundred thousand were muskrats. For both these animals effective substitutes to the leghold trap are readily available. In England (where wolves were eliminated centuries ago) the main use for the leghold trap (or "gin-trap" as it was called) was to control rabbits, which threatened gardens and farm crops. Yet, the British ban on leghold traps was passed only in 1958, by which time myxomatosis, a disease in rabbits, intentionally introduced into the country, had rendered the traps unnecessary.[41]

The remaining countries that have banned leghold traps include such unlikely fur-trapping nations as Hong Kong, Israel, Jordan, Belize, the British West Indies, Jamaica, Trinidad and Tobago and the Seychelles Islands. None of them sacrificed much fur income for their moral stand against the trap.[42]

On 14 February, 1983, *der Stern* ran a special "exposé" on fur trapping. Quoting from an interview with George Clements, *der Stern* reported:

> Few professional trappers are left in North America. Uncontrolled trapping and deterioration of the environment have caused a severe shrinkage of fur-bearing animal populations. . . . Also, the proceeds from the skins have dwindled due to the large production of the fur ranches where millions of animals are kept in the narrowest of space. . . .

More than two million *der Stern* readers were promised more "facts" about fur ranching in a forthcoming book, to be published by the magazine, called *The Penitentiary of the Animals*.

The flood of inaccuracies in such supposedly responsible European publications as *der Stern* would be comical if it were not for the damage they can cause to the livelihoods of people who can little afford it. While it is true that in the United States there are many "part-time" trappers (it is estimated that up to two million Americans do some trapping), about forty thousand people in that country still earn the greatest part of their living from trapping. (One wonders, moreover, why doing something part-time or as a hobby necessarily invalidates it.) In Canada, the proportion of trappers who make most of their living from furs is far higher than in the United States. There are about a hundred thousand registered trappers in Canada, of which up to sixty per cent are estimated to be native Indian, Inuit or Metis.[43]

Contrary to the *Stern* report, trapping is not "uncontrolled" in Canada. Registered trap lines are the basis of wildlife management. Obviously, it is in the trappers' own interests not to overharvest their territories. Fur-bearer populations, moreover, have natural cycles. When populations become low, it ceases to be economically sound to trap these species in certain areas so they are allowed to recover.

Wildlife populations are not shrinking in North America, as the annual sustained harvest of the world's largest numbers of fur bearers should make clear. This has not happened by accident, but through careful monitoring and management programs. Beaver, for instance, were overharvested and became virtually extinct in some areas in the 1930s. (During the depression, large numbers of unemployed workers tried their hand at trapping, with disastrous consequences for traditional conservation methods in, for example, Quebec Indian hunting territories.) The beaver were later reintroduced where necessary, and protected; and they are now as plentiful as they ever were all over their North American range. In northern Quebec, government biologists conduct detailed aerial surveys to help Cree hunters identify every beaver lodge in their trapping territories and to determine how many may be harvested each year.[44]

Charges that fur bearers in Canada are overharvested, or not well-managed, are simply false: beaver, muskrat, wolf, fox, bear, raccoon, ermine and mink are all being harvested under sustainable yields.[45] One reason fur bearers in Canada are underharvested, no doubt, is that there are simply so few people in many regions. It should be stressed, however, that wildlife populations are nonetheless monitored.

In the case of beaver, it may be as simple as counting lodges in aerial photos. Species like lynx, which travel great distances, are less easily counted (as anti-trapping advocates like George Clements are quick to point out), but even in such difficult cases scientists have certain tools at their disposal: age and sex-distribution sampling can allow them to develop a good idea whether populations are increasing or decreasing, for example. And by changing the open season for trapping different species, the wildlife managers can influence this population growth. (If the trapping season is opened when fox or wolf cubs are just beginning to get around on their own, for instance, a high proportion of younger animals with less experience will be trapped than if the season is opened earlier.)[46]

It is true that, in the United States especially, increased human population has whittled away wildlife habitat in many areas. In general, however, and especially in Canada, it is believed that fur-bearer populations in North America are now at least as high as they were when Europeans first came to the continent. The explanation for this seemingly impossible situation is that human intrusion into virgin regions of the north may often increase wildlife habitat, if the human population doesn't become too dense. Clearing forests for agriculture may increase "fringe" area, where deer and other herbivores prefer to graze.

More important, roads through marshy areas, which make up much of northern Canada, where great shallow lakes are in the process of being grown over, may radically boost potential fur-bearer habitat. Ditches on each side of the road serve to drain the surrounding land enough that the trees upon which beaver feed can grow. Beaver may dam the runoff ditches and other animals are attracted to the ponds they create: otter, mink, muskrat. Mice come into the newly drained land, and their predators, foxes and coyotes, can follow. In this way, low levels of human settlement, such as characterize much of Canada, can increase fur-bearer populations more than enough to compensate for higher levels of trapping.

Der Stern's assertion that "the proceeds from skins have dwindled" is perhaps intended to suggest that fur trapping, like Marx's state, is "withering away" and might well be given a final push. Between 1970 and 1979, the value of wild furs traded in the United States rose by 1,122%, and the number of animals trapped through this period more than doubled.[47]

DESTROYING THE CONSUMER MARKET FOR FURS

George Clements claims that he is interested only in more humane trapping methods, but most animal-rights advocates make it clear that they will be satisfied only with a complete halt to the use of animals for furs. Peter Hyde, for example, is past president of the Ottawa-based Animal Defense League and secretary general of the International League for Animal Rights:

> We are convinced that the notion of a humane trap is a fallacious notion, because animals come in so many different sizes that it has, up to now, proven impossible to design a trap that would kill instantly any animal that entered that trap. Although many years have been spent, and hundreds of trap designs inspected, examined and tested by the Federal-Provincial Committee on Humane Trapping, they have not yet found a humane trap. We are convinced that they will not. And if they did find a "humane" trap, it would still be a question of an animal's life being taken when there is no need for it to be taken, because the collection of these pelts is purely to serve the interests of the vanity trade. . . .[48]

Michael Giannelli, scientific advisor for the Fund For Animals, agrees:

> The Fund For Animals is against fur trapping completely, and the Fund For Animals is also against the raising of fur animals in so-called ranches. I think that the slaughtering of fur-bearing animals for human vanity is one of the most disgraceful chapters in human exploitation. There is no necessity for it obviously, but it takes place because there is still a great commercial market for it.[49]

Foreseeing victory or at least a temporary standoff in the anti-sealing campaigns in the near future (in the form, perhaps, of a moratorium for several years on the hunting of white coats), the animal-rights movement has begun to move the fight against fur trapping into the foreground. In August 1983, an "Animal Rights Symposium" was held in Vancouver, British Columbia. The public program focused on the use of animals in scientific laboratories (the symposium was timed to coincide with a convention of the International Council on Laboratory Animal Science.) But during three days of closed "business meetings," other topics were raised: data banks, fundraising and publicity, "putting animals into politics" and "the fur industry – proposals for action." Peter Hyde, who attended those meetings, described the approach that would be used:

The experience that has been gained in the anti-seal hunt campaign has shown very clearly that if one is going to protect fur-bearing animals from being used in the trade, you have to go after the secondary market. You have to create a situation where it becomes a socially unacceptable thing to wear the fur of another creature. And that is our ultimate objective – to arrive at a situation where people will no longer buy the product.

Henry Salt, in fact, had already concluded in 1894, that the consumer market should be attacked: "It is not the man who kills the bird, but the lady who wears the feathers in her hat, who is the true offender." In support of his position, Salt quoted Keats:

For them the Ceylon diver held his breath,
And went all naked to the hungry shark;
For them his ears gushed blood; for them in death
The seal on the cold ice with piteous bark
Lay full of darts; for them alone did seethe
A thousand men in troubles wide and dark;
Half ignorant, they turned an easy wheel,
That set sharp racks at work to pinch and peel.[50]

In their campaign to destroy the consumer market for furs, animal-rights groups encourage articles like those that appeared in *der Stern* in 1983. They also publish their own materials. A group called Beauty Without Cruelty prints a pamphlet that members can hand out in the streets. On the cover is a photograph of an attractive long-eared Persian lamb. "Please excuse me for approaching you," says the text. "I see you are wearing fur. I wonder if you know how it is obtained?"

Inside are more photographs: "The last mink in his small cage is waiting for his fate." "Why do these little mink have their heads in jars? They are being killed to make coats for men and women." Photographs of skinned mink carcasses in garbage bins: "Knowledgeable people believe that ranched furs constitute an even greater cruelty than trapped ones." "The animals are killed as quickly as possible by homemade electrocution boxes, painful gassing, cyanide, decompression, or cheap injection, by unskilled employees. . . ."

The greatest concentration of fur farms is in Scandinavia. Eighty-three per cent of ranched foxes and forty-five per cent of all mink come from farms in Denmark, Finland, Norway and Sweden. These are countries like Canada, where climate and soil conditions offer few agricultural opportunities. (First raised in Canada, blue and silver foxes have been bred through more than eighty generations in Europe.) Most fur ranchers are also conventional farmers, and the ranches complement other farming activities. The notion that fur ranching is particularly cruel is rejected by representatives of Scandinavian agricultural and humane organizations:

> Farm-produced fur-bearing animals are for the most part beasts of prey, namely mink and fox. It is characteristic of beasts of prey that they cannot develop or reproduce normally if conditions are not optimum with regard to both cages, food, and care. . . . The farming of fur animals in Norway is subject to the Welfare of Animals Act, as are other forms of animal husbandry. The Act provides detailed regulations on the housing, feeding, medication, and general care of these species, as well as the transportation, exhibition, killing and pelting. . . . Offenses are reported to the police and prosecuted by the courts of justice.[51]

Following the showing in Europe of a film critical of fur ranching, the Swedish division of the World Wildlife Fund and the Federation of Swedish Animal Protection Societies issued a statement:

> Only a person who is interested in animals, and who likes them, becomes a fur farmer. These criteria are essential, for two reasons: working with fur-bearing animals is no easy job; it is both hard and time-consuming, and the farmer is very tied. They are live animals that must be cared for and fed every day – weekday, weekend, or public holiday. It takes a real interest in animals to work up the best material. The farmer who has no interest in his animals, or no feeling for their welfare, soon suffers himself in the form of poor financial return. In our opinion, one cannot condemn or cast suspicion on a trade which is carried out as seriously as is the case with fur-breeding, and which is so closely regulated by rules and control measures.[52]

The pamphlet published by Beauty Without Cruelty also describes trapping: "The little animal struggles, terrified, and tries to free himself by biting at the cold hard metal. He may lie there for weeks, since there is no possible way to enforce regular checking of trap lines. . . ."

In the Canadian north, trapping is done when pelts are at their prime, in midwinter. A trapped animal doesn't live long in winter conditions, even if the trapper doesn't arrive quickly. Even when there are no legal time limits, most professional trappers visit their sets every day, if not out of compassion, then from economic necessity. For an animal left too long in a trap may be chewed at or eaten completely by another animal, destroying the value of the pelt.

But Beauty Without Cruelty is out for sensation: "It has been confirmed that some animals in foreign continents are killed by the insertion of a red-hot rod in the anus. . . ."[53]

Do you want to be the cause of such suffering? Of course you don't.

But the buying and wearing of fur encourages and subsidizes all of this. It is well known by now that synthetic furs provide as much warmth as real furs. Many arctic explorers wear quilted parkas or fake furs in sub-zero temperatures. . . .

As if this vision of arctic explorers bedecked in fake furs wasn't silly enough (shades of the E.F. Timme Company again?), the pamphlet, ever polite, concludes: "If you are not wearing fur, but instead one of the excellent make-believe furs, please excuse my mistake."

Beauty Without Cruelty was organized, we are told, to educate the public with facts, and to provide information about substitutes for animal products. On the back of their pamphlet is a photograph of another Persian lamb, "bled and skinned with a pocket knife." Once again, the men in the photograph are visibly "foreigners," probably Afghans. One final photograph in the pamphlet deserves mention because it shows a rabbit in a steel-toothed trap. Traps with teeth are no longer manufactured in North America, and are not used by trappers today.[54]

This is only a throw-away pamphlet, designed to grab attention in the street. Perhaps it is too much to expect responsible argument in such a medium.

Beauty Without Cruelty founder and chairman Muriel, Lady Dowding contributed an article to the landmark animal-rights book *Animals, Men and Morals*, edited by the Godlovitches of Oxford University. In it, Lady Dowding runs on in much the same fashion as does her handout:

> As it takes as much as a hundred skins to make up a single mink coat, the trapper likes to ensure his catch. One of his weapons is a steel-toothed leghold or "gin" trap, an instrument used to secure the four million animals that die by it annually in Canada. . . .[55]

She packs an extraordinary amount of misinformation into two sentences. As has been explained, traps with teeth are no longer manufactured or used in North America. As well, a very fine female mink coat uses at most forty to forty-five skins; a coat from male skins uses about twenty-four skins. Ninety-nine per cent of mink coats made today are from ranched mink, which are not trapped.

It is also worth noting that, as in the sealing controversy, Canada is singled out by the animal-rights authors, although it is by no means the main trapping nation. About three to four million wild pelts are trapped in Canada each year; about eighteen million are trapped in the United States. The USSR harvest is not known, but is estimated to be somewhere between the Canadian and United States figures. As in the sealing campaign, it must be assumed that Canada is singled out not because it is the only producer (and in spite of the fact that Canadian wildlife-management policies are considered to be some of the best in the world), but because Canada is less able than the United States and USSR to resist such attacks.

But Lady Dowding is not through informing her countrymen about the barbarities that occur among the "foreigners" in Her Majesty's overseas dominions. Ermine and sable, she says in her article in Godlovitch, are trapped by rubbing grease on a steel bar, so the animals' tongues will stick to the cold metal. Trappers in the Canadian Northwest Territories, where these two animals are trapped, point out that such a practice would be both absurd and illegal, since authorized trapping sets must be used. They could only guess that some cagey old trapper had spun Milady a tall tale.[56]

Lady Muriel appears to have a weakness for colorful stories. Broadtail lamb, she writes, is produced by inducing abortions in ewes, by "beating them with iron rods – up to a hundred blows per ewe." Needless to say, any herder who made a habit of such a practice would not have a flock for long. To sacrifice breeding females to produce a single tiny skin makes no sense, even to "foreigners." "Broadtail" lamb was produced when ewes aborted naturally, usually during severe Asian winters. Most "Persian" production now, however, is from Southwest Africa. (It is marketed as "Swakara.") One-quarter of the lambs are selected for breeding, and the rest are killed within a week of birth. They are first rendered unconscious by electroshocks. According to Doctor D. Matthews, chairman of the South West Africa SPCA:

> No abortions or premature births are induced on Karakul ewes by any artificial means, kicking, beating, chasing, et cetera, to produce broadtail pelts. The method used for slaughtering the lambs is humane and has been approved by veterinary authorities. . . .[57]

"Only those utterly lacking in sensitivity can fail to be horrified by the facts I have presented," Lady Dowding concludes. "There is on the market a wide selection of simulated fur fabrics . . . some of them so like the 'real thing' they cause embarrassment to those ladies who wouldn't be seen 'dead in a ditch' wearing animal furs. . . ."[58]

Apart from the simple inanity of such statements (one would indeed have to be quite "lacking in sensitivity" to mistake "fake furs" for the real thing), the question of synthetic furs must be considered, if only briefly. The ecology movement, from which much of the support for animal rights stems, presumably grew out of a sentiment that technological society has become too removed from direct contact with nature. Whatever else one may think of it, the fur trade does make use of a natural, renewable, nonpolluting resource. To tell people to buy synthetics is to tell thousands of trappers (many of them native Indians) that they should live in cities and work in factories rather than stay in the woods. It is difficult to see how such a shift can help heal the nature/culture split, which the ecology movement began by criticizing.

One of the earlier "modern" animal-rights texts is Gerald Carson's 1972 book, *Men, Beasts and Gods*. Among his other inaccuracies,[59] Carson claims that "about twenty-five percent of the [trapped] animals gnaw off their legs in the struggle to escape."[60] Monica Hutchings and Mavis Caver (who must spend most of their time driving about Europe and North Africa in search of animal atrocities) state: "trappers claim to lose about one-third of animals caught in steel-toothed 'leg-hold' gin-traps, because they chew off paw, foot, or toes."[61]

One country where Hutchings and Caver apparently didn't drive is Canada, or they would know that "toothed" traps are no longer manufactured or used. "Teeth" are not needed, and they can damage fur. (New experimental models are being produced by Woodstream that are "padded" with plastic and offset, so that a small space is left even when the trap is closed, to lessen the shock of impact.)

"Wring-offs" (when animals chew their own paws to free themselves) do occur, trappers admit, but very rarely. This usually happens when inexperienced trappers use a trap too large for the animal they are taking, and the trap breaks the bone. Only certain species will "wring off" at all: mink sometimes, but rarely martin, fox or lynx. Trappers surveyed on this question (by a fellow trapper and fur collector) estimated that they lost less than one per cent of their catch in this way. Some said they had lost none at all.

If a trapper leaves his sets unattended for too long, however, predators can take the trapped animal. This may account for some of the stories and photos of "wring-offs" that are so prevalent in anti-trapping publications. Precisely because this can happen, serious trappers visit their traps frequently, usually once a day.[62]

In summary: animal-rights advocates would have us believe that trappers visit traps once a week or less; that twenty-five to thirty-three per cent of the catch is lost to wring-offs (without counting what would be taken by predators); and that sixty to seventy-five per cent of the catch are "trash" animals. No one could remain a trapper very long under such conditions.

Considerable space has been allocated to documenting the inaccuracies of anti-trapping arguments. The most serious disservice of such writings, though, is that they totally disregard the skills, knowledge and hard work of people who still earn their livelihood in what to most of us is "the bush." Animal-rights advocates would have us believe that trappers simply "take" furs, the way an armed thug might relieve an elderly woman of her life's savings. Despite the increased security and comfort that have come with new technology – snowmobiles, bush planes and shortwave radios – life in the north woods in mid-winter still requires strength, skills and knowledge, not to say respect and real love of nature. These qualities are quite unknown to most westerners, locked into their hermetically sealed cities, totally dependent upon "the system" for food, shelter, warmth, transportation and entertainment, not to mention regular paychecks.

In our age of media, moreover, there is a tendency to assume that charges that go unanswered must be true. Trappers, however, have had little access to the media. They are far from their detractors who, whether academic "philosophers" or professional fund raisers, earn their livings by manipulating the opinions of others. The plethora of philosophers in the animal-rights movement is in fact remarkable. Does this indicate the critical moral importance of this issue today? Or does it, perhaps, reflect something more down-to-earth? Bernard Rollin, himself a philosopher, has explained why:

> Until very recently, philosophers felt little responsibility *qua* philosophers to deal with social and existentially relevant issues . . . a few years ago, however, economic forces began to shake philosophers out of their dogmatic slumbers. Suddenly there were no jobs for philosophers – student enrollment in philosophy classes declined as students became vocationally oriented; graduate programmes dried up. . . . Philosophers panicked and began to . . . write on medical ethics, violence, reverse discrimination, animals, etc. . . . Some philosophers adapted beautifully. . . .[63]

"WEARING FUR IS A MARK OF IGNORANCE OR INDIFFERENCE" – Beauty Without Cruelty

Animal-rights proponents argue that once people "know the truth," they will reject fur trapping. One informative pamphlet is entitled "If You're Dressed To Kill – You Have!" A cartoon on the cover shows a woman in a lynx coat, from which a single bloody paw extends, still caught in a trap complete with jagged metal "teeth" (despite the fact that toothed traps are no longer produced). The authors don't have Lady Dowding's excuse of living far from the scene, because the brochure was published by the University of Victoria Animal Rights Society.[64]

The University of Victoria brochure deserves mention for introducing a new bit of misinformation. In case you think you're spared from guilt because you bought a ranch-raised fur. . . .

> Wrong! Firstly, in the fur trade the term "ranch mink" refers to a particular colour of fur, not to the method of obtaining it. It is quite possible that a "ranch mink" fur coat was in fact obtained from sixty wild animals that had suffered all the prolonged tortures of a leg-hold trap, snare, or Conibear. . . .

There is, indeed, a color called "dark ranch;" it is a very dark brown. It is called "ranch" because it does not occur in the wild. One of the accomplishments of some sixty years of breeding has been to develop a range of colors not found in nature, except in the occasional mutations upon which the breeder's art is based. While wild mink are medium reddish-brown, ranched mink vary from almost white to almost black. These color strains have been developed using the same principles of selective breeding as define our familiar breeds of dogs, beef and dairy cows and roses. The dyer's art has added a still wider spectrum of tints and blushes – but a "dark-ranch" mink is always ranched.

Undaunted by such distinctions, the University of Victoria pamphlet claims that ranching is in any case no less cruel than trapping:

> Imagine that you are locked into a dark shed with a thousand other people held in a cage so small you can barely turn around . . . killed by personnel with no medical or veterinary training . . . animals may be poisoned, gassed, electrocuted, or have their necks broken. If you believe this is humane decide which method you would prefer.

The logic of this "proof" hardly merits commentary. (After all, how would you like to be a bat and live in a dark cold cave and eat live insects that wriggled as you swallowed them, or to be a tapeworm living in someone's intestines?) Its appeal may be based on an unconscious protest against the conditions of modern human life, where many are now shut up most of the day in windowless offices, schools and factories, "with thousands of other people."

Fur farming is usually a family-run operation, and is complementary to plant growing. Straw provides bedding for the animals; the manure goes back to the fields. Food used to feed the animals is almost all unsuitable for human consumption. In Finland, about thirty-seven per cent of "fodder" is waste from fish-packing plants; another fifteen per cent is slaughterhouse waste. Eleven per cent is industrial-grade fish, and four per cent is fishmeal. A certain proportion of carcasses of the mink and foxes themselves may also be added to the mix. By using by-products from fish, poultry and slaughterhouse operations, fur ranching contributes to lowering the price of the fish and meat consumed by humans. Not least important, fur ranching in Scandinavia, as in Canada, is usually practised in areas where harsh climate and poor soil make other farming ventures financially and often agriculturally difficult.

Finally, unlike animals raised for human consumption, fur bearers are spared the trip to the abattoir, a voyage that is often more stressful than the actual killing operation. Killing is never pleasant, but the notion that people who kill hundreds of animals each season are unskilled (whether or not they have "medical" training) is obviously nonsensical. A usual method of killing mink or foxes in Europe is to run the exhaust from a gasoline engine through a filter (such as a large water barrel) to cool and clean the gas before it is pumped into the killing area. Increasingly, today, pure bottled gas is replacing the older methods. In Canada, a common method has been electrical stunning, followed by dislocation of the neck. These methods, when properly used, are quick and painless. In Germany, however, gassing fur bearers is considered completely unacceptable, for historical reasons that have nothing to do with the fur trade.[65]

A final note on ranching: animal-rights "commandos" recently "liberated" twelve hundred mink from the "concentration-camp" conditions of a farm in England. The rancher turned on the automated feeding system, and almost all the mink promptly returned to their cages.

ABORIGINAL TRAPPERS AND HUNTERS

An often-repeated anti-trapping argument is that "trapping has little importance to most people today . . . few trap full-time, most do it part-time or as a hobby. The average [British Columbia] trapper makes $800 a year."[66]

> One also hears emotional "sob-stories" about trapping being "essential for the livelihood of native people" . . . Canada has one of the highest standards of living in the world. No one is forced by poverty to make a living by torturing animals. Trappers get a mere pittance for their furs. . . .[67]

Claims that trapping is a traditional occupation of the indigenous population, says one animal-rights pamphlet, are "particularly disgusting, since it takes advantage not only of animals but also of our native people."[68]

144

The native people of Canada don't agree. In response to the growing anti-trapping threat, Indian people from across Canada met in Winnipeg, Manitoba in February 1984 for the first Aboriginal Hunters and Trappers Conference. This conference, which was attended by chiefs of many bands, by the Native Council of Canada, by the Assembly of First Nations, by the Inuit Tapirisat and by the Metis National Council, resolved

> to combat the anti-trapping movement for the preservation of the Fur Industry, trapping rights for Aboriginal and Canadian trappers, and especially to safeguard the Native way of life, culture, heritage, and traditional values, and Aboriginal rights. . . .[69]

The Mathias Colomb Band, of Missinippi River, Manitoba, declared:

> Trapping has always been a way of life for Indian people. . . . It still offers us food, because most fur-bearing animals that we trap are a good source of meat. All beaver and muskrat that are caught are used as food . . . and certainly fried lynx chops are a delicacy. Today we sell the fur, and for many of us, trapping is our livelihood, our mainstay, and we value that traditional lifestyle as part of our heritage. . . . We don't squander, we don't pollute, and we certainly don't needlessly destroy; and if anything should be considered a national issue, it is these three topics that must be addressed, rather than the harvest of fur-bearing animals.[70]

About eight thousand Cree people still hunt and trap throughout the vast James Bay territory of northern Quebec. They, too, are clear in their opposition to the anti-trapping movement:

> The Crees reject the notion that the leg-hold traps are inhumane. . . . The reasons given by those who propose to ban the use of these traps are based on incomplete understanding of the trapper's way of life. Trapping is part of the Cree way of life. It is an essential part of Cree culture. It is a major source of food, and provides one of the sources of income within an extremely limited economic base. . . .
> Furthermore, Cree rights to hunt, fish, and trap are guaranteed by the James Bay and Northern Quebec Agreement, by the James Bay and Northern Quebec Native Claims Settlement Act, by the Federal Constitution of 1982, and by several acts of the Quebec National Assembly. The Crees vigorously defend their rights to hunt, fish and trap, and to apply the techniques and means which were in use at the time these agreements were signed.
> The Crees find it hypocritical that anyone should tell them about the humane use of animals. Cree tradition and belief is based upon a relationship with animals far more intimate and complete than the rather limited and inconsistent positions taken by people who repre-

sent themselves as supporters of humane killing. . . . The Cree relationship with animals is one of respect and conservation. The Crees depend upon the animals of the region, and their knowledge of this dependence has led them over several thousand years to respect the mutual nature of this dependence. . . .

It is particularly important to let our European friends know that the application of a ban (on the leg-hold trap) will cause serious damage to native people who depend upon hunting, fishing, and trapping; and that their efforts, however sincerely they may be based upon humanitarian motivations, will be one further example of damage caused by the European invasion of our land, and the application of foreign ideas not compatible to our way of life. . . .[71]

How, then, do ecologists and others who have expressed the need to develop a new contact with nature justify undermining the last vestiges of traditional Indian life in North America? Patrick Moore, director of Greenpeace, answered the question this way:

These are the most difficult case-by-case situations to deal with. . . . Sure, the Indian people are doing the dirty work of going out and killing the animal, but they have been co-opted into an unacceptable economy as far as we're concerned, that is the skin trade in wild-animal pelts. You have to look at an animal and say, well was that animal primarily for the food requirements, and did they just sell the skin on the side, you see? Those are not easy questions, and this is finally what it comes down to in the seal hunt too. You look at the native people taking seals in the Arctic, and those skins are going into the same fashion industry that the skins from the big commercial Newfoundland hunt are going into. And you have to make hard decisions there in the real world. . . . I agree there could be a fair amount of inconvenience and a fair amount of disruption of economies of people. But I think if it's thought through carefully, that can be minimized.[72]

"Luxury industry," "co-opted," "dirty work." The language used by animal-rights advocates tells us much about their own cultural blinkers. Hunting animals has never been, for Indians or Inuit, "dirty work." The anthropologist Frank Speck, who lived with the Naskapi of Quebec, said that for the Indian, hunting is a "holy occupation."

The notion that Indians were "co-opted" into the fur trade by cunning voyageurs and Hudson's Bay Company men is useful for those who would ban fur trapping today. Recent historical research, however, is beginning to show that Indians controlled the terms of trade far more than was formerly believed. Historians Dan Francis and Toby Morantz, of the McGill Centre For Northern Studies, were so impressed by what they found when they went back to original

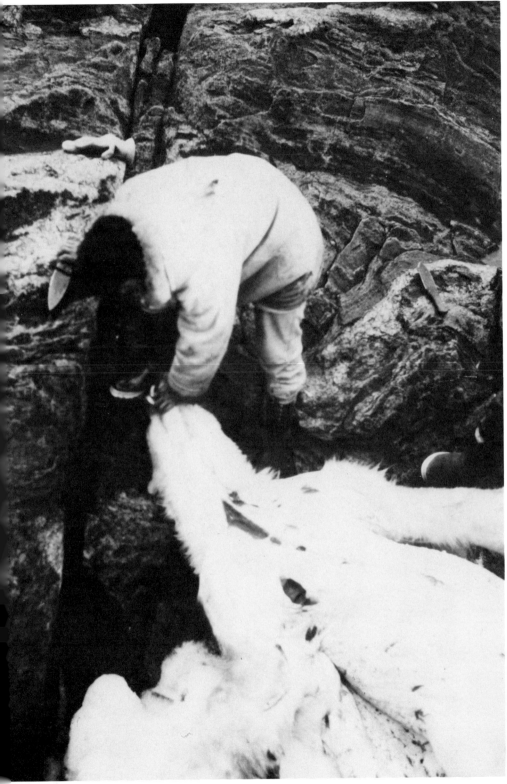

A hunter skinning a polar bear.

Removing a bobcat from a winter trap.

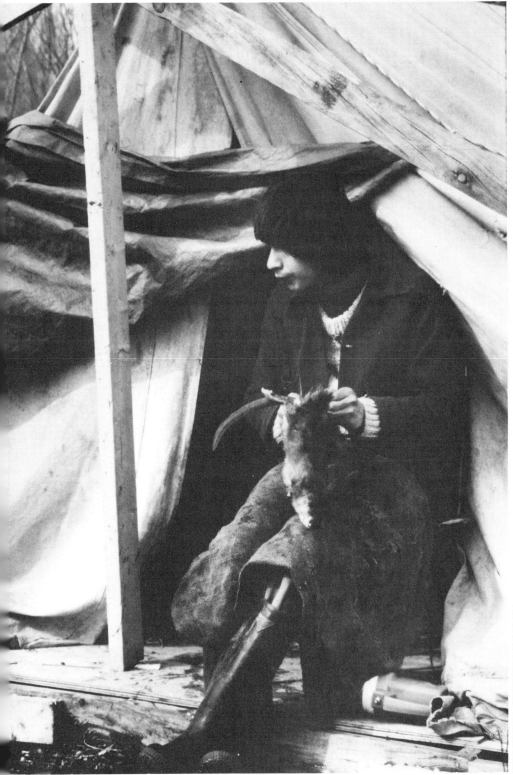

An Indian youth skinning a muskrat at the entrance to his camp.

Harvesting a humanely killed beaver. Notice the trap has taken the beaver correctly, ensuring a quick kill.

Clifford Shasha Weskum, a Wemindji Cree hunter, with a beaver. The animal is hung in the hunter's lodge so the fur may dry off.

The Conibear trap was designed to kill animals instantly, and often does. Here it is being used underwater—further insurance that the trapped animal will die quickly.

A recently captured ermine.

Bill Conley's shed at Wallace Lake, Manitoba, February 1971.

William Moore's camp, Artery Lake, Manitoba.

Hudson's Bay Company records that they decided to call their book about the James Bay fur trade *Partners in Furs*.[73]

Records of post managers reveal repeatedly this dependence of the traders on the Indians' hunting skills, and they often refer to their efforts to persuade Indians to secure for them more food – food which the Europeans were quite incapable of gathering for themselves.

> The Captain and his gard came and told me there was no geese to kill and they wanted some trust [supplies] to go to their winter quarters. I was willing to have as many geese killed as possible, so I told them that who ever ould stay a week longer to see if anymore geese was to be got, I ould lett them Nessacarys have for to go, and tham that ould not stay I ould trost tham nothing, so they ingaged again to stay . . .
> – Eastman House post journal, 1749[74]

Later on, post managers, especially in the interior, were often Metis, sons of European traders who married Indian women; these managers considered themselves to be, and were, Indians. In their research, Francis and Morantz found many ways in which Indians controlled their relations with the traders. They would not accept that the terms of trade be changed from year to year; therefore, although prices in London fluctuated, in Canada they remained very stable for long periods. The rituals of trading also followed Indian rather than European conventions. Upon the Indians' arrival at a post, the manager would distribute presents of cloth and tobacco, and the first day would be spent feasting. Only after that could trading begin. Some managers even instructed their employees to sing for the visiting Indians – certainly not a usual British business practice at the time.[75]

Such feasts and rituals could not be ignored by the traders, because, as post journals often lament, the Indians refused to trade if conditions didn't suit them:

> I am very much decived wth our bordring Indians for as we had plenty of Partridges I was in hopes they would ventur inland & kill a good many Beaver and Martin, but to ye contrary I find it, for as I have often mentioned, if they can catch plenty of fish or partridges or dear, they will never look out for any beaver or martin. I cannot find anything that will induce them to catch many more furs than what will trade them a kettle, hatchet, or Ice Chizel, when they are in want of them.
> – Thomas Mitchell, Eastman House post journal, 1741.

Indians had everything they needed from their environment, at least until they became dependent upon guns and ammunition, and no company inducements would change their work patterns. Another advantage they had over the traders was the fierce competition between fur companies, especially between the Hudson's Bay Company and the Montreal traders, before they amalgamated in 1821. Indians became skilled at playing one group off against the other, to secure better prices for their furs:

> This year is much superior to the last. Our consignment now amounts to 10,518¼,[76] and had we not been deserted by four of our [Indian] leaders, our trade this year would have been near thirteen thousand. Two of those leaders which have not been here this year reside near Mistacenne, which place will ever be of great injury to the trade of Eastmain, and it is our humble opinion that if some settlement of more than common consequence is not established there, your Honour's trade from that quarter will be much impaired. One of the other leaders which have not been here is from the south and we have been informed that he is made a leader at one of the Canadian settlements in that quarter. The other comes from the Nord. and I am fearful that he is gone to Minnaquogan. We had a leader from that place here this Spring with 5 canoes all of whome were entire strangers not having been here before, and I am in great hopes that we shall be able to keep them on our side. My plan has always been to treat the natives with mildness and affibility and whenever an opportunity offered, to impress them with a sense of our own friendly disposition. . . .
> – Report to London from Eastmain master, George Atkinson, Eastmain post, September 1791.

Or again, from the Fort George post journal, 1824:

> Much of the success in trade depends on the opinion which they [the Indians] entertain of the traders. . . .

Or very clearly, from Master James Foggett of Neoskweskau post, October 14, 1806:

> The guns that came up this summer, the Indians all refuse them, being so bad locks on them, which is a great hurt to this place for this year's trade. . . .

Indian hunters were not quite as naive and helpless as our high-school history books have led us to believe. The fur trade, in fact, was one of the few aspects of European civilization that Indians were able to turn to their own advantage, and in which they could participate on their own terms. Guns, horses, traps and, more recently, bush planes and shortwave radios might be adopted, but they were integrated into a lifestyle that remained bush-oriented and Indian.[77]

Trapping is still a crucial component of the economies of many aboriginal communities in Canada. Registered trap lines, moreover, often represent the Indians' strongest *de facto* claim to their traditional hunting territories – and their stake in the future.[78] Anti-trapping writers cite low cash earnings from trapping. What they do not explain is that the value of the meat collected and consumed in conjunction with trapping may exceed the money received for furs.

The cash is needed, however, to capitalize the subsistence hunt. Cash is the one "resource" not easily come by in the bush.

> Studies in the last ten or fifteen years have shown, somewhat to the surprise of southern Canadians who thought that Indian hunting as a way of life was dying, that modern communities of native people in the sub-Arctic and Arctic regions of Canada are relying for very often half of their total economy, half of their total income or more, on hunting, fishing, and trapping. It should be pointed out that in these areas where there is little alternative employment and little prospect of stable and permanent employment in the foreseeable future, the economic value from hunting, fishing and trapping is irreplaceable.[79]

Peter Usher, a Canadian social scientist, has said that the Inuit are "poor people whose tables are always laden with meat." The same could be said for many native communities in Canada. Hugh Brody, who surveyed land use in Indian areas of British Columbia, found that in one community, wages, pensions and other non-subsistence-sector annual income amounted to barely $3,500 per household. Furs brought the families that much again. But the value of the meat harvest consumed by the hunters and their families was conservatively estimated to be equivalent to almost $6,000 per household. Even on a reserve that was considered to have abandoned traditional life, hunting and trapping still represented about forty per cent of real income.

Colin Scott has shown that among the Cree of James Bay, too, the total value of the subsistence hunt far exceeds the cash received for furs. In other words, apparently small amounts of money received for furs permit hunting people to engage in subsistence activities that bring them highly nutritious food worth far more than the furs, and permit them to live within the context of the preferred, and traditional, lifestyle.[80]

Today, anti-trapping campaigns coincide with the interests of powerful industrial projects, which seek to undermine traditional hunting societies. Logging companies covet prime wildlife habitat; hydroelectric projects flood thousands of miles of northern Indian land, in order to sell cheap electricity to southern and American cities. Pipelines and geological exploration for gas and oil cut roads through the bush. Roads open the way for towns and all-terrain vehicles, and to thousands of white hunters with little or no commitment to the land. Brody estimates that in northeastern British Columbia, white hunters now take in a one-month season more than four times the number of moose the Indians kill in a full year.

The Indians depend on these animals for their survival: elimination of fur income would be a major blow to Indian hunting societies, and a boon to industrial developers. Sales of "cheap" electricity from hydro projects are actually cheap sales of land, usually Indian land. The province of Quebec had no intention of compensating the aboriginal people of northern Quebec for the vast territories flooded by the James Bay projects. Only after land-use studies helped establish that native people had never ceded their rights to their land, and had never stopped earning their living from it, did the province make concessions, after a bitterly contested legal battle.[81] Indians in British Columbia weren't compensated for land they lost to the Bennett Dam project.[82] Northern development is all too often just the latest chapter in a long history of disregard for aboriginal rights. But talk of protecting rights or encouraging Indian culture makes little sense unless the economic foundation of that culture is recognized:

> Concessions are made to Indian leaders so long as they do not demand a real recognition of the Indian economy. Pluralism is a North American ideal, but in practice it does not have room within it for a multiplicity of economic systems. Exotic languages do not get in the way of pipelines; hunting and trapping economies might.[83]

And so we come face to face with the central contradiction of the animal-rights philosophy: by undermining the economy of people who depend on wildlife for their survival, animal-rights advocates clear the way for interests that are not compatible with the needs of wildlife. For this reason, it is doubtful whether the animal-rights movement is in the interests even of wildlife.

"If we don't use the animals, then we'll lose them," says Ray Demarchi, a wildlife biologist with the British Columbia Ministry of the Environment. When logging companies wanted to fell some of the last remaining old-growth forests on Vancouver Island, they were stopped only because it could be argued that the forest provided cover for deer that brought hunters – and money – into the region. Demarchi fears that animal-rights activists will undermine the groups who can protect natural habitats from what he sees as the real enemies of wildlife: "the dammers, the ditchers and the developers."[84]

The greatest threat to wildlife is mushrooming human populations. The goal must be to build a coalition strong enough to stand up against ever-increasing human demands on land. Doctor Richard Van Gelder, curator for mammals at the American Museum of Natural History, argues that trappers and hunters have a vital role to play in this defensive action:

> If we're going to save wildlife, we'll have to have a sizeable lobby for it, which is why I like to see multiple use of most areas where there's wildlife . . . then when that land comes up for potential destruction, for agriculture, there's a lobby of recreation people, a lobby of trappers, of hunters, of the foresters, all of whom can say, "Look, this land is already producing more than it could for food production; let's leave it alone." I think that's really the thing that will maintain wildlife. If it's just recreation alone, it's going to have a tough time surviving a choice of whether we can go play with the animals or look at the animals, versus whether we're going to let these ten thousand or a hundred thousand people starve. Because no politician is going to keep land idle, so to speak, for recreation, when there are people starving.[85]

CITES 1983: Friends of Animals and Banning the Leghold Trap

A signal that the animal-rights movement was preparing to push the campaign against fur trapping to the fore came in April 1983, at the general meeting of CITES in Botswana. A resolution was introduced to ban trade in furs caught in leghold traps, which would have amounted to a virtual ban on wild furs. The official sponsor of the resolution was Gambia, which had originally sponsored a resolution to list harp and hooded seals in Appendix IIb. (See Chapter Five.)

Behind Gambia's participation in both resolutions is a British national, Eddie Brewer, director of the Wildlife Conservation Department of Gambia, who is sympathetic to the animal-rights cause.

Gambia is a former British Crown colony and became independent in 1965. It consists of a two-hundred-mile-long by twelve-mile-wide strip on either bank of the Gambia River: less than four thousand square miles in all. The country's main exports are peanuts, bee's wax and palm kernels. The fur trade – and traps – have little importance in Gambia, as Brewer freely admitted in a letter to the authors of *Facts about Furs*, published by the Animal Welfare Institute:

> In over 21 years I have only encountered two jaw traps in use, and when a consignment arrived in Gambia in the early 'sixties the customs officer had them taken out to sea and dumped. . . . As far as I am able to ascertain, they have never been widely used here – and it is refreshing to learn from almost every person I have spoken to in rural districts, that such traps are considered excessively cruel.[86]

As the traps were banned in most cases in order to protect people, not animals, it is not surprising that villagers consider them "excessively cruel." Given its size, Gambia has even less reason than most African countries to be concerned about trapping. Eddie Brewer's interest springs from the work of his daughter Stella, who spent many years in neighboring Senegal reintroducing chimpanzees into the wild. The Primate Protection League was one of the sponsors of this program, and through this group Eddie Brewer met other animal-rights organizers.

Gambia's resolution was declared *ultra vires* by the technical committee, which evaluates which motions should be considered by the CITES plenary session. The mandate of CITES is to protect endangered species, and the motion didn't address a conservation problem. In the plenary sessions, however, Gambia recruited a handful of other small, non-fur-trapping nations and insisted the question be debated. Once again, it was Sidney Holt, the representative for the Seychelles Islands, who dominated the debate on the seals resolution, who led the attack, citing initiatives taken by the International Whaling Commission to eliminate cruel practices.[87]

In response to the Gambian resolution, the Canadian delegation pointed out that without pressure from CITES or any other international organization, Canada had, for a decade, been actively pursuing the world's first scientific research to measure the stress suffered by animals in different trapping systems. The Fur Institute of Canada was established to continue the work of the Federal-Provincial Committee on Humane Trapping. Once this work was far enough advanced, it would be possible to set international standards for traps.[88]

The Gambian resolution was then put to a vote, and defeated thirty to six. However, twenty delegates abstained, which would indicate that the issue might easily resurface at the next CITES meeting, in Buenos Aires in 1985.

More important than the actual vote was the strong indication that animal-rights organizers were preparing the ground for a major

159

offensive against fur-trapping, to take advantage of the momentum created by the EEC ban on white-coat imports. While Gambia was the official sponsor of the anti-trapping resolution at CITES – only member nations can submit resolutions – the driving force behind the resolution was an "observer" from the Friends of Animals, Bill Clark. Friends of Animals (FOA) has been a leader of the anti-fur lobby since the 1960s, when it lobbied against the use of spotted cats in the fur trade.

An American living in Jerusalem and a Friends of Animals organizer, Clark was seen as a leader of the animal-rights contingency that gathered in Botswana. When it appeared that the CITES delegates wouldn't adopt his motion, he lobbied to set up a parallel international body for the express purpose of banning trade in furs trapped by leg-hold traps. He called several meetings, which were attended by a number of delegates and non-governmental organizations, and announced that Switzerland had agreed to become the repository nation for the new group's documents and administration.

A Canadian non-governmental delegate asked Clark why his group didn't take on the central animal-rights issue, meat eating, which causes far more animal death than the fur trade. Clark responded that a campaign against "kosher killing" had been considered, but they'd decided that the risks of being branded "anti-Semitic" were too great. "Ah, so you don't really have the courage of your convictions," the Canadian taunted. "We go where we can, and we take what we can get," Clark replied.

Like in the sealing campaigns, the animal-rights strategy on fur trapping is to push on as many fronts as possible, to see where most progress can be made. After the defeat of the Ohio amendment in 1977, Friends of Animals circulated an ordinance for the prohibition of trapping in individual towns, cities and counties. In their booklet, "Tips To Hunt Saboteurs," they suggest introducing municipal ordinances "in the interest of public safety," barring the use of all weapons: rifles, shotguns, even bows and arrows. Another FOA booklet advises:

(1) Patronize only businesses, doctors, lawyers, veterinarians, who don't hunt. Ask them to display the "I Don't Hunt" slogan;

(2) Keep your children out of the Boy Scouts or other youth groups until the policy of promoting hunting is changed to promote protection;

(3) Ask the PTA to press for nonemployment of teachers who hunt, and to bar speakers from the Game Commission or sports clubs;

(4) Consider changing your church – or your religion – if the leaders hunt or sponsor fund-raising banquets on the flesh of wildlife;

(5) Ostracize socially those who hunt. . . .

FOA has also lobbied to change the allocation of "Pittman-Robertson" funds. These are taxes from guns and ammunition sold in the United States – some $60 million per year – which now pay for wildlife management and conservation. FOA wants these funds to be taken away from wildlife managers, whom it sees as in the service of hunters and trappers.[89]

There are indications that even conservative, well-established animal-welfare organizations are being pushed to take more radical positions by the aggressiveness of the animal-rights campaigns. A national vice-president of the Humane Society of the United States (HSUS) has stated:

> I say the fur industry must die, every last shred of it. And if we have tried to accommodate ourselves to the industry and said, "Think Mink," in the hopes that ranch-raised furs meant less suffering than wild-caught furs, we can forget that one. The only way to get people to stop wearing fur is to get them to wear no furs at all. Jobs be damned! The contention that animals are a natural resource is not a scientific doctrine, but a biased political assumption.[90]

A hint that Greenpeace might take more interest in the fur industry came in 1983, when the organization charged that the Soviet Union continues whaling in order to supply "fodder" to a giant mink-raising complex on the Chukchi peninsula, in the Bering Sea. A "spy voyage" by Paul Watson's *Sea Shepherd* brought back photographs of long conveyor belts leading from the beach to rows of wooden sheds that might well have housed fur bearers. The Soviet Union is believed to raise more mink than any other country, although the exact figures have never been published.

Greenpeace has been uncharacteristically quiet about the fur industry, perhaps because Vancouver, where Greenpeace is based, is also the headquarters of George Clements' Association for the Protection of Fur-bearing Animals (APFA). However, with the two major campaigns of the past decade – whales and seals – now virtually "won," Greenpeace may soon be tempted to branch out into fur trapping, as they moved into Brian Davies' seal campaigns in 1976.[91]

George Clements of the APFA says that he is being pressured to "radicalize" his campaign. He has always claimed to oppose only the leghold trap, and not trapping in general, but government "inaction" he says, may force him to push for the abolition of the whole fur industry.[92] The real cause of Clements' new urgency may really be too much government action. As the establishment of the Fur Institute of Canada makes clear that a major institution dedicated to developing the most humane traps possible is becoming operational, it is to be expected that the debate will move to a more overtly animal-rights stance, that animals shouldn't be killed at all. In fact, we have already seen the beginnings of such action.

The Fund For Animals, Trans-species Unlimited and the Animal Defense League of Canada joined forces to sponsor demonstrations on October 22, 1983 at the headquarters of Woodstream Corporation, the trap manufacturer, in Lititz, Pennsylvania, and its plants in Niagara Falls, Ontario and Westminister, California. The object of the demonstrations was declared to be:

(1) to generate mass-media attention and public awareness of the cruelties of trapping;
(2) to present elected representatives with a clear public mandate to pass legislation against the leghold trap;
(3) to demand that Woodstream call a complete halt to the production of leghold traps. . . .[93]

Supporting organizations, according to a press release, included People for the Ethical Treatment of Animals, the Humane Society of the United States, Friends of Animals, Animal Liberation Inc. and Beauty Without Cruelty.

On April 7, 1984, the largest anti-fur demonstrations ever took place in Washington, Los Angeles and Chicago, with smaller ones in other cities. The coordinator was Mobilization for Animals (honorary president, Brigitte Bardot;[94] honorary chairman, Peter Singer), an umbrella group that claims to unite some four hundred animal-welfare and animal-rights groups around the world. Announcements for the anti-trapping rallies stated:

The only beneficiaries of trapping and mass extermination programs are the fur industry and "wildlife management" bureaucrats. No industry, agency, or individual has the right to torture and kill sensitive living creatures for financial gain and personal vanity. . . .

The stated goal of Mobilization for Animals is to "create a world where no animal will ever again be the victim of suffering inflicted by humans." Peter Singer suggests that rather than allow hunters and trappers to control animal populations, programs should be developed "to reduce the fertility of animals."[95]

The Canadian Fur Industry

In animal-rights texts, the "fur industry" is commonly spoken of as if it was a single monolithic entity, the rich and powerful manipulator of what everyone knows is a "luxury" – if not a "vanity" – trade. The image of the fur-industry Goliath challenged by the animal-rights Davids is perhaps a mythic holdover from the heyday of the great Company of Adventurers who sailed into Hudson Bay; that company controlled about half the territory of present-day Canada. (Although the Hudson's Bay Company still buys furs, its main role now is to auction furs belonging to trappers and ranchers, for which the company takes a commission.)

The fur trade in Canada today is a loose association of thousands of small-scale, usually independent operators. Some hundred thousand trappers collected about $47 million worth of wild furs in 1982–1983. (Furs are collected through winter, which spans two calendar years.) Another $44 million was produced by fur ranches.[96] Collectors and dealers still buy pelts from trappers "in the country," but increasingly, organized trappers' associations (like the Ontario Trappers Association [OTA] or the Cree Trappers Association) allow trappers to sell their furs directly at auction, where they are purchased by fur "manufacturers."

Most fur garments sold in Canada are manufactured in Canada (about eighty per cent in Montreal), and about half the production is exported. It may seem unremarkable that a fur-rich country like Canada developed a strong, export-oriented fashion-fur industry; but, in fact, the growth of the manufacturing sector is quite recent. Traditionally, Canada exported raw furs (as it still does), which were made into clothing in the fashion houses of Europe, London, and especially after World War One, New York. Until the end of World War Two, the Canadian manufacturing sector was limited, and worked mostly with less expensive furs like muskrat and lamb, while fine furs like mink were more often sent to New York.

At the start of the century, Jewish artisans from the fur-working centers of Europe came to Canada and established the nucleus of a creative and energetic manufacturing center. Later, when Jewish refugees were trying to flee Europe after World War Two, these furriers (along with Jews in various other trades) pledged jobs for refugees who had training in the trade. In this way, thousands of skilled European fur craftsmen reached Montreal and Toronto (some also went to Winnipeg).

The trade was strengthened by a second wave of immigration of Greek furriers, most from the northern mountain village of Kastoria, from "castor," meaning "beaver." Canada became, in the process, a world-class fashion-fur manufacturer, and began to export not only raw furs but also finished coats. As well, raw and dressed pelts were imported to feed a growing manufacturing sector.

For, while Canada is a major fur exporter, at least as many unworked pelts are imported as exported: raccoon and muskrat from the United States; ranched mink and foxes from Europe and other furs from around the world. After being worked into finished garments, many are re-exported, a tribute to Canadian workmanship.

By 1981, the value of fur garments produced was up to $260 million, yet the industry remains small-scale, with an average of seven employees per shop, fewer employees per shop than even forty years ago. There does not appear to be any great advantage in large operations.[97] The largest manufacturers may dominate the market, and fashion, but virtually any skilled furrier can, at any time, rent a small space, set up a blocking table and a fur-sewing machine, manufacture coats and be competitive in the marketplace.

This situation is very different from almost any other industry, for the fur industry remains virtually artisanal. Processes cannot be greatly automated. Every pelt is unique and must be individually handled, graded, cut and sewn. Every step in the production of fine furs still depends on the judgment and skill of specialized craftsmen.

For these reasons, the monolithic term "fur industry" as it is used by animal-rights groups is misleading. About half the production of the manufacturing sector is divided among more than 270 individually owned and operated shops. Retailers, too, have traditionally been independent. More than eighty per cent of retail sales are made from privately owned, family-run, one-store businesses. From trappers and ranchers to manufacturers and retailers, the Canadian trade is made up of thousands of small-scale independent businesspeople. This has given the trade flexibility and strength, but it is also the reason the trade has been incapable, to date, of responding effectively to the threat posed by animal-rights groups.

A major strategy of the animal-rights attack on the fur trade is to foster the impression that those involved in it contribute nothing, that they merely "exploit" nature. This is one of the reasons that trap opponents object to the word "harvest" as applied to wildlife. A farmer, they say, at least works and improves his land, while the fur trader just "takes."

Most people understand that working a trap line in the northern woods in midwinter is not the easiest way to earn one's livelihood. Chapter Three described the aboriginal hunter's relationship with his prey and with nature. The work of the fur craftsman, however, is probably even less well-known than the way of the Indian.

Most Greek-born furriers in Canada come from Kastoria, a town of fur workers. Virtually every house has a fur machine and children learn to operate them at a young age; for Kastoria is the center of a remarkable world-wide recycling operation. From fur ateliers around the world, pieces trimmed from pelts being made into coats are collected and shipped in large bales to Kastoria. There, in the Macedonian mountains, the pieces are meticulously sorted by fur type and color. (Mink paws, for example, are sorted into back and front paws, because the fur texture is different.) The sorted pieces, often as small as a human finger, are carefully sewn together into "plates," each large enough to make one coat. The plates are then usually exported.

Not only the plates, however, require painstaking sewing. As most animal pelts are considerably shorter than the length required for a full coat, long narrow diagonal slices are made in the skins, so that they may be "let out" and sewed back together into longer, narrower bands. In a mink coat, where up to forty-five skins may have to be "let out" like this, there will be thousands of precise cuts and seams, to produce supple, free-flowing lines, rather than the bulky effect that results when skins are simply tacked together without the "letting-out" process.

From beginning to end – from trapper or rancher to pelting and careful preparation of skins for the "dressers," to matching, cutting, "blocking" (wetting and stretching the skins to a pattern) and sewing – a great deal of skilled labor goes into the production of a fur coat, which is why they are expensive.

The point of mentioning these processes is to emphasize that furs, for which animals have died, are treated with skill, consideration and craftsmanship – in brief, with respect.

The death of animals is not treated lightly, nor are their "gifts" abused, as animal-rights groups would have us believe. On the contrary, the experience, skills and traditions of cultures as diverse as those of Cree hunters and Kastorian furriers come together to produce, with these furs, some of the most meticulous craftsmanship to be found in clothing today.

Animal-rights advocates have declared that they will make it "socially unacceptable" to wear furs. But fashions change. Ironically,

Placing a pelt on a stretcher to dry.

NATIVE PRESS

Preparing the hide: scraping.

Beaver pelts prepared for drying.

ENÉ FREMOLEAU

An ironing machine is used to condition the fur and to provide lustre and sheen.

A worker "spots" foxes to simulate lynx fur.

one hundred years ago, when Henry Salt was writing, an English accountant was impressed by the sound health philosophy of a German zoologist, Dr. Gustav Jaeger; the accountant translated Jaeger's books and opened a special "Jaeger" clothing store in London. Doctor Jaeger's theory was that humans should wear only animal hairs next to their bodies. Vegetable fibers like linen and cotton were to be avoided. The store in London, then called "Doctor Jaeger's Sanitary Woolen System," sold clothing made of cashmere from goats in the Himalayas; of angora from Asia Minor; of alpaca, vicuna and marino sheep. The store was an instant success. The vegetarian George Bernard Shaw, who is often quoted by animal-rights groups, bought a suit there. Oscar Wilde wrote in *The Times*:

> Animal materials such as wool are made by nature to protect animal life, and will not prevent but assist the evaporation of the emanations from the body. . . .[98]

The explorer Sir Henry Stanley wore "Jaeger" clothes to Africa, and Scott, Ziegler, Wellman and Shackleton all wore them to the Antarctic. Jaeger "natural" clothing is still sold around the world, although, since the 1950s, they also manufacture clothing made of synthetics.

Woolens aren't furs, it may be protested. However, it has been shown that the stress a sheep suffers when it is cut from the rest of the flock to be sheared may be greater than that of being slaughtered in an abattoir with its fellows. (The problem of evaluating levels of animal suffering is considered in more depth in Chapter Seven.) More to the point, in an age when many fear that the ceaseless expansion of industrial society is leading us ever farther from any real contact with nature (and ever closer to ecological cataclysm), one would think that the fur industry would be embraced with the same zeal as was Doctor Jaeger's Sanitary Woolen System a hundred years ago.

Trapping is a mainstay of the remaining traditional Indian hunting societies. It is a bulwark against further encroachments by hydroelectric and gas interests into wildlife habitat. It provides employment for thousands of people who still wish to live close to the land. And not least, the manufacturing sector it supports has remained artisanal in scale and quality. Not only trappers, but fur workers, too, represent values that the ecologists pretend to respect.

The remarkable decentralization of the fur trade is its biggest obstacle in trying to respond to the potentially devastating campaign launched by animal-rights groups.[99] It remains to be seen if public opinion will abandon the fur trade as blindly as it turned against sealers. People, of course, see what they wish. Even the meticulous craft that goes into sewing a fur garment was seen by Henry Salt as part and parcel of the conspiracy against which he was struggling:

A fur garment or trimming, we are told, appearing to the eye as if it were a uniform piece, is generally made up of many curiously shaped fragments. It is significant that a society which is enamoured of so many shams and fictions, and which detests nothing so strongly as the need of looking facts in the face, should pre-eminently esteem these articles of apparel which are constructed on the most deceptive and illusory of principles.[100]

7

Animals in Research and on Factory Farms

Those who work for the abolition of vivisection, or any other particular wrong, should do so with the avowed purpose of capturing one stronghold of the enemy, not because they believe that the war will then be over, but because they will be able to use the position thus gained as an advantageous starting-point for still further progression ....
– Henry Salt, *Animals' Rights*, 1894

It is impossible to understand the campaigns against sealing and fur trapping without considering the animal-rights critique of the treatment of animals in scientific laboratories and modern intensive "factory farms." Peter Singer's *Animal Liberation*, the most influential of the new animal-rights texts, concentrates its full attack on these two areas because, says Singer, they cause more suffering to animals than does any other human activity.[1]

The quota for harp seals in the Canadian hunt in recent years has been about 186,000, although less than 60,000 were taken in the past two seasons. About forty million wild animals are annually trapped for fur, worldwide, with perhaps another thirty million raised on ranches. More than two hundred million animals are used for research and product testing. Hundreds of millions of cows, pigs and sheep and about three billion poultry birds are consumed annually in the United States alone.

Equally important, says Singer, research and factory farming are two areas where everyone is directly involved, for everyone profits from animal exploitation. If these two areas of animal abuse can be eliminated, Singer says, surely the others – the fur trade, hunting, rodeos and circuses, zoos and aquariums – would not survive long.[2]

Organized resistance to vivisection, which includes any research that intentionally hurts or injures animals, began more than a hundred years ago in England, with the protest against the work of the Paris School. (See Chapter 3). In the past twenty years, however, the anti-vivisection movement has developed a new militancy: scientists have been recruited into the movement, and vivisection is now criticized as not only cruel but scientifically unsound. Donald Barnes is the director of the Washington office of the National Anti-Vivisection Society. For sixteen years he was a research psychologist with the United States Air Force at the School for Aerospace Medicine, at Brooks Air Force Base, San Antonio, Texas. His lab irradiated monkeys in order to predict the behavior of pilots during a nuclear war. He began to question his work when he was asked by his superiors to do an experiment that, as a scientist, he believed was not worth doing:

> The boss told me to go ahead and do the experiment because he had promised it to one of the funding agencies, and it was a political maneuver. So I had to refuse to do that. This brought about a confrontation between me and my superiors, as you might well imagine, in the course of which I had more and more reason to look at the total gamut of my experiences as an experimental psychologist, and I saw a lot of things I didn't expect to see. I realized that of the thousand or so monkeys that I had personally seen trained and irradiated and observed, that none of the data – and I say this very thoughtfully – absolutely none of the data that came from those experiments could have any relevance for man or other animals. At that point I was appalled at my own lack of ability to see the ethical question, and also appalled at the fact that my training didn't lead toward the ethical question, but in fact away from it. . . .
>
> I'd been conditioned to see these animals as tools for research, as surrogates for man. Calling them "subjects," calling them "preparations," using their numbers, seeing them scream in pain during training as a necessary part of the experiment – I was completely conditioned. I call it "conditioned ethical blindness."[3]

Traditionally, anti-vivisectionists argued that animals shouldn't be made to suffer because, like humans, they are sentient beings. The new argument adds that insofar as animals are not like us, they don't make good experimental models for human problems. Donald Barnes, for example, worked with Rhesus monkeys, which have a histamine-release factor sufficiently different from human levels to make them poor models for radiation research. Upon radiation, the amount of oxygenation to the brain triggered by histamine release determines the level of consciousness, and therefore the level of behavioral functioning:

> But even though this fact was brought out, it was suppressed, because these animals, Rhesus monkeys, had been used for so long, labs were set up for them, and people simply shrugged that data

aside because it's an ongoing program. That's where their budget comes from, that's where their salaries come from.[4]

The work Donald Barnes was doing is particularly objectionable because its goal was to fight wars more efficiently. Similar criticism, however, is leveled against less dramatic elements of medical science. Like Donald Barnes, Robert Sharpe gave up a career as a research scientist; today he is scientific director for the International Association Against Painful Experiments on Animals. He believes that the emphasis on animal experiments in medical research has shifted attention from the human patient:

> Recently in Britain a drug called Oparin, which was used to treat arthritis, was withdrawn from the market. This drug was promoted by the drug company Eli Lilly as having the potential to cure arthritis on the basis of curing artificially induced arthritis in rats. When it came to treat human arthritis, it was the same as all the twenty-three previous similar drugs in that area – it didn't cure it. Not only that, but Oparin killed many people. It killed them because the drug was not metabolized in the body very rapidly in elderly patients. The trouble is, the researchers had concentrated on animals, who metabolized the drug differently, instead of concentrating on the metabolism in elderly volunteers. That's what I mean by subtly transferring the emphasis onto animal experiments instead of carefully considering human observations. . . .[5]

Another example, says Sharpe, is shock research: for years dogs were used in this work, but it was discovered they weren't very good models for people. Then rats were used. But rats and people are different. Warming up a human shock victim helped the patient, but it was fatal for rats. Because animals react so differently, says Sharpe, dangerous drugs slip through the most extensive animal tests, and potentially useful ones may be lost.

Penicillin, for example, is lethal to guinea pigs, and drugs like digitalis, the early anaesthetics and quinine would probably not pass the animal-testing stage if they were introduced today. Salicylates (aspirin) cause malformations in rats, but not in mice or humans. On the other hand, Thalidomide was extensively tested on animals for six years before it was marketed.[6]

The animal-rights critique leads quickly to a more profound questioning of the role of medicine in our society. Without animals to test and develop thousands of new drugs to "mask symptoms of disease," or to try out sophisticated artificial hearts and valves, it is argued, medicine would be forced to explore less violent approaches; acupuncture, naturopathy, homeopathy and the use of the mind to control disease. In Britain, work is being done to control cancer using diet and psychotherapy.[7] More accent could be placed on disease prevention through better diet and living habits. The World Health Organization estimates that eighty to ninety per cent of cancers are, theoretically at least, preventable, and at least forty percent of male cancer deaths have been directly linked to smoking. And yet, Robert Sharpe objects, governments have taken no steps to ban smoking, and few to limit cigarette advertising.

Even if experiments with animals could be proved to benefit humans, however, animal-rights advocates would still consider it unacceptable:

> This is fundamentally a moral issue ... during the last war, Nazi doctors carried out quite atrocious experiments on Jews. There's no doubt that benefit came from those experiments, but no one would justify the holocaust because of those benefits.[8]

Using the same criteria that are commonly used to justify experiments with animals, animal-rights spokesmen point out, more culturally advanced or intelligent aliens from another planet could justify making use of humans for their own experiments.

Having rejected the sacrifice of animals, even for medical advancement, their use for testing cosmetics and household products is strongly opposed. Millions of animals die each year in tests like the LD–50 ("Lethal Dose – 50%"); animals are force-fed various products until half of them die. For the Draize eye-irritancy test, cosmetics and other products are placed in the eyes of living rabbits (rabbits' eyes cannot tear to wash them out), to observe the extent of the damage caused.

Animal-rights critics claim that such tests have little validity for humans. The massive killing doses administered in the LD–50 (acute toxicity) tests, moreover, tell nothing about the cumulative long-term effects of ingesting smaller quantities (chronic toxicity). It has been said that the only possible use for LD–50 results would be to tell mice what dose of different chemicals they need to commit suicide effectively.[9] Changes that might make these tests more useful, however, such as long-term studies of the effects of small doses, would not necessarily reduce the suffering of test animals.[10]

The numbers of animals used for product testing have mushroomed due to pressure from consumers' groups to insure product safety. However, because chemicals introduced into the environment interact with other substances in often lethal and unexpected ways, thorough testing is virtually impossible. It is estimated that some five hundred thousand toxic substances are in common use. To consider the interaction of this many substances only in *pairs* (of course there are certainly more complex interactions) would require testing 125 billion combinations.[11] Animal-rights theorist Bernard Rollin argues that, even without considering animal suffering, the sheer impossibility of insuring safety may make it necessary to consider restraining the introduction of new products. Manufacturers might be required to prove that a new product is appreciably superior to existing substances in order to manufacture it, Rollin suggests.

In addition to censuring medicine, the pharmaceutical and tobacco and other industries, in other words, the animal-rights groups' position on animal tests leads to a fundamental questioning of the role of innovation as a driving force of economic growth and social change in modern society. Thus Peter Singer in *Animal Liberation* complains: "Don't we have enough of these products? Who benefits from their introduction, except the companies that hope to make a profit from their new gimmicks?"[12]

Pressure from anti-vivisectionists has led to some reduction in the use of animals for certain tests. Henry Spira's campaign against the Draize test and his threat to launch a massive boycott against the cosmetic industry pushed Revlon to donate $750,000 to the Rockefeller Foundation to sponsor research for a replacement to the eye-irritancy test. Spira also revealed that up to five United States government agencies might conduct the same animal tests, with no communication among them. Government agencies are now required to insure that tests aren't repeated needlessly.[13]

The American Pharmaceutical Manufacturers Association is asking governments to re-evaluate the purpose of LD–50 tests. This is one case in which concern for profits is in no way opposed to the goals of animal-rights groups, as animal tests are invariably expensive. Testing a product for carcinogenic (cancer-causing) properties, for example, is lengthy; about two years using rats or seven years using dogs. It is also expensive, costing up to $500,000 to test a single product. The recently developed Ames test, using a special strain of salmonella bacteria instead of animals, is equally effective in many cases. It takes only three weeks and costs about $500.[14]

For some tests, however, such as detecting teratogens (toxins that cause changes in the developing fetus), no substitute for animal tests has yet been found. Rollin spotlights the complex moral considerations that underlie all such discussions when he points out that instead of animals, human embryos destined for abortion could be used, and would be the best subjects for study, although the vast majority of society would never accept this solution.[15]

United Action for Animals (UAA), headed by Eleanor Seiling (who provided Peter Singer with access to her files on laboratory experiments as research for his *Animal Liberation*) now employs a professional lobbyist in Washington to push for legislation like H.R. 556, the Research Modernization Act. This act would have required that thirty to fifty per cent of federal money used in research be directed to developing alternatives to the use of animals.[16] But when Henry Spira called off his planned boycott of the cosmetics industry after Revlon donated funds to find alternatives to the Draize test, he was accused by more militant animal-rights leaders of "selling out."[17]

This brings us back to a central problem of the animal-rights philosophy: as was seen in the campaigns against sealing and fur trapping, correcting abuses in one area does not necessarily end the protest, but may lead to an intensification of the attack on other fronts – because animal-rights groups are fundamentally opposed to any use of animals for human ends. Because the attack tends to be directed against one specific problem at a time, however, the full implications of this philosophy are rarely considered.

The attack against the "Scientific Inquisition" (the term coined by Salt in 1894)[18] follows a pattern very similar to that used against sealing and the fur trade. The first step is to cast doubt on the character and moral integrity of scientists. People with any tender feelings toward animals, we are told, are "weeded out" of scientific programs, beginning with the first high-school dissection class. Far from "scientific," laboratory science is said to cruelly act out "social fantasies,"[19] to be based on "primitive magic,"[20] and is unfavorably compared to "the ancients who tried to divine the future from the entrails of animals, which were at least mercifully killed first."[21]

Scientists are described as being more interested in securing jobs and grants than in knowledge,[22] and it is argued that their work rarely has any value in any case. An ironic statement by H.F. Harlowe, for twelve years editor of the *Journal of Comparative and Physiological Psychology*, is often cited: "Most experiments are not worth doing, and the data attained are not worth publishing."[23]

The main tactic of animal-rights groups, however, is to describe particularly unpleasant experiments, often with supporting photographic evidence. H.F. Harlowe's gruesome methods of inducing psychopathology in monkeys are often described,[24] as are the experiments reported by Donald Barnes. These cases are presented as typical, at least regarding the callousness of the researchers, and all laboratory science is condemned by association. Examples are usually chosen from experiments on cats, dogs or monkeys, as often as not with electrodes protruding from their skulls. In actual fact, only about one per cent of the animals used in laboratories are dogs, cats or primates.[25] More than ninety per cent are mice, rats or guinea pigs. Singer does include mice and rats in his survey of experiments, but it is the photographs of dogs and monkeys that attract the most response.

(One cannot help but recall the "Warning" packets of horror photo-graphs Brian Davies' IFAW uses in the anti-sealing campaigns.)

With the photographs and graphic descriptions of painful experiments, anti-vivisectionists use statistics to drive home their message: "only one experiment in four is ever published"[26] (and therefore may be repeated countless times by other investigators, with no contribution to knowledge); "two-thirds of laboratory animals are used to test non-medical products, such as toiletries and cosmetics;" "less than one-third of all licensed experiments on living animals can be seen to be medical."[27]

This "less than one-third" is of some importance, because a survey conducted by the RSPCA in 1974 revealed that about three-quarters of voting-age Britons disapproved of testing cosmetics, toiletries or weapons on animals. However, eighty per cent accepted their use for medical purposes, and seventy per cent for testing drugs. Another survey, by *Glamour* magazine in 1981, showed that eighty-four per cent of those surveyed opposed the use of animals to test cosmetics.[28]

The figure of less than one-third medical use is discussed by Richard Ryder, in his important critique, *Victims of Science*; it has been argued that Ryder misinterpreted Home Office reports in arriving at this figure. In Britain, since the 1876 Cruelty to Animals Act, experiments using animals must be licensed. The 1975 Home Office reports on which Ryder based his figures specified that one-third of experiments were for cancer research, diagnosis and legally required testing of drugs. Two-thirds were not described, and Ryder assumed they were nonmedical. The 1978 report, however, was more detailed, and stated that fifty-six per cent of the experiments were "performed to select, develop, or study the use, hazards, or safety of medical, dental, or veterinary appliances;" twenty-two per cent were to study body structure or function and twenty per cent were to fulfill legal obligations of testing nonmedical products such as food additives, herbicides and cosmetics. Less than one per cent of all experiments conducted in the United Kingdom in 1978, however, were to test cosmetics or toiletries.[29]

Animal-rights groups' statistics on animal testing, like those used in the campaigns against sealing and trapping, are often misleading. By claiming that three-quarters of the population oppose the use of animals for cosmetics testing, and that two-thirds of tests are "non-medical," they construct a "scientific conclusion" that most people oppose the use of animals in laboratories. They can then go on to suggest that only pressure from greedy scientists and insidious business lobbies prevents governments from banning animal testing altogether. In fact, most people still do accept the use of animals for medically oriented research,[30] and most research is health-oriented.

Only a very small proportion of research is for "vanity."

On a simpler level, animal-rights groups use figures for shock value: eighty-five thousand primates per year used in United States labs; half a million dogs; two hundred thousand cats; fifteen to twenty million frogs; forty-five million rodents; perhaps two hundred million animals, in all, worldwide.[31] Combined with the photographs and descriptions of particularly horrible experiments, these figures conjure up a frightening picture.

To a large extent, however, the horror is a creation of media. Advanced communications allow us to tabulate a global picture of ourselves as never before. Human population has grown, and continues to grow, so quickly that almost any global statistic takes on menacing proportions: the number of potatoes consumed each hour, the number of humans who are born or die each day.

In this global context, the number of animals used in laboratories falls into perspective. With a world population of more than three billion, two hundred million laboratory experiments worldwide means that one animal is used for every fifteen or twenty people; more than ninety per cent of these animals are mice, rats or guinea pigs.[32] Without trying to minimize the importance of controlling animal testing and eliminating experiments that are vicious, sadistic or useless, the fact remains that most people would accept that one mouse for every fifteen people (or one mouse per person every fifteen years) is not too high a price to pay for medical research and product-safety testing.

Most of us, of course, prefer to think that it is a mouse or rat that is sacrificed for our benefit, rather than a dog or a cat. Only about one per cent of animals used in research are cats or dogs, but that still amounts to some seven hundred thousand cats and dogs per year in the United States laboratories. However, this is about 3.5% of the number of unwanted dogs (about twenty million) that are killed each year by the humane societies in the United States. A recent Humane Society of the United States (HSUS) report, moreover, states that more than one million animals a day are killed on Ua.ited States streets and highways by automobiles. Cars and trucks kill more than three times the number of squirrels, rabbits, raccoons, opposums, skunks, dogs, cats, deer and farm animals as are used in research of all kinds.[33]

Even on a theoretical level, lines are not so easy to draw as animal-rights advocates would have us believe. The Canadian Council on Animal Care (CCAC), in their *Ethics of Animal Experimentation*, hold that experiments involving prey killing or fighting should be generally "restricted, and used only when, on the basis of expert opinion, it is anticipated that their utilization will undoubtedly contribute knowledge or benefit to humans or animals."[34] However, Marian Stamp

Dawkins, an Oxford biologist, questions whether it is that simple. She asks: If a scientist were simply to watch animals in the wild kill their prey, how many people would object? Still fewer would protest if this scientist merely examined carcasses left behind after, say, a fox raided a gull colony. But what if the researcher takes a more active role? What if he releases a hawk near a flock of pigeons? And what if, for closer observation, he builds a large aviary, and releases pigeons and hawk into it? "At what point does a scientist cease to be an observer and become responsible for 'cruelty,' when that 'cruelty' is inflicted not by him but by other animals?"[35]

Dawkins' example shows the difficulty of setting down hard-and-fast rules about experimentation and, therefore, of establishing control mechanisms to administer laboratory science. In Canada, the use of animals in laboratories is under the supervision of the CCAC. In every institution where animals are used, there is a Local Animal Care Committee, including at least one professional veterinarian and one "non-user" (in universities this person is often a faculty member from one of the humanities). Every experiment to be done on a living animal must first be submitted for approval to the local committee; the committees are evaluated every three or four years by a team from a central pool of ninety scientists. Local committees have the power to stop any experiment that is believed to cause undue or unjustifiable pain or that has strayed from the research proposal. The CCAC board is made up of representatives from fifteen government and scientific agencies, and includes one member from the Canadian Federation of Humane Societies (CFHS). This system has recently been adopted in the United Kingdom and is being considered for use in the United States.

From a militant animal-rights perspective, the CCAC is little more than a sham, since the system is self-regulating: most of the representatives on the council and the local committees are animal users and colleagues of those whose work they are assessing. Without an outside adjudicator with legal powers, it is argued, the CCAC is merely a public-relations trick. Doctor Harry Rowsell, executive director of the CCAC, insists, however, that the flexible moral force of the present system is preferable to a rigid set of government regulations, which can easily become little more than a licensing system that cuts scientists off from dialogue with the outside community.[36]

In a society like ours, in which there is no longer a clear moral consensus about the nature of our relationship with animals and our environment, law can rarely have any positive effect. Doctor Rowsell is concerned that the increasingly militant animal-rights groups' call for strict controls may lead to polarization of the public and scientific communities. That Doctor Rowsell's fears may well be justified was illustrated by two recent events.

In August 1983, the city of Vancouver hosted a conference of the International Council on Laboratory Animal Science (ICLAS). The convention was a symposium-cum-trade-fair, and in addition to a full schedule of scientific presentations, major suppliers of laboratory animals and equipment (a multimillion dollar industry) set up exhibitions and sales booths on the mezzanine of the Hotel Vancouver. At the Four Seasons Hotel, animal-rights organizers countered with an "Animal Rights Symposium," featuring speakers from the Fund For Animals (FFA), the National Anti-Vivisection Society (NAS), the International League for Animal Rights (ILAR), and the International Association Against Painful Experiments on Animals (IAAPEA).

Mutual suspicion was intense. At the ICLAS convention, extra security was called in and journalists' credentials were doublechecked. Rumors flew that animal-rights commandoes would "try something" to disrupt the convention.

A few blocks away, Peter Hamilton, whose Vancouver-based Lifeforce had sponsored the animal-rights symposium, screened films that he had made by "infiltrating" laboratories. Hamilton scored a coup by arranging for the mayor of Vancouver to inaugurate an "Animal-Rights Day" in Vancouver. Unfortunately, other than a few journalists who covered both events, the two groups never addressed each other or took the opportunity to answer each other's charges.

No one at the animal-rights symposium, for example, heard Washington State University veterinarian Leo Bustad's closing address to the ICLAS convention. Doctor Bustad reminded researchers that how they treated their laboratory animals would have definite effects on the results of their experiments. Animals that are not well cared for, that are separated suddenly from their mates or fellows or that do not have contact with other animals or humans will succumb more quickly to stress, disease or toxins. If laboratory animals are not treated with respect, as living beings, Doctor Bustad pointed out, they are not normal animals, and the results of tests done with them may be very misleading.

Consideration for their animals should lead scientists to be very cautious about submitting them to painful procedures, said Doctor Bustad; but one must also evaluate the cost of not doing a given experiment. Many animals were sacrificed to develop polio vaccine but, thanks to them, people today no longer live in dread of that crippling disease.

"People used to be afraid to let their children go swimming in the summer," Doctor Bustad reminded those too young to remember some of the battles the "Scientific Inquisition" has won for mankind. He also pointed out that animals, too, have profited from the advances of medical science, particularly immunology.

Leo Bustad's ideas are a bridge across the gulf that separates scientists and animal-rights groups. Yet Peter Hamilton of Lifeforce chose to dismiss Bustad, charging that he had conducted irradiation experiments on animals. Doctor Bustad is building another bridge between humans and animals through "people-pet partnership" programs. Doctors sometimes "prescribe" pets for the elderly, as it has been shown that the companionship of an animal can often be more beneficial than drugs. If we take a cat in our laps and stroke it, our blood pressure goes down measurably; so does the cat's. Animal companions and helpers are also being provided for the handicapped; horseback riding has had extraordinary results with some crippled and even autistic children. Training dogs for the handicapped has had a calming effect on prisoners with histories of violence. (The most alienated prisoners appeared to appreciate that the animals weren't aware of their records.)[37] But once again, animal-rights groups opposed Doctor Bustad, charging that such programs would lead only to more animal abuse and neglect, and "are good news only for the veterinarians."[38]

Yet the scientific establishment can be equally dismissive. In the spring of 1984, a group of students prepared a presentation on the animal-rights critique of laboratory science for a graduate seminar at a Quebec agricultural college. The presentation was low-key and brief, barely outlining the animal-rights position; but in the question period the defensiveness of the faculty was evident. The students were accused of being "one-sided," of having shown too much sympathy for the animal-rights position; the mere acknowledgment that some people did criticize laboratory science was taboo in this milieu.

The students' original proposal had been to visit local commercial research labs, perhaps with a video camera, to verify the truth or exaggeration of animal-rights groups' charges. They were quickly warned off such a venture by their advisors, and with due regard for their diplomas and professional careers the plan was quietly dropped.

Such defensiveness and repression is probably the most dangerous problem facing laboratory science today. It is remarkably similar to the attitude of the fur industry: the belief that, by sticking one's head deep enough into the sand, the problem will go away. Yet this very failure of the fur trade or scientists to respond directly to their charges is used by animal-rights advocates as "proof" that their arguments are irrefutable.

THE FACTORY FARM

Now it must be admitted, I think, that it is a difficult thing to recognize or assert the rights of an animal on whom you propose to make a meal. . . .
– Henry Salt (*Animals' Rights*)

Factory farming is the "sleeper" of animal-rights issues. While sealing, trapping and, sometimes, laboratory animals have attracted most of the media attention to date, these campaigns make little sense unless they lead to a rejection of meat eating. As Peter Singer has stated, it is the raising of animals for food that causes by far the greatest number of animals to suffer. It is also the form of animal exploitation in which almost everyone is directly involved.[39]

The strategy for the attack on "factory farming" is familiar from the other animal-rights campaigns. Farming, we are told, is "agrobusiness." Twenty large corporations control poultry production in the United States, and a single egg battery will house more than a million laying hens. Pillsbury, Safeway, Kentucky Fried Chicken and Armour have laying batteries; Ralston Purina raises broilers; Greyhound Corporation raises turkeys; IT&T keeps pigs; insurance and oil companies run feedlots where up to a hundred thousand cattle are fattened at a time.[40]

Farmers today no longer care for animals, it is said, but only for profits. The more pigs or chickens that can be squeezed under one roof, the higher the profits; therefore living space is reduced to the degree that a chicken may have only half a square foot or less of cage space. Overcrowding and boredom leads to "vices," like feather pecking and cannibalism, so battery chickens are regularly debeaked. Pigs' tails are docked so they won't be bitten off by other pigs.[41] Pigs and calves are raised on concrete or slatted floors, for ease of manure removal; as a result, many animals suffer foot and leg damage. Veal calves are fed liquid diets and deprived of roughage to keep their flesh pale – in fact, anemic. In Henry Salt's time, the main suffering of food animals came when they were transported to slaughter (often over long distances without food or water); today, the conditions in which they are raised are said to be most oppressive.

Intensive methods have lowered the cost of meat and made it more widely available than ever before. Before World War Two, table chickens were still relatively rare. From 1950 to 1972, per-capita meat consumption in the United States, already high, doubled.[42] Thanks to "factory" methods and careful breeding, only half as much food is required now to produce a dozen eggs as was needed at the start of this century.[43] Broilers are now raised in only seven to eight weeks, during which time they increase their weight forty-three times.[44] (This means, incidentally, that they grow to the maximum density of two or more per square foot – a figure often cited by animal-rights groups – for only a few days before they are slaughtered.) Pigs are now killed at fifteen to thirty weeks of age, veal calves at twelve weeks old.

The critique of factory farming begins by discrediting the farmer as a "businessman," concerned only for "profits." (The growth of a strong antibusiness ideology in our society is a phenomenon that warrants a full examination of its own.) The next step is to drive the case home with "horror" pictures of animals in long shedlike buildings, confined in narrow stalls and cages, with lurid descriptions of the suffering this "must" imply:

> It is impossible to farm animals for food without imprisoning, mutilating, and eventually slaughtering them, and no one can ignore this price that has to be paid for the pleasure of eating meat.[45]

But is it really so easy to evaluate what farm conditions are suitable for animals, and which ones cause suffering? Marian Stamp Dawkins shows that the problem is not always as simple as we have been led to believe. Obviously an animal limping or crying out in pain may be presumed to be suffering, but does an absence of symptoms "prove" an absence of suffering? Farmers can cite high productivity or weight gain as proof of the well-being of their animals, but animals are often now raised to their slaughter weight so quickly that they may simply not live long enough for any ill-effects they may be suffering to be exhibited in overt ill health.[46] On the other hand, neither do many of the concepts commonly introduced by animal-rights groups necessarily give us a clear idea about the nature of an animal's experience.

The most common animal-rights argument, whether it is openly stated, is that because factory-farming conditions are not "natural," they must cause suffering. A German federal animal-welfare law, passed in 1972, states that anyone keeping an animal should "provide accommodation that takes account of its natural behavior." The Bramwell Committee, which investigated the conditions of farm animals in Britain, came to similar conclusions: animals have "natural instinctive urges," and "natural behavior patterns;" therefore, "the degree to which the behavioral urges of the animal are frustrated under the particular conditions of confinement must be a major consideration in determining its acceptability or otherwise."[47] Because wild poultry exhibit certain behavior, in other words, such as living in small groups, flying, preening, roosting in trees and laying their eggs in isolated nests, it is assumed that the repression of such "drives" must cause suffering.

Dawkins argues, however, that there may be little justification for using the behavior of wild animals as a model for domestic animals. Humans have "tinkered" with animal genetics for thousands of years. Dogs have been bred for certain traits for at least twelve thousand years; goats and sheep, pigs and cattle seven or eight thousand years. Chickens have been bred for at least four thousand years.

Wild jungle fowl, raised under domestic conditions, produce about sixty-two eggs per year, which is considerably more than they lay in the wild. Domestic White Leghorns lay an average of 181 eggs. This increase has been achieved by breeding birds that mature earlier and "go broody" less often. In the process of selecting for more eggs and other traits, other physical and behavioral characteristics have also inadvertently been changed, so that broiler and laying breeds differ from each other more than "primitive" breeds such as Brown Leghorns differ from the ancestral jungle fowl.[48]

In addition to such genetic changes, the conditions of an animal's early life have a strong influence on that animal's development and behavior. Newly hatched birds and other animals will "imprint" on humans (or even on flashing lights or boxes), and zoo animals often try to mate with their attendants. Dawkins found in free-choice experiments that battery-raised chickens often preferred the battery shed to an open grassy run, at least when they were first exposed to the choice.[49]

Even totally wild animals at times appear to prefer captivity to "freedom." In 1964, a group of African buffalo were herded into a compound to be moved to a national park. While in captivity, they were regularly fed and watered, and when the time came for them to be released, they kept returning to the compound. Gerald Durrell reported that when a revolution prevented him from shipping out animals he had collected in Paraguay, he released them; but most wouldn't leave his camp. Parrots that had been in captivity for three months chewed through wood and wire to get back into their cages.[50]

The flaw in the critique that factory farms aren't "natural" is that it implies that life in nature is free of suffering. A study of songbirds found that adult robins and sparrows, which live about eleven years in captivity, survive only one or two years in the wild. This presupposes they escape the even higher mortality rates from hatching to maturity:

> We ourselves would be shocked if half our friends died each year, and in fact mankind experiences a death-rate of this magnitude only under unusual circumstances, such as the Black Death in 1348, or in some of the actions by commando units in the late war. But in wild songbirds, this is the natural state of affairs.[51]

Animal-rights authors who bemoan the fact that some sheep are being brought indoors into intensive regimes forget that free-range sheep may suffer more: being half-eaten alive by blowfly maggots in summer and dying of cold or starvation through the winter. In all, Dawkins concludes, there is too much suffering in a wild animal's life for that to ever be used as a standard for humane farming conditions.[52]

There are other problems with trying to use animal behavior as a measure for evaluating suffering. Domestic animals, for example, show far less escape and anti-predator behavior than do wild animals, but does this mean that they suffer because they have lost this natural reaction? On the other hand, captive or domestic animals often exhibit "vacuum" or "displacement" behavior: hens may peck the floor of their cages although there is no food there; a cat will play with a ball of fluff when there is no prey to pursue; a dog turns around and around before lying down, although there is no long grass to flatten on the living-room carpet. Yet none of these activities necessarily means the animal is "suffering." Again, if a hen shows signs that she is frustrated at not having a nest in which to lay her egg, does this mean that she is "suffering," and if so, how much?

Frustration is not unique to domestic animals. Rutting stags may pace up and down in front of each other for hours, uncertain whether they should fight; and the more closely the two animals are matched, the longer they'll keep it up. Even some obviously abnormal behavior does not necessarily mean that the animals are suffering. Desmond Morris observed zoo monkeys throwing their feces at human visitors – often with great skill. The monkeys seem to be quite enjoying themselves.

To make the problem even more complicated, naturalists have observed that animals appear to seek a certain level of stress or suffering. Wild herbivores in Africa will frequently, of their own accord, move in so close to predators that they are captured.[53] (One cannot help but think, in this connection, of the Amer-Indian concept of animals "giving themselves" to the hunter). Herring gulls will approach foxes and, in experiments, came closest to a stuffed fox when a dead gull was lying near it. The gulls may be drawn to "learn" about gull-killing predators even if some risk is involved.

Often, monkeys that had been trained to press levers to see films repeatedly chose to watch pictures that obviously frightened them. Their ears went back and they urinated in fright, but they repeatedly pressed the same lever. (Perhaps this is the same impulse that makes humans watch horror movies and read murder mysteries.) Animals' need or desire for a certain level of stress makes "suffering" all the more difficult to define, and standards for human farming conditions elusive.

Attempts to replace subjective interpretations of what animals "must" suffer under certain circumstances with a scientific standard have taken the cue from the pioneering work of Hans Selye. (He measured stress physiologically, testing for certain hormones like ACTH – adreno-cortico-trophic-hormone – and cortisone in the bloodstream.) Tests have revealed that, when pigs were chased around a yard or sheep were subjected to such routine procedures as loading into a truck, dipping or being chased by a dog, the ACTH and cortisone levels in the animals' blood rose. Isolating a sheep to shear it caused far greater production of stress hormones than slaughtering it when the animals remained together.[54]

The problem once again is that there is no clear understanding of what level of stress is compatible with the overall well-being of an animal, or at what level stress should be considered suffering. Animals, like people, appear to prefer some level of stimulation, even if it may be considered painful. The animal-rights concern totally to eliminate stress is, therefore, an empty concept.

The desire to eliminate suffering, even if it means eliminating all stimulation, is not a problem limited to animals. One cannot miss the anthropomorphism in much of the animal-rights critique of farming. For their descriptions of factory farms sound very much like a criticism of modern life in human communities:

> Characterized by extreme restrictions of freedom, enforced uniformity of experience, the submission of life-processes to automatic controlling devices and inflexible time-scheduling ... and running through all this is the rigid and violent suppression of the natural.[55]

The "family structure" as well as the "social structure" (the herd or flock) of intensively raised animals is broken, we are told. The individual has difficulty finding his place in the social order, and violence often results. An animal is forced to "conform as one of the mass, for twenty-four hours a day, every day of its life;" its "individuality [is] ignored" and it is regarded "purely for its product potential."[56]

The most fundamental step in industrializing agriculture is bringing the animals indoors, where every aspect of the environment can be controlled for maximum efficiency and productivity.[57] "One-half of pigs now live out their lives indoors." "Mothers and young are separated at an early age." "No form of animal raising allows the animals to grow up and become part of a community of animals of varying ages, as they would under natural conditions."[58]

This all sounds suspiciously like a description of human life in a modern city, with underground malls connected by subways to temperature- and light-controlled offices and apartment blocks; working mothers and day-care centers; old-age homes and retirement communities where children are not admitted. The criticism depends on the assumption that human needs are a model for animal needs.

Meanwhile, what animals think or feel about their conditions, if they think or feel about them at all, is rarely considered. There are, however, ways of allowing animals to "vote with their feet." Pigs and other animals have been trained to operate switches in order that they can choose for themselves the lighting and temperature they prefer.[59] Chickens, given the choice, preferred an outside run to battery cages, although those that had been raised in cages were less quick to opt for the outdoors. But they would go freely into the cages if that was where food was placed. This suggests that chickens may find cages less oppressive than humans assume.[60]

In one experiment, chickens were given their choice of flooring by being allowed to choose which cage to stay in. The Bramwell Committee had recommended that the floors of battery cages be changed from the traditional fine-gauge hexagonal wire, which the committee thought must be uncomfortable for chickens to stand on. In its place, the committee proposed heavier, flattened, rectangular mesh. Such a change would have been quite expensive, since this flooring had a tendency to crack the eggs. When hens were given a chance to choose for themselves, they opted for the fine wire the committee members had rejected. Photographs taken from beneath the floor revealed that the fine mesh supported the chickens' feet better than the suggested alternative.[61]

Marian Dawkins warns against evaluating animal welfare by human standards and of interpreting animal behavior in human terms. A rat or hamster in its "freeze" posture may appear sleepy or content; yet it is frozen in fear as if in front of a predator. (In Chapter Five, we saw that the white-coat seals' "deep-dive reflex" has often been taken as a sign that the animals were happy or "smiling." We also saw that it is a lack of knowledge about the physiological "swim reflex" that is almost certainly at the root of many tales about seals "skinned alive.")

There are more than a million animal species: many have very different ways of expressing their feelings than humans do. Their needs are also very different. "Imagine how horrible it must be to live in a battery shed (or mink ranch) with thousands of other animals..." is the most common introduction to the animal-rights critique of factory farming. "The tapeworm's peptic Nirvana is not for me," Julian Huxley has said. A child sees a "poor, cold, dirty frog" in the garden, and wants to bring it into the house to clean and warm it up, not understanding that frogs prefer a cool, damp environment. The frog's Nirvana is not for us, either, and this is why one must remain wary, when Singer and other animal-rights writers describe intensive farms as "slave-labour camps" where the inmates "cling tenaciously to life" until the end when, "in contrast to the prisoner who gets a special meal before being hanged, the condemned hens may get no food at all."[62]

VEGETARIANISM AND ANIMAL RIGHTS

If horror stories about conditions on factory farms have not convinced you to give up eating meat, the new "militant vegetarianism" of animal-rights groups makes its appeal in human terms. Vegetarianism, it is claimed, is healthier and cheaper, and it is the only way to avoid the array of chemicals and antibiotics that is routinely fed to livestock. Most important, meat eating is "a choice of diet which is in effect condemning many humans to starve."[63]

The argument goes something like this: it is "obviously" cheaper and more efficient to feed humans with grains than to feed that same grain to the animals that are then eaten by humans.[64] The figure usually quoted is that it takes about ten pounds of grain to produce a pound of meat. A pamphlet published by Lifeforce citing data from the United Animal Defenders states that "the area needed to produce meat for one human could produce nutritionally superior vegetables for eighty people." Peter Singer says that from ten to twenty times the protein per acre is produced by plant foods than by meat.[65] Feedlot cattle in the United States are said to consume ninety-seven per cent of the country's legumes, ninety per cent of the grain, eighty per cent of the fish supplies. The United States produces seventy-five per cent of the world's soybeans, says Peter Singer, and ninety-five per cent of it is fed to animals.[66] (Other authors place the grain consumption by animals in the United States closer to sixty per cent.)[67] In all, it is said,

> ... the food wasted by animal production in the affluent nations would be sufficient, if properly distributed, to end both hunger and malnutrition throughout the world.[68]

These are certainly impressive arguments at first glance; they do not, however, stand up to much analysis. First, they are based on the assumption that world hunger is a problem that can or should be solved simply by producing more food. Apart from the rather bizarre idea that entire nations would sit by their airports waiting for their daily rations to arrive, the argument ignores the larger problems, of which hunger is actually a symptom: constantly rising population resulting in lowered quality of life, breakdown of traditional social structures, pollution, rapid destruction of wildlife habitat and of other wild spaces. Much of the world social order is seriously out of balance, and it is doubtful whether the answer is to ship more grain around the world.[69] There are far more people on earth today than ever before, and even if constantly rising populations could be fed, high populations present more than a food problem: they cause waste problems and social problems. Perhaps there is a limit beyond which we might choose not to go, even if it were possible, for the sake of a quality of life we prefer.[70]

It is also doubtful that grain "liberated" from the production of cattle in the United States would go to feed the world's hungry. If this grain were not used to feed cattle, it would not be grown at all. The meat-raising industry doesn't merely consume grain – it is closer to the truth to say that it "creates" it.

Nor is it accurate to assume that meat production is necessarily always inefficient or "wasteful." "Militant vegetarians" often claim a conversation rate of ten to one for plant food to meat, but this describes the gross material consumed by animals, not the digestible part of their diet. When only digestible food is considered, the ratio falls to about three to one for good dairy cows or pigs; about five to one for egg production; and between three to one and twenty to one for other meats.[71] Moreover, theoretical conversion rates may not be the same as real rates, where the land used to raise sheep or cattle is not suited to growing grain or potatoes or other produce, as is the case in much of Canada. Real rates also differ from theory insofar as grazing animals do much of the work of gathering their own food. Finally, if animals are consuming what in human terms is considered "garbage," the transaction may be efficient indeed.

Animal raising is far less "illogical" than militant vegetarians would have us believe. Ruminates have traditionally made use of marginal lands unsuited for other use. They consume plants that are high in cellulose and roughage, which cannot be digested by humans. They harvest and convert to human use wild grasses which, although indigestible for man, may be higher in energy and protein than grains or potatoes. Finally, they synthesize in their rumen certain amino acids and B vitamins vital to human life but not easily found in a completely vegetarian diet. Nonruminates are scavengers and convert garbage and waste or byproducts from other parts of the farming operation. Not least, animal manure can be fed back into the plant cycle as fertilizer.

Traditionally, animals also serve as a "buffer" of security for farmers (who form most of the population in many parts of the world). They consume surpluses in times of plenty, and are eaten when crops are poor or during the winter. It is in the very regions that are too crowded or too poor to have such animal "shock absorbers" that the spectre of sudden famine is still most terrible.

In sum, animal production is a vital link in a balanced agriculture and is complementary to plant growing. In many parts of Canada and Europe, mixed farming continues. It is true that large feedlots have become important, especially in the United States; but in Canada, most cattle still graze on pasture land, and a great part of Canadian agricultural holdings are suited to nothing else. And while modern feedlots in the United States are a long way from the balanced mixed-farming pattern described here, so are vast monocultures of soybeans and cereals. Monocultures of any kind make severe overdrafts on the soil and attract insect pests and disease, all of which call for increasingly high applications of chemical pesticides and herbicides. We do not, as militant vegetarians would have us believe, get off the pesticide chain by eliminating meat, as a casual glance at government guides to commercial fruit and vegetable growers makes very clear. More to the point, barely two per cent of the world's land mass is suited to vegetable or cereal production; forty per cent is grazing land.

The general condemnation of meat raising as advanced by Peter Singer and others is oversimplified at best. Meat eating may sometimes (but not always) be more "expensive" than pure vegetarianism, but it may also, on a societal level, be sounder.

From the standpoint of the native people of Canada, the ideals of militant vegetarianism are ethically loaded, and anything but "new." It is only quite recently, it should be remembered, that meat eating has played a very important part in the diets of most Europeans.[72] In North America, the dividing line was very clear: "savages" ate meat; "civilization" consisted in clearing the land (of timber, animals and indigenous hunters) and planting cereals. As Henry Salt explained:

> Animals were first slaughtered by uncivilized migratory tribes under the stress of want, and ... the practice thus engendered, being fostered by the religious idea of blood-offering and propitiation, survived and increased after the early conditions which produced it had passed away.[73]

The "habit" of meat eating, Salt assumes, has had "a very detrimental effect on the study of man's moral relations to the lower animals." Thoreau had no doubt that:

> ... it is part of the destiny of the human race, in its gradual improvement, to leave off eating animals as surely as the savage tribes have left off eating each other when they came in contact with the more civilized.[74]

Thoreau appears to have overlooked that wars, Inquisitions and purges of the "civilized" nations have no doubt "eaten" more of their fellows than savages ever did – without often showing the same respect for their victims' remains. The Europeans who came to America rarely gave much thought to the nature of the civilization

they found there. Agricultural and industrial, the Europeans identified culture with buildings, books and bureaucracies, and concluded
that there was no civilization in America.

Hugh Brody points out that this opinion was also convenient, as it
justified European expansion into what could then be considered
"unoccupied" land.[75] Rather than facing the implications of stealing
land, the Europeans could pride themselves on bringing culture to a
barbaric land. That Indians rarely showed much appreciation for this
cultural "gift" was further evidence of their inferiority: "not only was
the [Indian] hunter poor, but he was too ignorant even to appreciate
the fact!"[76]

Brody suggests that the values and vision of agricultural-industrial
people are so different from those of hunting people that it is virtually
impossible for them to comprehend each other. Agricultural people
value the virtues of careful planning, thrift and the accumulation of
material goods. The Indian disregarded these "virtues" because his
needs were provided for by an environment that made very different
demands of him: flexibility, attentiveness to the movements of
animals, cooperation and sharing with others.

The cultural values of the Europeans included a deep-rooted prejudice against meat. (European culture considers "bread" the staff of
life.) Scurvy was one of the most lethal enemies of the first explorers
who came to America. Early symptoms of the disease are depression
and lethargy, which European medical authorities of the day attributed to "the bleakness of the northern terrain and the long gloomy
darkness of an Arctic winter."[77] Entertainments and exercise were
prescribed as a cure.

Although the meat-eating Indians were healthy, meat was believed
to aggravate the disease: soups and watery gruels would solve the
problem. By the 1800s, fresh fruit was found to prevent scurvy, but it
wasn't until the twentieth century that western medical authorities
acknowledged what North American native people had known all
along: fresh meat also prevents the disease.[78]

Even today many Europeans have difficulty accepting that people
who eat only meat can be in good health. The militant vegetarianism of
animal-rights groups, in other words, is merely the latest, albeit
extreme, manifestation of a long-standing European bias against
eating meat. Indian hunters would take issue with Peter Singer's
unabashed declaration that "flesh taints our meals."[79]

The anti-meat bias of animal-rights writers today serves the same
ideological function in North America as it always has: to deny the
validity and integrity of native Inuit and Indian culture. It is unlikely,
of course, that animal-rights activists will convince many Europeans
or white Americans to give up their Sunday roast. But the guilt it stirs

up may lead them to decide that we should "at least" ban fur trapping and hunting.

This, then, is the new threat to the survival of the remaining indigenous hunting people of Canada, whose lands are once again coveted by the ever-expanding tentacles of "advanced" – and maybe one day even vegetarian – industrial society.

> Stereotypes of Indian life now conveniently obscure any possible conflict of interest between the worldwide importance of hydro-carbons and hydroelectricity, and a few communities of Indians who have supposedly ceased to need even the little they once may have had.[80]

PART THREE

BUILDING A NEW RELATIONSHIP WITH NATURE

Ecologists warn us that without a new attitude toward the rest of creation, the rapid expansion of human population and industrial technology spell doom for wildlife and for the natural environment upon which we ultimately depend.

But the apparent "successes" of animal-rights campaigns do not lessen our increasing alienation from nature; rather they are a symptom of our disease.

The issues raised by animal-rights groups do, nonetheless, provide an opportunity to begin a reassessment of our relationship with nature.

8

Building a New Relationship with Nature

Self-actualization for our species is, I fear, distant. It would require our acknowledgement of belonging in nature, our development of actual (as opposed to artificially conditioned) self-respect as sentient beings, and it would require open acceptance, from the inside out.

– John A. Livingston (*The Fallacy of Wildlife Conservation*)

According to Michael Giannelli of the Fund For Animals, the exploitation of animals for any purpose reveals that "human beings as a species have not yet reached a level of being civilized and ethically evolved enough to respect the fact that we share this earth with other animals."[1] The earth is not ours to use up as we wish. Animals are biologically related to us, they suffer like us and they fear as we do: "They are not tools – they should not be tools – simply to be exploited in whatever way we happen to see fit."[2]

Animal-rights authors argue that the justifications for the exploitation of animals today are of the same order as those that were used to support slavery, racism and the subjugation of women. Man's conviction of his own superiority, which Peter Singer, following Richard Ryder, calls "speciesism," is so prevalent that it is often difficult to identify:

> It's analogous to the fish swimming in water. The fish is not aware of the water, because he lives in it. We live in a sea of Speciesism.[3]

Having defined speciesism in this way, animal-rights advocates take on a pose of historical inevitability. The various scientific revolutions, it is said, have progressively dethroned humans from their assumed role of unique superiority: the Copernican revolution showed that the earth wasn't at the center of the universe; Darwin proved that man was biologically related to other life forms on the planet; Freud taught that our behavior is greatly influenced by "irrational" or unconscious forces; and Einstein pulled the rug out from under our most basic assumptions about time and space. Despite all this, says Giannelli, "we still act as if we were the special darlings of the universe, entitled to exploit the earth in any way we see fit."[4]

The growth of the modern ecology movement revealed that, despite all his technological tricks, man was still part of nature and could abuse it only at his peril. Beginning with a concern with pollution, pesticides and endangered species, however, we have seen ecology transformed into "animal rights." The seal hunt is now said to have been a moral, rather than an ecological issue, and according to Patrick Moore of Greenpeace, the public reaction to that campaign shows that values and attitudes about nature are in transformation: "What is happening is that people are just automatically accepting that animals have rights. Once you accept it, there's no questioning it any more, it's no longer a debate."

Only people who have vested interests still hold "backward opinions" and "would still like to treat animals as a commodity that can just be bartered and traded," says Moore. "Their children will change and come into line with the new way of thinking, which is more fitting, makes more sense and is just all around more appropriate."[5]

Maureen Duffy, in the landmark collection of animal-rights articles *Animals, Men and Morals*, reduces hunting to a "masturbation fantasy," comprising two distinct parts, the chase and the kill.[6] The point of hunting, she says, is "to conquer by catching or killing." The desire to kill "lurks" in all of us, says Duffy, and she cites troops "going berserk" and killing villagers in Vietnam as proof.[7]

Moreover, she recalls Freud's theory that the original totem animal symbolizes "the father." The hunt, Duffy concludes, is the ritual slaughter of the patriarch by the sons. The fox and the otter, which are still hunted in England where Duffy writes, both have long tails and elongated bodies, "and no great insight is needed to divine what they represent." Rabbits, on the other hand, referred to traditionally in English ballads as "poor puss," "coney" or "cunny," are female, as are deer. Deer and rabbit hunting, according to Duffy, are "symbolic rape."[8]

Amer-Indian people too, often compare hunting animals to the sexual relations between men and women (see Chapter Four), but not, notably, to either rape or masturbation. Duffy's critique tells as much about problems between humans in contemporary society as it does about our relations with animals. Ironically, Duffy also claims to be appalled by the destruction of Amer-Indian societies in the past; yet she is apparently oblivious to the way in which she perpetuates that destruction through animal rights. For today, as in the past, the willingness to destroy Amer-Indian society is predicated on a judgment that hunting cultures are somehow less sophisticated or "civilized" than those of factory workers, bureaucrats and academics.

But what of the animal-rights tenet that we have no "right" to kill animals at all? Doctor Richard Van Gelder, curator for mammals at the American Museum of Natural History in New York, believes that this idea is based on a misunderstanding about the role of death in nature:

> The point is, death is a part of life. If nothing died, the world would come to an end in about twenty minutes, because all the oxygen would be absorbed and tied up by the living things. So that's the first premise, that you cannot have a deathless society. The second premise is that anyone who is alive is of course preempting the oxygen, the space, the food, the water, of some other living thing. And that's what it's all about. It's basically competition. The question is whether we're going to have the competition in a form of equilibrium in which various species continue to live without being wiped out. . . . [9]

The error that animal-rights groups make is to jump from the perfectly valid idea of trying to save species from extinction to the unjustifiable conclusion that it is possible to avoid taking any individual life. It's possible to choose certain species – whales for instance – and say we won't kill any of them, especially because the part of the human economy they represent is very small. (Most societies have had restrictions on which animals may be killed or eaten.) Cows, however, play a major role in human nutrition; what are we to put in their place? And if we then say let's stop killing plants (as the Fruitarian Network has proposed) then there's not much left. "It's very easy to pick out one animal and say, let's stop killing it, but as an overall philosophy, I'd rather say, let's maintain them." [10]

But if the idea of killing no animals is unrealistic, how does one explain the large number of people who are apparently eager to subscribe to this idealized view of nature? Van Gelder believes it's because "the farther we get from nature, the better it looks." He notes that most support for anti-vivisection groups in England historically came from "wealthy, elderly, urban women," the very people who had the least direct involvement in handling animals. Many people today think that animals in the wild are like the ones they see on television. Every year people are hurt or killed in the national parks because they walk up to bears or buffalo to pet them or take their pictures:

> I see it on my tours to Africa. When I take people there they say: "Oh, I want to see lions, but I don't want to see them killing or eating." Some of us call this the "Disney Concept." I think we have a wishful-thinking idea of nature, and I don't think that's good. [11]

In fact, says Van Gelder, when most people talk about nature, they're usually thinking about an environment that has already been profoundly altered by man:

> Their idea of nature is their country place in the Adirondacks or in Connecticut, where they might see a deer occasionally, but they don't want to think about the fact that they have deer because the wolves and mountain lions have been killed off long ago. If you say, well, if you're so interested in wildlife, let's bring back the wolves and mountain lions – which was a question raised in the Adirondacks, in New York – then no, no, they didn't want those, because they would kill their lovely deer.

The importance of media in modern society is undoubtedly a major factor in the rapid rise of animal-rights groups in recent years. Divided as it is into short segments punctuated by commercial advertising, television demands visually powerful images that will grab the fickle viewer's attention instantly. Advertising has become the fine art of banging a story into thirty- or sixty-second slots. In such a context, the baby-seal confrontations were made to order. A ten-second shot of a bloody white-coat seal on the north Atlantic ice fields is television. Lengthy expositions on game management and complex mathematical population models are not.

Fur trapping, too, is readily visible and identifiable. The suffering that results when nature uses her own methods to control populations is not so obvious. Television messages must be short and punchy, and the animal-rights groups have supplied a product that suits the medium: shock value, horror stories and a simple solution: "stop the suffering."

THE STORY OF MIRACLE

In January 1983, one of the young orca ("killer") whales at Sealand of the Pacific, in Victoria, British Columbia, was killed. Her name was Miracle, and she drowned after becoming caught up in the netting of her pen, which had been cut, apparently in a bid to "liberate" her. It was a particularly unfortunate end, for Miracle had been found as an infant, wounded and near death, off the coast of Vancouver Island; she was saved only after nearly a year of intensive care. That Miracle and Sealand became the victims of animal-rights protests is ironic, says Sealand manager Angus Matthews, because aquariums (which, like zoos, are an aspect of the media) were largely responsible for encouraging the idea that animals, especially whales, shared human qualities, including intelligence:

In 1962 to 1963, when killer whales were first being considered for display in aquariums, everybody was terrified they were going to get eaten by them. Everybody knew somebody who'd had a boat split in half by one. Every fisherman could tell you about the nets being ripped and that if you dropped anything over the side a whale would have it right away.[12]

There was even a campaign to eliminate killer whales. North of Campbell River, just three miles up from Menzies Bay on Vancouver Island, where Miracle was found, the government had set up a post to machine-gun the orcas. In the 1950s and 1960s fisheries patrol boats were regularly instructed to shoot killer whales whenever they saw them; and in 1958, the United States government bombed killer whales near Iceland (at the invitation of the Icelandic government) as a form of air-force target practice. The animal, says Matthews, had been badly "misunderstood," as the name "killer whale" implies.

Then whales got into the aquariums. The first orca in captivity was named "Namu" – it came from Namu, British Columbia – and was sold to the Seattle Aquarium. Ted Griffin, Namu's trainer, found that he could get into the water with the whale and not get eaten. People couldn't believe it, says Matthews, and came from miles around "to see Ted Griffin not get eaten by the whale."

And then we started a whole new image of the killer whale which was overcorrecting for the old image. In an attempt to prove that they were cute and adorable and superintelligent they were taught a number of behaviors, which included sticking your head in their mouth and scratching their tongue, and all those old lion behaviors, which were designed often to show that the trainer was courageous as much as anything. But really to show that the animal didn't deserve its old reputation.[13]

All this was done, with the best of intentions, through the early 1970s, says Matthews. In 1974 Paul Horn, the jazz flautist, became friendly with some of the staff at Sealand; Horn played the flute to one of the whales, Haida, who quickly responded to him. Horn later included Haida in one of his albums, which set off, as Matthews put it, "a whole series of flute players and kayak rowers, and everyone under the sun trying to get close to the killer whale and relate with the killer whale . . . we developed this whole incredible era of killer-whale hugging." One of those who took his kayak into the ocean to "relate" with the whales during this period was Robert Hunter, soon to be president of Greenpeace.[14]

The pendulum had swung so far the other way, says Matthews, that

We generated an awareness about these animals which probably attributes skills and abilities to them which they may not deserve . . . somewhere along the line we lost track of the fact that they're a wild animal, they're the top predator of the ocean, and the reason they're at the top of the food chain in the sea is that they're the best hunting machine going.

Matthews feels that through the 1970s, aquariums were giving the public too much of what they wanted, "because the public loved it – they wanted to believe these animals could be hugged." Instead, Matthews believes, it's important to balance what the public appears to want with what's really in the best interest of wildlife:

We realize now that we have to take a step backwards and say, no, that's not quite the way they are. They eat seals, they eat sea lions, they're very proficient hunters, they hunt in packs like wolves. Their intelligence has been overrated, because we've equated it to the intelligence of humans. Their intelligence should really be looked at as sophistication in their environment – they're very sophisticated and proficient in their environment. We should admire that, not intelligence as we understand it, because people always get off on the wrong track.[15]

Aquarium displays, in fact, allowed people to see whales as some sort of "perfect being." One could speculate long on the need for such a model of perfection in an age when religions have been pushed from their pedestals and many feel what George Steiner has called "nostalgia for the absolute."[16] Matthews admits that what he'd really like to do is put a harbor seal into the pool one day with Sealand's killer whales "so people would see what they're built for – what they do best!"

The attack on Sealand was the result of a progression of activism. In 1973, a pair of dolphins at SeaLife Park in Hawaii were released into the sea by their trainers. In 1974, Paul Watson and Patrick Wall, in a daring operation, freed two hundred dolphins that had been rounded up for slaughter by Japanese authorities because they had been found near fishermen's nets. Few people with any interest in wildlife could help but approve of that action, Angus Matthews admits.

But in November 1982, two beluga whales, which were being used to recover unexploded missiles at the test range of the Canadian naval base at Nanoose, on Vancouver Island, were "liberated" by divers, who swam in from the channel to cut the netting of their pen.

Interviewed at the time of the incident, Angus Matthews stated that freeing the whales was an irresponsible gesture. Beluga whales are not native to British Columbia waters, and their usual food is not available there. Moreover, orca whales, which *do* inhabit the straits, feed on beluga whales. The animals were accustomed to traveling with their trainers and, had they not found their way quickly back to their pens after a brief tour of the bay, they might have perished. While admitting that he didn't like the whales doing military work, Matthews felt that the animal-rights activists were doing the same thing they accused others of: exploiting the whales for their own purposes.

Matthews believes that his outspoken criticism of the Nanoose incident probably incited the attempt to free Miracle the next month. Patrick Moore charges that aquariums like Sealand are "concentration camps" because of the high number of captive whales that have died. Matthews counters that aquarium whales are "ambassadors" from the wild; many people have their first contact with wild animals in zoos and aquariums, and "you don't close the school just because you've graduated."

Boat trips to observe marine mammals in their natural habitat are fine, Matthews believes, and both Greenpeace and Sealand are major tour operators. However, there are tour facilities for only about ten thousand people each season along the Pacific coast of Canada and the United States. By contrast almost four hundred thousand people a year, most of them schoolchildren, visit Sealand. Furthermore, naturalists are warning that large numbers of observation tours may be more disruptive than the removal of a number of young animals from whale pods (families) from time to time.

The controversy over captive whales is a good example of the dangers of anthropomorphism, Matthews believes. Some people can think about animals only by associating them with their own problems. They assume that animals accept a situation the way humans would. Rarely do they think to turn the telescope around the other way:

> An animal looks at us and says, well, you get up at 8:30 in the morning and eat a bowl of Cornflakes, and you get on a bus and go to work and stay there all day, and then you come home and put your feet up and watch the news and go to bed. That, to an animal, is probably the dumbest day you could put in....[17]

The display of marine animals in aquariums had a considerable effect on the two biggest animal issues of the 1970s: the "save-the-whales" campaign and the anti-sealing campaigns. The popularity harbor seals and sea lions gained through their performances in installations like Sealand contributed to both species becoming completely protected in west-coast waters. (There was a west-coast bounty on harbor seals until 1968; there still is one on the east coast.) The population of California sea lions is believed to have doubled in the past five years and may triple its present numbers in the next five. Commercial fishermen have already begun to complain, and if the sea lions affect the sport-salmon fishery – a major west-coast industry – a confrontation will certainly result. This time, however, it won't be across the continent in isolated Newfoundland; it will be in Greenpeace's own backyard.

Vancouver is perched at the brink of one of the world's last frontiers, with the Pacific Ocean on one side and the vast spaces of the Canadian Rockies on the other. Patrick Moore likes to say that Greenpeace, which began in Vancouver, is the wilderness screaming back at civilization: "Enough ... you can't come any farther!"[18]

Insofar as Greenpeace has adopted an animal-rights position, however, the group may serve quite different interests by perpetuating the modern myth that mankind can live outside nature:

> A general and tacit evasion of the crudities of our root contacts with the planet permeates our mode of organization of work. . . . Foodstuffs and fibers must still be brought forth from the dirt, animals must still be killed and gutted, minerals must be wrested from rock veins, smelted and forged. . . . In our automated world, this intimacy with the physical processes of existence is not in good taste.[19]

These lines were first published in 1961. They formed part of the rising wave of "ecology consciousness" that questioned the logic of a constantly expanding technological society. Both ecology and animal-rights spokesmen argue that man has cut himself off from nature. The thrust of animal-rights groups, however, has been to make that gulf wider still. When we are most conscious of our dependence on nature, our respect for it is greatest, as is illustrated by Amer-Indian culture.[20] It is industrial man, confident in the myth that his machines and his own intelligence have "freed" him from nature, who feels entitled to abuse it. Animal-rights groups serve only to accelerate this tendency. Stanley Godlovitch, for example, criticizes conservation even when its only object is to preserve for the future "the pleasure of walking through forests, observing wild animals," because this is still "for human benefit" rather than a recognition of the "intrinsic rights" of the animals.[21]

Modern society projects the illusion that man has lifted himself "out" of nature. We cool our houses in summer and warm them in winter; electricity turns night into day. Even in the center of the largest city, however, the energy of spring is felt by the human inhabitants. The cycles of the moon, which pull the oceans' tides, tug also at fertility cycles. Despite all our technology, we remain profoundly tied to natural rhythms which, René Dubos concludes, may mean that there are definite limits beyond which human culture cannot stray, whatever our ambitions.[22] Our very minds have been formed through millions of years of contact with the natural environment. For all our marvelous advances of knowledge, we still remain quite ignorant of the parameters of our own real needs.

Far from being a critique of industrial society, the ideas of animal rights are the logical extension of the myth that modern man is no longer dependent on nature. As Jeremy Rifkin has noted, "the death of another living thing is always a painful reminder of the debt we owe for the next breath we take."[23]

Harald Traue, who is a clinical psychologist in Germany – where the animal-rights movement has been particularly influential and where urbanism is also notably pronounced – believes that the animal-rights philosophy reflects a society that has become cut off from natural life processes. People in cities live within a narrowed perspective, and Traue thinks this is affecting how we perceive life.[24]

As death has been compartmentalized and hidden away, the fear of it has become greater than ever before. Death has become a "dirty word" in a society that has lost much of the spiritual orientation that traditionally helped humans accept, if not make much sense of, death. Seen in this light, the call to stop killing animals may be a projection of our own fear and denial of death – as if we would banish death from the world.

A society that denies death finds itself in some uncomfortable dilemmas. There are hospital wards full of terminally ill patients who are not allowed to die naturally even though they are in pain. In the current debates over abortion, many who defend the right to end a pregnancy feel obliged to deny that the fetus is really alive or a "real person," rather than accepting that we do have or at least exercise the right to kill under certain circumstances.

Yet many animal-rights supporters are young, independent, well-educated working women[25] – the group most likely to defend a woman's right to choose to have an abortion. There is a contradiction here, and the implications have yet to be fully appreciated. Germaine Greer now argues that modern contraception reduces women to sexual passivity, repressing their natural role as mothers: IUDs transform the uterus into a "poisonous abattoir," and attempts to introduce contraception into third-world countries are cultural imperialism.[26]

Human population growth, however, is the major threat to wildlife today. Animal-rights doctrines obscure the fact that "what happens to animals also happens to us." Like all animal populations, if humans don't control their numbers voluntarily, they will be limited in other ways – by famine, disease and violence.

202

We have a lot to learn from animals, and I wish that some of the people who object so much to wildlife management would take the trouble to learn some of the principles of what occurs in nature rather than objecting blindly on emotional grounds to some of the things which are done.[27]

There is a range of social, political and psychological influences that confuses any discussion about redefining our proper relationship with nature. One of the obvious, yet far from resolved, questions that haunts the debate is that in virtually every society, the killing of animals has been primarily a male domain. In psychoanalysis, meat is often associated with the father while milk is the province of the mother. Jewish laws make a strict division between the eating of meat and milk, and in the winter camp of Cree hunters the men's trapping and hunting gear is stored on the opposite side of the tent from women's cooking and household utensils. Certain parts of animals are traditionally reserved for consumption by either men or women.[28] The growth of the animal-rights philosophy is certainly more than an expression of the increasing economic and political power of women in society; but it is worth noting that the emotion accompanying the debate about animals, particularly "baby" seals, which are an archetype of the infant, has such a powerful mass appeal at the very time that abortion is such a troubling issue.

Balancing real human needs with the overall welfare of the biosphere is probably the greatest challenge facing society today. But animal-rights activists would have us believe that "there is no dilemma," that "reformists face no moral problem."[29] Albert Schweitzer would not agree:

In a thousand ways my existence is in conflict with others. The necessity of taking life and harming life is imposed on me. When I walk along a lonely path my foot brings pain and death to the tiny forms of life that populate it. To preserve my life, I must defend it against the life that injures it. I become the persecutor of the little mouse that lives in my house, a murderer of the insect that wants to build its nest there, a mass-murderer of the bacteria that endanger my life. I get my food by the destruction of plants and animals. My happiness is built upon injury to my fellow creatures.[30]

The realization that animals suffer is not a solution, but only the first step in the recognition of our problem. Every society must explain and direct man's transactions with the natural environment. Animal-rights groups bring to the fore a question that must be addressed anew, because the tremendous advance of urbanism and industry has changed the conditions of that interaction. Animal-rights groups, however, pose only half the question. We must acknowledge that animals are sacrificed, but the groups provide no structure within which to situate our relationship with the natural world. They pretend, instead, that we can withdraw from that relationship completely. They allow men to cherish the illusion that they may live without harming or killing at all.[31]

The religious values that justified the sacrifice of animals for human welfare and placed limits on their use no longer satisfy the ethical requirements of an increasingly specialized society in which innovation rather than tradition is rewarded; now values focus on the individual more than on family, neighborhood or the larger community. Judaism, not unlike traditional Amer-Indian philosophy, encouraged respect for God's creation: man's needs would be satisfied only so long as nothing was wasted or needlessly destroyed. Christianity, while lacking a detailed code to regulate humans' treatment of animals, encouraged compassion and raised to the highest level the realization that life is founded on the suffering and sacrifice of others: Christ crucified.

The emergence of animal-rights groups is a symptom of the breakdown of the values that used to regulate our relations with the natural world. The key to developing a new vision of our place in nature, however, may be found in the fact that we do still use animals. Schweitzer argues that because animals are sacrificed for our benefit, we must acknowledge a growing debt to them. He doesn't rule out the use of animals in laboratories (which of itself would not end suffering), but insists that scientists remain constantly alert to be sure their work is justified by the anticipated results:

> By the very fact that animals through these painful experiments have contributed so much of value to suffering mankind, a new and special bond of solidarity has been established between them and us.[32]

We cannot end suffering, Schweitzer insists. That is our real dilemma. We can only try to become conscious of the real impact of our actions and then choose as best we can. Thus Schweitzer can choose to save a baby kingfisher, although he realizes that to feed it he must kill fish every day. He can choose to kill a favorite pet boar that has become a menace in his village, and serve it for supper. Yet he can also choose to stoop in mid-conversation to rescue a worm that has been washed onto the sidewalk.

> The ethic of reverence for life prompts us to keep each other alert . . . it keeps us watching together for opportunities to bring some sort of help to animals to compensate for the great misery that men inflict

Cleaning fish immediately after catching.

NATIVE PRESS

Preparing fish for two days of smoking and five days of drying.

RENÉ FREMOLEAU

upon them, and thus for a moment we escape from the incomprehensible horror of existence.[33]

The farmer who has just mowed thousands of flowers into hay for his cows, says Schweitzer, must take care not to lop the head from a single flower with his stick on his way home.[34]

What is to be our standard in making such decisions? Animal-rights advocates have often proposed an expanding circle of moral sympathy. It begins with the closest family, grows to encompass other nations and races and finally other species.[35] (The Way of Confucius also describes progress in stages: loving one's kin, loving all people and finally loving all creatures.[36]) This progression suggests that an "absolute" solution cannot be achieved all at once or, perhaps, ever. It offers, rather, a set of priorities. As one might be wary of someone who talks of saving the world while he is incapable of feeding his own family, so there is something suspect about destroying the livelihood of other, politically less powerful people in the cause of reducing animal suffering. Brian Davies likes to argue that more people support the IFAW's view of sealing than make up the population of Newfoundland. This is a sad parody on the ideals of democracy. Professor Ronald Dworkin, who holds the Chair of Jurisprudence at Oxford and is known for his defense of the moral basis of legal rights, has written:

> A man has a moral right against the state if for some reason the state would do wrong to treat him in a certain way, even if it be in the general interest to do so.[37]

It is doubtful whether the campaigns of animal-rights groups have been in anyone's interest.

Following Schweitzer's lead, it seems reasonable to propose that even fur trapping, which is to many the least acceptable form of animal use, may not necessarily violate a sincere "reverence for life" so long as it is done with respect for the animals. Even Henry Salt was prepared to allow that "there is a certain fitness in the hunter – himself a product of a rough, wild era in human development – assuming the skins of the wild animals he has conquered." But it does not follow, says Salt, that "because an Eskimo may appropriately wear fur, or a Red Indian feathers, that this apparel will be equally becoming to the inhabitants of London or New York."[38]

With the increasing specialization of society, which is far more urbanized now than in Salt's day, people have little contact with the natural environment and therefore, perhaps, less appreciation of where natural products come from. This is equally true of tomatoes and soybeans as of furs. Thus, even biased anti-trapping films and brochures serve the function of reminding people of "the real cost of a fur coat." The point of showing animals in traps, however, should not be so that the reaction upon seeing furs will be "nausea," as Amanda Blake of the Fund For Animals has suggested.[39] On the contrary, furs should be treated with respect, because of the suffering required to secure them.

The careful craftsmanship that goes into the preparation of a fine fur garment (see Chapter Six) can be seen as a form of respecting animals. We must insure that we are using the most humane trapping systems possible: here animal-rights groups deserve credit for pushing government to initiate programs like the Fur Institute of Canada, which will make possible improvements based on the scientific study not only of traps, but of the whole environment of trapping.

Most anti-trapping films, however, have sought to denigrate the character and values of trappers. A better model are the films of Arthur Lamothe, about the Naskapi Indians of northern Quebec. Here the killing of animals is neither hidden nor prettified, but is situated within the culture and belief of hunting peoples.[40] Unfortunately, the debate over trapping has polarized and neither side is prepared to face the central issues. Animal-rights groups portray those who use or collect furs as "criminals" and "immoral"; the fur trade has tried to play down the fact that animals are killed at all.

Our culture has yet to come to grips with the central problem raised by the ecology movement: that the constant expansion of industrial society threatens wildlife and the natural environment. Fur trapping can actually protect the environment by supporting a group of people in whose interests it is to defend wildlife habitats from further encroachment by machine technology. Furs, properly appreciated, might also help remind city dwellers of the world outside their concrete palaces.

If nothing else, the growing debate about animal rights provides a forum in which the question of our proper relationship to nature can be formulated. Not least important, the threat posed by animal-rights groups is forcing the people who still live closest to the land – fishermen, trappers, native hunters – the people who have traditionally been quite isolated, to reach out and communicate with others like themselves, to protect the way of life they value. Before he became executive director of the Canadian Sealers Association, Kirk Smith worked with film in industry and community organizing. In St. John's he met fishermen and sealers. He began talking with them on the docks; he filmed their discussions and played them back at small gatherings. The discussions that resulted were also filmed, and played back to larger groups. Slowly the fishermen began to see that they shared common problems – and that they could express them. The Canadian Sealers Association was born as the sealers came to see that they were a group, with a story to tell and a worthwhile life-style to defend. First there were workshops, which used videotapes; then Smith went to local television stations, and from there to the national and international media. Sealers and fishermen are learning to use the media for their own purposes. The recent formation of the Aboriginal Hunters and Trappers Federation (and, still more recently, a pan-aboriginal conference in Yellowknife, Northwest Territories, in August 1984, which ended with the creation of an "Indigenous Survival International Committee") may signal a more influential role for native people in the fur trade they have done so much to build.

Finally, the debate over the use of animals exposes the extent to which the primary sector is still important in many regions. Most people in Europe, and many in southern Canada, do not realize that large parts of Canada are still inhabited by communities of native hunters who continue to derive their living largely from the land, much as they always have. One of the most unfortunate aspects of the animal-rights movement is that it unconsciously serves the interest of the mining, oil and gas and hydroelectric industries, which would like nothing better than to clear traditional hunters and trappers from the land.

It is far from certain, however, that the destruction of the last traditional hunting societies is in the interests of either wildlife – or southern Canadians. Much of the nonrenewable resources, power and timber, extracted from the Canadian north, are exported south to the industrial centers of the United States, one of the most wasteful civilizations that has ever existed.[41] It may be in all Canada's interests to slow such foreign-oriented "development."

Meanwhile, hunting societies may yet teach us valuable lessons about living in harmony with our environment. For Canada is not the United States, and certainly not Europe. Vast expanses of this country are suited for nothing but fishing, hunting, trapping and gathering, as well as mining, lumbering and ranching – activities directly related to the natural environment. Native people have charged that animal-rights groups' attacks on sealing and fur trapping are nothing but the most recent expression of European imperialism, the attempt to impose foreign values on the people who live here. In Canada, in recent years, there has been much discussion about the distinctive character of the "Canadian," as opposed to the European or American national identity. The government has sponsored programs to encourage Canadian cinema and television production in the name of protecting and developing this special identity. If the rights of native and all Canadians to make use of the special natural endowments of this land cannot be defended, however, it is difficult to imagine what these debates have really been about.

The object of this book is not to discredit the ecology movement. Quite the contrary – it is because the ecology issues raised by Greenpeace and others are so important that the danger of ecology being co-opted by animal-rights groups is so grave.[42] Kirk Smith of the Canadian Sealers Association does not consider animal-rights supporters to be the "enemy." Our society, he says, is groping for the cultural roots we have lost. He feels that what has happened is a necessary part of a process that will bring us a new balance. Yet, if we lose our relationship with wildlife and with animals generally we lose an opportunity to understand ourselves. We will also be losing one of the few things that stand between us and the environmental apocalypse the ecology movement so rightly warns about.

Notes

Notes – Chapter 1

1 Aldo Leonard, quoted in Paul Shepard and Daniel McKinley (eds.), *The Subversive Science*, p. 414.

2 Richard Van Gelder, *Animals and Man: Past Present Future*; also Shepard and McKinley, *The Subversive Science*, p. 100.

3 Shepard and McKinley, *The Subversive Science*, p. 212.

4 Interview with Patrick Moore, recorded by the author, July, 1983.

5 Interview with Michael Giannelli, recorded by the author, August, 1983.

6 Ernst Haeckel, *The Wonders of Life*, New York, Harper and Bros., 1905.

7 By 1984, eighty-six nations were signatories to the Convention.

8 John A. Livingston, *The Fallacy of Wildlife Conservation*, p. 66.

9 Jeremy Bentham, *Introduction to the Principles of Morals and Legislation*. Quoted in Salt, p. 113.

10 William Lecky, *History of European Morals*.

11 Henry Salt, *Animals' Rights*.

12 Stanley and Roslind Godlovitch and John Harris (eds.), *Animals, Men and Morals*; Peter Singer, *Animal Liberation*. Seven of the thirteen contributors to the Godlovitch collection studied or taught at Oxford or Cambridge, England. The Godlovitches, however, are Canadians, and Singer is Australian. There is a definite colonial flavor to the animal-rights movement, as we shall see.

13 Originally, Greenpeace was an "ecology" group, and their mail-outs still use that term, but the borders between ecology and animal-rights philosophies have been blurred by support for issues about zoos and aquariums.

14 "The Animal Rights Movement in the United States: Its Composition, Funding Sources, Goals, Strategies, and Potential Impact on Research," prepared by the Harvard University Office of Government and Community Affairs, based on research by Phillip W.D. Martin. September, 1982, p. 2.

15 Dr. Lars Karstad, of the New Brunswick SPCA, after the 1968 hunt: "I did not see any instances of intentional contravention of regulations; ninety-seven per cent *at least* were unconscious before skinning began." Quoted in Calvin Coish, *Season of the Seal*, p. 105.

16 "The east-coast harp-seal hunt is *not* an issue of what is a humane or inhumane way of killing. The real issue is that at the present rate of extermination, the harp seal will be *extinct* in five years." Greenpeace spokesman, from CP report, January 27, 1977, St. John's *Evening Telegram*; quoted in Coish, *Season of the Seal*, p. 146.

17 "Is ecology a phase of science of limited interest and utility? Or, if taken seriously as an instrument for the long-run welfare of mankind, would it endanger the assumptions and practices accepted by modern societies, whatever their doctrinal commitments?" Paul B. Sears, "Ecology – A Subversive Subject," *BioScience* 14(7): 11, 1964.

18 Traditional ballad, recounted by Ray Demarchi, wildlife biologist with the British Columbia department of the environment, in a recorded interview with the author, August 1983. Phrase about "ditchers, dammers, and developers" is attributed to Carmen Purdy, president of the Canadian Wildlife Federation.

19 Harvard University Study, p. 10.

20 Singer, *Animal Liberation*, p. 167.

21 Recorded interview with George Wenzel, anthropologist with McGill Centre for Northern Studies and Research, September 1983.

22 Albert Schweitzer, *The Animal World of Albert Schweitzer*, p. 190.

Notes – Chapter 2

1 Recorded interview with Richard Van Gelder, September 1983, by the author. Also: Hochett and Ascher, "The Human Revolution," in Shepard and McKinley, *The Subversive Science*, pp. 13-41.

2 Recorded interview with Jack Ornstein, Philosophy Department, Concordia University, Montreal, September, 1983.

3 E.S. Turner, *All Heaven in a Rage*, quoted in Singer, *Animal Liberation*, p. 203.

4 René Descartes, *Discourse on Method*, pp. 43-44.

5 Quoted in Gerald Carson, *Men, Beasts and Gods*, p. 41.

6 Lynn White, Jr., "The Historical Roots of Our Ecological Crisis," *Science*, 10 March 1967 (155): pp. 1203-1209.

7 See: Singer, *Animal Liberation*, p. 208; also: Michael Peters in Godlovitch, *Animals, Men and Morals*, p. 229; Gerald Carson, *Men, Beasts and Gods*, p. 38; John Harris in Godlovitch, p. 102.

8 Henry S. Salt, *Animals' Rights*, p. 10.

9 Descartes, *Discourse*, p. 44.

10 A dog was hanged as recently as 1906 in Switzerland, and well into the twentieth century parish priests in Quebec were said to excommunicate insects from farmers' fields, perhaps with the help of government agricultural manuals, which described annual insect cycles. "Bugs and Beasts Before the Law," in Carson, *Men, Beasts and Gods*, p. 25.

11 Norbert Wiener, *The Human Use of Human Beings: Cybernetics and Society*.

12 Jeremy Rifkin, *Algeny*, p. 11.

13 Terence Hegarty, "Alternatives," in Godlovitch, *Animals, Men and Morals*, pp. 89-90.

14 Descartes, *Discourse*, p. 51.

15 Quoted in Salt, *Animals' Rights*, pp. 10-11. See also: Shepard and McKinley, *The Subversive Science*, p. 5; Animal Welfare Institute, *Facts about Furs*, p. xi; Gerald Carson, *Men, Beasts and Gods*, p. 13; Singer, *Animal Liberation*, pp. 194-195; Godlovitch, *Animals, Men and Morals*, p. 178, p. 215; and White, "Historical Roots," pp. 1203-1207.

16 Singer, *Animal Liberation*, p. 53.

17 White, "Historical Roots," p. 1206.

18 Salt, *Animals' Rights*, p. 90.

19 Milton R. Konvitz (ed.), *Judaism and Human Rights*, p. 249. I am indebted to Alan Livingston for bringing this book to my attention.

20 Quoted in Samuel Belkin, "Man As Temporary Tenant," in Konvitz, *Judaism*, p. 254.

21 Eric G. Freudenstein, "Ecology and the Jewish Tradition," in Konvitz, *Judaism*, pp. 265-274. Pollution control, such as sewage disposal, even during wartime, is laid out in Deuteronomy 23: 13-15. Sheep and goats were forbidden by the Talmud within cultivated areas of Palestine (p. 270). No furnaces were permitted within the walls of Jerusalem, and tanneries, cemeteries and even threshing floors were required to keep specified distances from settled areas. The Old Testament stipulates how latrines must be dug by traveling armies: "And you shall have a place outside the [military] camp, thither shall you go out, and a spade shall you have with your accoutrements, so that when you sit down outside you shall dig therewith, and turn back and cover over again that which comes from you" (Deuteronomy 23: 13-15).

22 Samson Raphael Hirsch, "Do Not Destroy!" in Konvitz, *Judaism*, p. 263.

23 Quoted in Carson, *Men, Beasts and Gods*, p. 14.

24 William Edward Hartpole Lecky, *History of European Morals (from Augustus to Charlemagne)*, Volume Two, p. 167.

25 Lecky, *History*, p. 162.

26 Lecky, *History*, p. 167.

27 Lecky, *History*, p. 170.

28 Schweitzer, *The Animal World*, p. 185.

29 Keith Thomas, *Men and the Natural World: A History of Modern Sensibility*.

30 Quoted in Schweitzer, *The Animal World*, p. 144.

31 Schweitzer, *The Animal World*, p. 144.

32 Schweitzer, *The Animal World*, p. 145.

33 Schweitzer, *The Animal World*, p. 146.

34 Schweitzer, *The Animal World*, p. 145.

35 Schweitzer, *The Animal World*, p. 187.

36 Quoted in Schweitzer, *The Animal World*, p. 154.

37 Schweitzer, *The Animal World*, p. 186. In this connection it is interesting to note that China has recently been charged with conducting a virtual "war on wildlife" since the 1950s. Wild animals are trapped not only for fur but to be shipped live to Hong Kong for human consumption. (Animal Welfare Institute, *Facts about Furs*, p. 52.) Tibetan refugees have also reported that wildlife in that country, once plentiful, have been decimated since the Chinese military occupation of that country: T.L. Danlock, "Wildlife in Tibet: Past and Present," *Newstibet*, September/October 1982, p. 4.

38 Schweitzer, *The Animal World*, p. 186.

39 White, "Historical Roots," p. 1205.

40 White, "Historical Roots," p. 1203. This contradiction in White is pointed out by Lewis W. Moncrief in "The Cultural Basis for Our Environmental Crisis," *Science*, October 1970 (170): pp. 508-512.

41 Moncrief, "Cultural Basis," p. 510.

42 Jean Mayer, quoted in Moncrief, "Cultural Basis," p. 512.

Notes – Chapter 3

1 Richard Van Gelder, *Animals and Man*, pp. 36-37.

2 D.H. Lawrence, "The Spirit of Place," in *The Symbolic Meaning*, pp. 25-26.

3 Van Gelder, *Animals and Men*, p. 41.

4 Van Gelder, *Animals and Men*, p. 40. Caribou were protected in Maine in 1870, and wapiti in Michigan in 1879, but both later disappeared. Wyoming (1890) and Montana (1897) both stopped the hunting of buffalo when they were already extinct in those territories.

5 Quoted in Dan Gottesman, "Native Hunting and the Migratory Birds Convention Act," *Journal of Canadian Studies*, Autumn, 1983: (18) 3, p. 82.

6 Quoted in Gottesman, "Native Hunting," p. 75.

7 Gottesman (p. 77) recounts several incidents that encouraged the notion that Indians were "wasteful" and irresponsible hunters. In 1878, three thousand Sioux fled United States military authorities into Canada; the North-West Police were sent into the Cypress Hills after them to prevent "wanton destruction" of buffalo by the new arrivals. After Rocky Mountain National Park was established at Banff, in 1887 (the first such park in North America), local Stoney Indians were repeatedly charged with "poaching." By contrast, Dr. W.T. Hornaday, of the New York Zoological Society, believed that "the white races of men believe in the doctrine of legitimate sport and sensible utilization" (Gottesman, p. 83).

8 Quoted in S.D. Grant, "Indian Affairs Under Duncan Campbell Scott," in *Journal of Canadian Studies*, Autumn, 1983: (18) 3, p. 30.

9 Aldo Leonard, in 1949, estimated that of 22,000 higher plants and animals native to Wisconsin, barely five per cent could be "eaten, sold, or put to economic use." Quoted in *The Subversive Science*, Shepard and McKinley, p. 407.

10 Recorded interview with Richard Van Gelder, by the author, September 1983.

11 The EEC Council of Ministers delayed their final decision until the study of the thirteen-nation North Atlantic Fisheries Organization (NAFO) was completed, in June 1983. Although NAFO upheld the Canadian position, and showed that the seal population was rising, the Europeans decided "for political reasons" to go ahead with their ban. European representatives from the EEC commission repeatedly told Canadian officials, "Look, there's no point in showing us the figures; for political reasons we have no choice but to impose the ban." (Personal communication with Canadian Fisheries officials.)

12 Lecky, *History*, p. 244.

13 Plutarch, quoted in Salt, *Animals' Rights*, p. 30.

14 J.H. Parry, *The Establishment of the European Hegemony: 1415-1715*, passim. Spices were more than a luxury. Until quite recently, not enough forage could be produced in Europe to keep many animals through the winter. In an age without refrigeration, spices—including salt—were needed to preserve the meat that was butchered each autumn.

15 Michel Foucault, *Madness and Civilization*, pp. 38-64.

16 Samuel Brody, "Facts, Fables and Fallacies on Feeding the World Population," in Shepard and McKinley, *The Subversive Science*, p. 59.

17 Salt, *Animals' Rights*, pp. 3-4.

18 Ortega y Gasset, cited in Paul B. Sears, "The Steady State: Physical Law and Moral Choice," in Shepard and McKinley, p. 369. See also Rene Dubos, *So Human an Animal*, pp. 29-30, for a discussion of the sense of "optimism" derived from expanding American frontier and from industrialization.

19 Singer, *Animal Liberation*, p. 7; p. 257. Also John Harris, in Godlovitch, *Animals, Men and Morals*, p. 97. Bernard Rollins calls Singer's book a "pioneering" work.

20 Salt, *Animals' Rights*, pp. 16-17.

21 Jeremy Bentham, *Introduction to the Principles of Morals and Legislation*, quoted in Salt, *Animals' Rights*, p. 113.

22 The same theme is foreshadowed in Jacob Grimm's romantic version of the medieval Jewish legend of the Golem. (Grimm's version was published in 1808.) A man made of clay is brought to life by writing the Hebrew letters that mean "it lives" on his forehead. The creature does his maker's bidding, but grows slightly larger each day. The Golem grows so large that the maker can no longer reach his forehead to erase one letter so that the letters will spell "he is dead." He finally orders the creature to bend over so he can reach its forehead. It obeys and the letter is erased, but the maker is killed when the creature collapses on top of him, a mound of inanimate clay.

23 Mary Wollstonecraft was, for a time, in the same intellectual "salon" in London as William Blake, Joseph Priestly and Thomas Paine. Like Paine, she crossed to France to observe the French Revolution first hand. She died giving birth to her daughter.

24 Quoted in Salt, *Animals' Rights*, p. 32.

25 Salt, *Animals' Rights*, pp. 30-31. At the time Salt wrote, the use of animals for traction was a major problem. Gerald Carson provides a good description of the lot of horses that pulled New York trolleys. Carson, "Horses Are Cheaper than Oats," in *Men, Beasts and Gods*, pp. 87-94.

26 Louis Pasteur, because of his work infecting animals with anthrax, rabies and other diseases, is added to this list by Richard Ryder in *Victims of Science*, p. 177. The material for the brief history of the anti-vivisection movement is taken from the appendix to Ryder's book.

27 E.S. Turner, *All Heaven in a Rage*; A.W. Moss, *Valiant Crusade, the History of the RSPCA*; John Vynyan, *In Pity and in Anger* (a two-volume history of animal experimentation); Godlovitch, *Animals, Men and Morals*; Antony Brown, *Who Cares for Animals?* (a history of the RSPCA); Monica Hutchings and Mavis Caver, *Man's Dominion: Our Violation of the Animal World*.

28 The intellectual and social credentials of the book are impressive. The widow of Air Chief-Marshal Lord Dowding contributed an article about the fur trade and cosmetics; novelist Brigid Brophy, who is married to the Keeper of the National Gallery, also is included. Ruth Harrison, author of *Animal Machines*, wrote an essay about factory farming. There is also German philosopher Leonard Nelson (1882-1927) of Gottingen University. Of the remaining ten contributors, no less than eight were educated or teach at Oxford or Cambridge.

29 See: Roslind Godlovitch, in *Animals, Men and Morals*, pp. 156-157. See also Duffy, in the same book p. 112, and Harris, in the same book, p. 99.

30 Quoted in Singer, *Animal Liberation*, p. 163.

31 Michel de Montaigne, *Essays*, p. 183.

32 Quoted in Salt, *Animals' Rights*, p. 45.

33 Salt, *Animals' Rights*, p. 45.

34 Godlovitch, *Animals, Men and Morals*, p. 7.

34 Godlovitch, *Animals, Men and Morals*, pp. 167-171.

35 Godlovitch, *Animals, Men and Morals*, pp. 229-230.

36 Singer, *Animal Liberation*, pp. 229-230.

37 The Animal Welfare Institute's Greek delegate was also a delegate to the International Council on Laboratory Animal Science. See Singer, *Animal Liberation*, p. 231.

38 Harvard University Study, p. 4. The MSPCA in 1980 invested $2 million in cosmetic and pharmaceutical companies that used live animals in tests: $366,000 in Bristol-Myers, which is cited by animal-rights groups' reports as one of the five major users of the LD-50 tests; $586,000 in Johnson & Johnson; $350,000 in Abbot. MSPCA also invested $325,000 in Dow Chemicals, which supports Biomedical Research, an animal-experimentation lobby group. An MSPCA chief executive officer was also reported to be on the board of a lab that used live animals for tests.

39 Doctor Robert Marshak subsequently resigned. He had also been affiliated with Biomedical Defense Fund Incorporated, which financed the appeal of Doctor Edward Taub, convicted in 1981 of mistreating his laboratory animals. (Harvard University Study, pp. 4-5).

40 Singer, *Animal Liberation*, p. 243.

41 Singer, *Animal Liberation*, p. 92.

42 Singer, *Animal Liberation*, p. 24.

43 Harvard University Study, p. 5. Some groups, for example, have rejected the use of public demonstrations believing that legal strategies are more effective. Attorneys For Animal Rights and the Society for Animal Rights did not support the April 1983 Primate Center demonstrations, claiming that rallies may attract mass audiences, but they do not help to define clear strategies.

44 Singer, *Animal Liberation*, p. 27. The defense department received more mail about the beagles than about the bombing of North Vietnam.

45 In 1973, a bill was promoted that would have made animal tests illegal if an alternative were available. That year some two hundred questions relating to animal-welfare matters were tabled in the British parliament (Ryder, in *Victims of Science*, p. 245). In 1974, there were several fire-bombing incidents in British labs (Ryder, p. 246). Also in 1974, an RSPCA poll found that three-quarters of the British public disapproved of using animals for testing nonmedical products.

Notes – Chapter 4

1 Robert Hunter, *Warriors of the Rainbow: A Chronicle of the Greenpeace Movement*, p. 28. Paul Watson participated in the Wounded Knee occupations in March 1973, as did Greenpeacer David Garrick, alias "Walrus Oakenbough," because "the Sioux Indians had originally gone to war against General Custer to defend the last of the buffalo from extinction." Hunter, *Warriors*, p. 155.

2 Colin Scott, from an interview recorded with author in June 1983. Doctor Scott is an anthropologist who has lived and hunted with the Cree of northern Quebec. He is a research associate, formerly with the McGill Centre for Northern Studies and Research and presently with McMaster University, Hamilton, Ontario. Unless otherwise indicated, the material for this chapter is taken from my interviews with Doctor Scott and with Thomas Coon, first president of the Cree Trappers' Association, now director of traditional pursuits with the Cree Regional Authority, Val d'Or, Quebec.

3 There are parallels here with the Adam and Eve myth: it was Adam's involvement with woman (society) that caused him to taste the "forbidden fruit." He realizes his "nakedness," is dressed in skins, begins to eat meat and is cast out of innocence. Colin Scott recounted and interpreted the Chischihp legend for me.

4 Colin Scott interview. See also Adrian Tanner, *Bringing Home Animals: Religious Ideology and Mode of Production of the Mistassini Cree*, pp. 178-179.

5 Hugh Brody, *Maps and Dreams: Indians and the British Columbia Frontier*, pp. 221-223.

6 Recorded interview with Thomas Coon, by the author, September 1983.

7 Scott interview.

8 Scott interview. See also Tanner, *Bringing Home Animals*, pp. 148-150.

9 Tanner, *Bringing Home Animals*, p. 136.

10 Scott interview.

11 Tanner, *Bringing Home Animals*, pp. 117-135.

12 The Indian (and Inuit) notion that refusing animal "gifts" may cause game to leave an area has some ecological support: fertility of animals tends to rise more quickly if the animals are heavily harvested and falls when they are not. (See Paul Errington, "Of Men and Lower Animals," in *The Subversive Science*, pp. 179-189.)

13 For this reference from the Hudson's Bay Company archives, I am indebted to Toby Morantz of the McGill Centre for Northern Studies.

14 Philip Drucker, *Indians of the Northwest Coast*, p. 155.

15 Brody, *Maps and Dreams*, pp. 186-187.

16 This section on geese is from the Scott interview. Thomas Coon has informed me that the Cree of James Bay have begun a project to codify traditional rituals and rites into "Aboriginal hunting by-laws," which can be taught even to Cree children in the schools. This project is expected to take several years to complete. (Personal communication with Thomas Coon, August 1984.)

17 Brody, *Maps and Dreams*, p. 43.

18 Coon interview. See also Tanner, *Bringing Home Animals*, pp. 162-170.

19 Scott interview.

20 See Brody, *Maps and Dreams*, pp. 35-36, on different values of agricultural/industrial versus hunting societies. Thus the importance of the Christian church, which provided the ideological blinkers required to invert reality – categorizing as "primitive" people who were so obviously better adapted to the land, in closer contact with animals and nature in general; people upon whom the Europeans were often dependent for food and mobility. Even today, Pentecostal and other Christian missionaries

continue their "work" in the north, discouraging feasting and suppressing the shaking tent as "evil." (Interestingly enough, they apparently don't question the efficacy of the ceremony but claim the animal spirits called up are "devils.")

21 Alan Cooke, "A Gift Outright: The Exploration of the Canadian Arctic Islands After 1880." "The Inuit, who taught the explorers what they had to learn about living and travelling among their islands, have other lessons to teach a crowded world that is running short of food. Not only do they gather harvests from land and seas that through time, will be richer than any oil field, they understand better than any other people how to share scarce resources of food and fuel, how to show patience, goodwill and cooperation in difficult circumstances, and how to achieve goals through mutual assistance. . . . If men everywhere learned the principles according to which Inuit harvest and share renewable resources and if they began to understand some of the other survival strategies of Inuit culture, then many of the horrors the future seems to hold for all mankind might be palliated or averted."

Notes – Chapter 5

1 Canadian Fisheries Department reports. Also Canadian Wildlife Federation Spring 1983 report.

2 The average annual income of Newfoundland fishermen who sealed in 1982 was $9,800.

3 Brian Davies interview on BBC Radio 4, 17 February 1984. For Greenpeace statistics see note 123.

4 Ron Hollander, "The Man Who Loves Animals," Town & Country, March 1984, p. 203. (Also personal communication with Tom Hughes, Ontario Humane Society, March 1984.)

5 Seth Rolbein, writing in the Cape Cod Business Journal, June 1984 ("Brian Davies and the IFAW: The Pricetag on Animal Welfare"), reported: "Davies is reported on public documents to be making close to $70,000 (US) a year and his expenses probably match or exceed that figure. . . ." Rolbein also points out that IFAW maintains three offices: two on Route 6A in Yarmouth Port, Mass., and one at Davies' private retreat at Barnstable Harbor. One building in Yarmouth Port was purchased by IFAW; it is an old Colonial house, valued at more than $150,000. There is a computer valued at more than $200,000, with office and program material worth more than $112,000, as well as a car worth $17,000, a Jet Ranger helicopter, and a fixed-wing plane (valued at from $355,000 to $500,000 in different reports).

6 "The Atlantic Seal Hunt: A Canadian Perspective," a Canadian Fisheries Department publication, Spring 1984. Rieber Incorporated agreed to buy sixty thousand pelts in 1984 (but no white-coat pelts). Because of poor ice conditions in the spring of 1984, however, less than thirty thousand seals were taken. Rieber had not purchased white-coat pelts in 1983 either, probably because of the growing threat of EEC action.

7 "Report on the Meeting of the Ad Hoc Working Group on Assessment of Harp and Hooded Seals in the Northwest Atlantic," International Council for the Exploration of the Sea. See also "Report of the Standing Com-

mittee on Fishery Science," Northwest Atlantic Fisheries Organization. Adult harp seal population is now estimated to be about two million.

8 See pp. 75-76, p. 94, notes 23 and 103 (this book). Also: personal communication with Tom Hughes, Ontario Humane Society.

9 Interview with George Wenzel, an anthropologist who has hunted with Arctic Inuit, recorded by the author, September 1983. Wenzel, a research associate with the McGill Centre for Northern Studies, is presently conducting a survey to measure and predict the impact of animal-rights groups' anti-sealing campaigns on the livelihood and culture of Arctic Inuit. The Council of Ministers approved a directive dated March 28, 1983, providing for a two-year ban on harp and hooded seal pup products, commencing October 1, 1983.

10 Coish, *Season of the Seal*, p. 20. Coish has brought together a very useful chronology of the anti-sealing campaigns up until the end of 1978. This chapter draws heavily on it for the sequence of events.

11 Coish, *Season of the Seal*, p. 28. As recently as 1952, five ships went down and seventy-nine men were lost. One or two men die each season, despite precautions and improved technology.

12 Coish, *Season of the Seal*, p. 31.

13 Seal oil, taken from the layer of fat next to the pelt, is still a valuable product, nonetheless, as it is resistant at higher temperatures than petroleum oils.

14 Doctors Sergeant and Fischer reported. Doctor Fischer, interestingly enough, stated that he wasn't worried the seals would be exterminated: "At some time they will reach a point where it will not be economic. Then the seals will have a chance to repopulate." Quoted in Coish, *Season of the Seal*, p. 60.

15 Coish, *Season of the Seal*, p. 64.

16 Personal communication with Captain Willie Deraspé, February 1984. Deraspé died suddenly on March 20, 1984 at fifty-two years of age, of a coronary attack, while flying from his home in the Magdalen Islands to Montreal, where he was to have appeared in a television debate against representatives of the IFAW. Deraspé, captain of and instructor on the sixty-five-foot E.P. *Québécois*, a Quebec Institute des Pecheries training and research vessel, had been very active in the past few years in trying to convey the fishermen's and sealers' point of view to Europeans as well as Canadians. He had accompanied Minister DeBané's party in December 1982, to lobby against the EEC proceeding with their proposed ban on seal products, and also to CITES in April 1983. A member of the newly formed Canadian Sealers' Association, he argued that sealers must learn to use media as effectively as animal-rights groups had, and that scientific arguments would not be enough to win what had become a political issue.

17 Personal communication with Tom Hughes, Ontario Humane Society. Hughes was on the first teams (with Brian Davies) that investigated charges of cruelty in the hunt in 1964.

18 Hughes. See also Coish, *Season of the Seal*, p. 74.

19 Quoted in Brian Davies, *Savage Luxury: The Slaughter of the Baby Seals* (Toronto: Ryerson Press, 1970), pp. 102-103.

20 Quoted in Cynthia Lamson, *Bloody Decks and a Bumper Harvest*, p. 92.

21 Coish, *Season of the Seal*, p. 107. The *Daily Mirror* photographer, Kent Gavin, was named British Press Photographer of 1968.

22 Quoted in Coish, *Season of the Seal*, p. 108.

23 Brian Davies, *Savage Luxury*, p. 157. Davies argued that Karstad's conclusion was meaningless, since it didn't prove that there had been no contravention of the regulations—even if Karstad had seen none. According to Davies, Karstad nonetheless refused to change his statement, but allowed Davies to delete it when publishing the report, if he so chose. To his credit, Davies published the report unabridged, as an appendix to his book.

24 Dr. Douglas Pimlott, "The 1967 Seal Hunt," *Canadian Audubon*, March/April, 1967.

25 Hollander, "The Man," p. 246.

26 Hollander, "The Man," p. 246.

27 Hollander, "The Man," p. 200.

28 Hollander, "The Man," p. 202.

29 The Godlovitches had reason to be conscious of the seal hunt, as both are from Montreal.

30 Quoted in Coish, *Season of the Seal*, p. 119.

31 Quoted in Hollander, "The Man," p. 203. The IFAW again talked of influencing Canadian elections, with a threat to pour up to $3 million to swing up to seven Ontario seats, especially against members of parliament who had a record of defending the seal hunt. See the interviews and debate between Jim Winters of Fisheries Canada and Stephen Best (now "political consultant" to the IFAW) on CBC Radio, "Morningside," April 30, 1984. See also IFAW (Canada) mail-out of June 1984, p. 4: "Our plan is simple. With your support we will mount a special anti-cruelty election campaign that will cost the Liberal Party votes, cost them more seats in Parliament than they can possibly win in Newfoundland with their 'Liberal' strategy of seal hunt politics...." The mail-out is signed by Stephen Best, "Canadian Campaign Coordinator." (In the event, no IFAW political campaign materialized for the September 1984 Canadian elections.)

32 In an interview with Patrick Moore of Greenpeace, Moore suggested that a solution to man's warlike nature might be to encourage development of the neutron bomb or some other weapon that would kill only people (if that's what people are committed to doing), but at least spare the rest of the biosphere.

33 Hunter, *Warriors*, p. 150.

34 Hunter, *Warriors*, p. 178.

35 Hunter, *Warriors*, p. 250.

36 Hunter, *Warriors*, p. 250.

37 Quoted in Coish, *Season of the Seal*, p. 132.

38 Hunter, *Warriors*, p. 265. This statement, and the "deal" with Newfoundlanders, enraged many Greenpeace supporters. A newly formed Toronto chapter (started with the help of a federal-government LIP – Local Initiative Project – grant) crushed their Greenpeace buttons and returned them to Hunter in a brown-paper bag.

39 Hunter, *Warriors*, p. 290.

40 Greenpeace spokesman in a CP report in the St. John's *Evening Telegram*, 17 January 1977. Quoted in Coish, *Season of the Seal*, p. 146.

41 Hunter, *Warriors*, p. 253, p. 376.

42 Coish, *Season of the Seal*, p. 144. Tom Hughes, of the Ontario Humane Society, commented that Weber's plan made about as much sense as suggesting that the Eskimos should all become stockbrokers.

43 *Der Spiegel*, 14/1983, "The Battle Over Seals and Fish," p. 149. As reported in *Der Spiegel*, Bardot arrived in Blanc Sablon, on the arm of her then constant companion, but missed the helicopter made available by Greenpeace, which was to take her on the ice. In a fit of anger, she returned to wherever she had come from. She never got closer to the "little balls of wool," which she described for *Paris-Match*, than the distance of several miles.

According to Cynthia Lamson, in *Bloody Decks* (p. 93): "Her [Bardot's] photo was taken with a stuffed seal, which later became the topic of controversy when press releases suggested the pup was alive."

Coish, in *Season of the Seal* (p. 162), quotes a CP report that "a stuffed seal pup was used as a prop by European photographers to stage the killing of a young seal on harbour ice." The report concluded that the same pup might have been used for the notorious Bardot photo.

Robert Hunter, in *Warriors of the Rainbow* (p. 372), also reports that a "toy" seal was used to stage shots by European film crews who were unable to find helicopters to take them to the Front, and were "desperate for film." Hunter, who was there, describes a visit by Bardot to the Greenpeace base camp on Belle Isle on March 18, but makes no mention of her visiting the sealing grounds.

Mark Small, president of the Canadian Sealers Association, told me that in any case, no one could hug a live wild seal pup without being scratched badly.

44 Hunter, *Warriors*, p. 380. Acknowledging that Brigitte Bardot's arrival was a publicity "tidal wave" for the anti-sealing campaign, Hunter recalls that Greenpeace was at first very divided about whether they should be associated with the famous "sex kitten." The women in the group were especially outraged. Suffering difficult conditions at the advance camp on Belle Isle, several Greenpeace members, including Paul Watson, didn't like the idea of being upstaged by the starlet's lightning visit.

45 Coish, *Season of the Seal*, p. 165.

46 Hunter, *Warriors*, p. 253. According to Hunter, hostility between Watson and Moore dated back to the first Amchitka protest voyage, when Moore tried to prevent Watson from coming aboard – without success.

47 Coish, *Season of the Seal*, p. 188.

48 Coish, *Season of the Seal*, p. 211.

49 Watson eventually set up an organization called the Sea Shepherd Society, which in 1981 declared income, from donations, of $120,000. In 1983, Watson made news by threatening to "blockade" the sealing grounds, with his ship the *Sea Shepherd*. In 1984, while on bail following appeal of his sentence for his activities during the 1983 seal hunt, Watson led "Project Wolf," a protest against the government's plan to kill four hundred wolves in northeastern British Columbia.

50 Quoted in Coish, *Season of the Seal*, p. 170.

51 Quoted in Coish, *Season of the Seal*, p. 211.

52 Coish, *Season of the Seal*, p. 166. The Canadian parliament responded with a unanimous affirmation of the right of Canadians to hunt seals off Canada's east coast. (Coish, *Season of the Seal*, p. 168.)

53 The Animal Protection Institute (API) in 1979 collected $1,102,290 in donations. According to a report of the Philanthropic Advisory Service (PAS) of the Council of Better Business Bureaus, in Washington, the API reached a settlement with the state of California in September 1978, after criticism about "incentives and bonuses" paid for funds raised by the organization. API has also actively supported legislation against the leg-hold trap.

54 Scientists who worked on the report were from the United States (which bans the import of white-coat pelts), the United Kingdom, West Germany, Holland and Denmark as well as from Canada and Norway.

55 NAFO study, p. 29. These figures, incidentally, are based on a harvest that includes at least eighty per cent pups. As mentioned above, scientists calculate that one breeding adult is equivalent to at least four pups because of the high natural mortality of young seals. It is one of the many ironies of the seal protests that the objection to harvesting "babies" is at odds with ecological considerations.

56 "EEC Commission's Report to Council on Seals." Quoted in "Canadian Commentary" (see note 58).

57 The Canadian "Commentary" also criticized the commission's interpretation of events at the general meeting of CITES, April 1983.

58 "Canadian Commentary on the EEC Commission's Report to the Council on Seals, Pursuant to Article 2 of Council Directive (83/129/EEC) of 28 March 1983." (Hereafter called Commentary.)

59 Quotas in Canadian waters for hooded seals were fifteen thousand in 1982 and twelve thousand in 1983, of which Canadian and Norwegian ships were each allotted half.

60 The Greenland hunt took an estimated five to six thousand hooded seals in both 1982 and 1983. Despite home rule, Greenland is considered part of Denmark for EEC purposes; Greenland is withdrawing from the EEC, however, in 1985.

61 EEC Commission report, quoted in Commentary, p. 8.

62 Commentary, p. 9.

63 Commentary, p. 9.

64 EEC representatives, according to Canadian fisheries officials who met with them, showed a remarkable ignorance of the hunt. The leader of the EEC delegation reportedly said: "Must you really kill so many of them? Wouldn't just a few for each sealer be enough?" Disgusted by the EEC attitude, fisheries minister DeBané stood up at the end of a formal luncheon for the representatives and announced: "Well, didn't we have a lovely dinner? We all ate some nice baby cows." (Personal communications with fisheries officials.) The Europeans were especially eager to do away with the use of clubs. The Canadians, for their part, did more than present statistics: they also proposed an international convention covering every aspect of the hunt.

65 Personal communications with Canadian fisheries officials. In meetings with Canadian fishery officials and with the West German Fisheries minister, Norwegian Fishery Minister Thor Listav complained that the first semiannual study had yet to be started as of June 1984.

66 The German resolution claimed harp seals couldn't be distinguished from truly endangered species, especially Mediterranean monk seals. However, there are estimated to be barely four hundred Mediterranean

monk seals left, and these are rarely seen, let alone commercially exploited.

67 Senegal and Gambia were for a time united into a federation: Senegambia. The Canadian ambassador to Senegal also services Gambia. See Chapter Six.

68 Not only small underdeveloped countries have made use of animal-rights research facilities: as has been said, the EEC relied heavily on IFAW materials to reach their decision to ban whitecoats.

69 Personal communication with Canadian delegates.

70 Holt has given similar performances at the International Whaling Commission. His grants totaled $3,928 in the first six months of 1982, according to IFAW's report to the IRS. Holt is also vice-chairman of the IUCN Species Survival Commission. The issue of "Flags of Convenience," delegates who are not actually citizens or residents of the countries they "represent," deserves further analysis.

71 The Canadian delegation had calculated that a secret ballot would favor them, but their chance to propose it came when the Colombian delegate complained that diplomatic pressure was being exerted against Latin American representatives. The Argentinian delegate complained that no one had tried to influence him.

72 The Europeans were so shocked by this reversal that they considered cancelling an "extraordinary meeting of the parties" that they had called for the following day, to vote an amendment to allow the EEC to be represented by a single delegate, with voting power for all. (The resolution was, in fact, passed the next day, with Canadian support. As one Canadian commented, "After all, *noblesse oblige*.") The United States delegation was rankled by the EEC proposal, and argued that, by this logic, it should have fifty votes.

73 Johnson visited the Magdalen Islands in 1982, before the official EEC ban on white-coat seals. After being shown around by local fishermen, who tried to explain their lifestyle and problems, Johnson told them: "Well, boys, I have to admit you've changed my mind." He then flew to the mainland where, before television cameras, he proclaimed: "They call it a hunt, but it's nothing but a slaughter, and something's going to have to be done about it." (Recounted in personal communication with the author by Deraspé.)

74 "Guide To The Scientific Literature on Harp and Hooded Seals," prepared by R.L. Drinnan and Associates, March 1983. (A 1984 Greenpeace letter states: "We are ecologists." Like IFAW's, however, Greenpeace's stand on seals has become an animal-rights position.)

75 Greenpeace "Guide," Volume Two, p. 8.

76 Greenpeace often cites the figures of Doctor D.M. Lavigne, whose seal-population surveys, according to ICES scientists, probably underestimate pup production in recent years. Lavigne has received funds for research from the IFAW ($4,354 in the first six months of 1982). He was one of the people who presented the IFAW position to Burger King during the 1984 "fish boycott" campaign.

77 Recorded interview with Patrick Moore, by the author, July 1983.

78 Hollander, "The Man," p. 203.

79 Recorded interview with Doctor Richard Van Gelder, with the author, September, 1983.

80 Interview with Doctor Harald Traue, recorded by the author, August 1983.

81 *Der Spiegel*, 14/1983, "The Battle Over Seals and Fish," p. 144.

82 *Der Spiegel*, "The Battle," p. 144.

83 Traue interview.

84 Quoted in Coish, *Season of the Seal*, p. 72.

85 *Der Spiegel*, p. 146.

86 *Der Spiegel*, p. 144. (Germany is the second-largest market for furs, after the United States.) Sympathy for seals has been general, and yet this is a country where side by side with "save-the seals" posters, grafitti warns Turkish workers: "FOREIGNERS OUT!"

87 George Steiner, *Nostalgia for the Absolute*, p. 32. Steiner is paraphrasing Lévi-Strauss on the destructiveness of European colonialism, but his words apply well in this case.

88 See the new book (*Sex and Destiny*) by Germaine Greer, the feminist writer, who now argues that birth control and abortion deny a woman's nature.

89 According to officials of the Communications section of the Canadian Fisheries Department, about eighty per cent of letters against the seal hunt which have been received are from women.

90 Recorded interview with Mark Small, September 1983, with the author.

91 Small interview. Note that the EEC ban included hooded-seal pups, called "bluebacks." In 1983, the harvest of hooded seals fell to 129. The 1984 harvest will be about two or three hundred, despite a total allowable catch of 2430. (The total allowable catch was based on conservative NAFO estimates of hooded-seal populations.)

   The Canadian government has recently named a Royal Commission on seals and the sealing industry, to be chaired by Quebec Court Justice Albert Malouf. Part of the mandate of the Commission, which begins work in September 1984, is to determine the impact of seal populations on fish stocks.

92 Quoted in Coish, *Season of the Seal*, p. 127.

93 Small interview.

94 Wenzel interview.

95 Wenzel interview.

96 These prices are taken from Don Foote, "Remarks on Eskimo Sealing and the Harp Seal Controversy," *Arctic* (20): 4, 1967, pp. 267-268.

   The prices for the 1976 to 1977 period are from George Wenzel, "The Harp Seal Controversy and the Inuit Economy," *Arctic* (31): 1, 1978, p. 5, table 1. I am indebted to George Wenzel for both references. The quotations that follow are from Wenzel interview.

97 Western activists have borrowed the notion of nonviolent resistance from the east, especially Gandhi. Greenpeace's legalistic interpretation of "nonviolence," however, has more in common with the doctrine of *Ahimsa*. Followers of *Ahimsa* will not kill a cow, but they will let it starve to death. Animal-rights advocates can speak of "nonviolence" without a blush as they destroy the livelihood of thousands of fishermen and native hunters.

98 From a mail-out published by Greenpeace USA, part of the 1983-1984 "Save the Seals" campaign, called "Kiss This Baby Goodbye." The newsletter is published by Greenpeace USA.

99 Open letter to Edwin Newman, president of the Native Council of British Columbia, 26 April 1983.

100 Best's letter to Newman.

101 Open letter from Jean Rivard, May 25, 1983.

102 Interviews with Janice Henke, in *Pilot* magazine. Henke, who is a New York State wildlife consultant, has been writing a book that will be titled Seal Wars, scheduled to be published by Breakwater Press, St. John's, Newfoundland.

103 Clubbing seems unsophisticated, but the Batelle Laboratory in Columbus, Ohio tested alternative killing methods for more than one year: they tried lasers, electric shock, decapitation, gas, poison, ultrasound and other weapons. The result: under existing circumstances, the stout club used is the surest killing method. The constant call for a "killing pistol" would appear to have more to do with our own fascination with technology than with humane killing. Colin Pratt, inspector for the International Society for the Protection of Animals (ISPA), accompanied a Norwegian vessel to the seal grounds and pronounced the hunt, with few exceptions, "satisfactory." *Der Spiegel*, p. 146.

104 James Morrow, vice-president of National Sea Products, the largest Canadian packer, told a St. John's *Evening Telegram* reporter on 8 March, 1984 that he had been contacted by customers who had threatened to cancel Canadian orders if the seal controversy didn't die down. Morrow named no customers.

105 IFAW sued DeBané (and the CBC) for comments he made on CBC Radio in the fall of 1983. The minister made similar charges in the spring of 1984, as the "fish boycott" peaked, just before the annual seal hunt. (See *The Globe and Mail*, 8 March 1984, p. 3.)

106 Quoted in a telex to DeBané by the Fisheries Association of British Columbia. Fish packers were upset that DeBané's accusations had "reopened the can of worms." In fact, however, on the CBC television show "On Camera," on 14 October, 1983, Stephen Best, then Canadian national coordinator for the IFAW, readily admitted that the boycott was "blackmail":
REPORTER: I want to ask you about another effort of yours, and that's to try and launch a consumer boycott against Canadian fish products. Again, to try to force the government to ban the seal hunt. Isn't that a type of blackmail?
BEST: Yes. It definitely is . . . no, it's not fair, not fair at all, it's a terrible strategy . . . .
The interviewer asked Best if it seemed fair that countries like Denmark had voted for the boycott even though Greenland seals come into the Common Market unobstructed because Greenland is considered part of Denmark. Greenland seals are already "in" the EEC.
BEST: It's one of the inconsistencies of international relations. . . . I don't deal with inconsistencies.

107 IFAW newsletter, February 1984.

108 Best has reappeared, however, as a spokesperson for the IFAW. On 30 April, 1984, he was interviewed on CBC's "Morningside." He now calls himself a "political consultant" for the IFAW.

109 Transcription from an Australian Broadcasting Corporation radio interview, 26 January, 1984.

In her interview, Sue Arnold also claimed: "The New South Wales government, by the way, has banned them from any further fund-raising activities in New South Wales." This action was apparently taken because IFAW Australia already existed, and laws of the state don't allow two charities to have the same name. The parent US organization has now registered the name "IFAW Australia," and Sue Arnold confirmed to me recently that her own group has changed its name to "Australians For Animals." According to the US office of IFAW, the Australian wing is presently "dormant."

On the question of receipts for donations: the IFAW office in Toronto informed me that receipts are issued, but only if donors specifically request them.

In her Australian Broadcasting Corporation interview (26 January 1984), Arnold also charged that she had seen considerable "high living" by anti-cruelty teams during the seal-hunt protests. In personal communication, she told me she believed that tighter control of IFAW funds would bring an end to these problems.

Jerry Conway, a Canadian Fisheries control officer based in Halifax, also recalls being impressed by Davies's gourmet tastes. During the 1981 sealing season, Conway stayed at the Kirkwood Motel in Charlottetown, Prince Edward Island, where Davies and his group were also staying. The motel had "laid on all the best" for their out-of-town guests, Conway recalls, but it wasn't good enough for Davies, who instructed the chef to send out for Cornish game hens for his supper.

110 BBC 4, 17 February, 1984, "You and Yours" (transcription).

111 Brian Davies, "You and Yours."

112 Tim Yeo, "You and Yours."

113 In November 1982, however, a report by the United States Philanthropic Advisory Service (PAS) of the Council of Better Business Bureaus Incorporated, had noted: "The International Fund for Animal Welfare does not meet CBBB standard calling for soliciting organizations to establish and exercise adequate controls over contributions. . . . In their opinion to the 1981 financial statements, the auditors state that 'it is not practical to extend (their) examination of public support beyond amounts recorded. . . .'

"In response to this finding, IFAW's auditors have advised PAS that the qualification (regarding examination of public support) does not relate to revenues received by domestic (i.e. US) locations, but rather addresses locations outside North America."

PAS reports are "not intended to recommend or deprecate" and are published "solely to assist you in exercising your judgement." PAS has since dropped its reservations about IFAW fund-raising controls, mainly, however, because questions about how money moves in and out of IFAW's international affiliates have been put aside, apparently. See Seth Rolbein, "Brian Davies and the IFAW: The Pricetag on Animal Welfare," in *Cape Cod Business Journal*, June 1984. Following publication of Rolbein's article, Brian Davies wrote to Rolbein on 22 June 1984: "Seth Rolbein . . . appeared to attach negative connotations to everything he saw. . . . Well, that's his right. . . . The organizational stresses and strains that come from a philosophy of 'the animals come first' allow the likes of Seth Rolbein of the *Cape Cod Business Journal* to nit-pick. . . . Well, so be it. . . . The animals came first before his story, and they come first still." (Published in *Cape Cod Business Journal*, letters section, August 1984.)

The PAS report, incidentally, stated also: "IFAW does not meet the CBBB Standard calling for soliciting organizations to have an independent governing board, in which no more than 20% of the total voting membership receives compensation. . . ." In responding to this finding, IFAW comments: ". . . Executive Director Brian D. Davies receives compensation as Executive Director; and although he is a member of the Board of Directors, he does not receive compensation therefore. Our organization was formed under these provisions in 1969 and we do not foresee any need to change our structure at this time."

114 IRS *Returns for Organization Exempt from Income Tax 1982*. Report for January 1 to June 30, 1982:

IFAW declared total income of (for 6 months):　　　　　$3,073,592

Of about $2 million "expenses," more than $1 million was for printing newsletters and postage.

115 Correspondence from the office of the minister of fisheries and oceans to Bay State Trappers Association, 6 March, 1984. IFAW responded on 20 July, 1984 in a letter to the Canadian minister of fisheries: ". . . Mr. Robert is correct in his criticism of the entry on page 2, part III(a). IFAW did not set up nurseries for baby seals in 1982 as was done the year before. Apparently when our attorney filled out the form, the wording was taken verbatim from the prior year's report and was not corrected. This was an oversight on our part." The letter was signed by Robert J.Govoni, IFAW controller.

116 "IFAW Saves Starving Stranded Seals." Brian Davies, IFAW Seal Rescue Report (undated).

117 Dr. J. Geraci, in a report to the director of field services of the department of fisheries and oceans, 8 June, 1981.

118 Personal communication with Jerry Conway, March 1984 and with Stan Dudka, August 1984.

119 Personal communication, Conway.

120 CP report, 12 March 1984, in Montreal *Gazette*. No one was in the helicopter when it was overturned. The four IFAW crew members had left for Charlottetown after being refused permission to refuel the Bell Jet Ranger (valued by IFAW at $375,000) by angry islanders. During the night, the guard of eight provincial police and five RCMP were unable to hold back the crowd of about a hundred who came to overturn the 'copter. The crew, headed by Dan Morast, returned to the scene the next day and shot video film of each other "climbing out" of the smashed helicopter as if it had just been overturned with them in it. (This last detail is not included in the CP news report, but was observed by witnesses and passed to the author in personal communication.)

121 *Toronto Star*, 24 September, 1984.

122 Personal communication with Fred Bearisto, August 1984. Bearisto quit IFAW at the end of 1982. He stresses that he doesn't want his actions to harm IFAW or its work, and he admits that the boycott may even have been effective. Personally, however, he still doesn't believe in third-party boycotts. Bearisto also insisted that he doesn't "look down" on sealers. If he'd been brought up in Newfoundland, he says, he'd probably have sealed, too, just as he hunted, because he was brought up in New Brunswick. "I don't hunt any more, either," says Bearisto, "but that doesn't mean that I think those who do are barbarians."

123 Greenpeace Canada is clearly looking around for other issues. In 1983, spending on "seal campaigns" was only $11,095, down from $118,679 the previous year. Campaigns against "whaling," by contrast, were up to $97,224, from $30,760 in 1982. It is instructive to note that "whaling" in this context no longer refers necessarily to protests against large-scale commercial hunting. In 1984 there have been reports of Greenpeace protesting the hunting of whales by aboriginal people in the Queen Charlotte Islands, on the coast of British Columbia. In 1983, "whale" campaigns included major protests against captive whales in institutions like Sealand of the Pacific. (See Chapter 8.)

While Greenpeace Canada was scaling down its "sealing" campaign, however, Greenpeace USA still allotted almost $1 million to seals, almost as much as all its other specified "program services" taken together. It is interesting, too, that in its financial statement for the year ending June 30, 1983, Greenpeace USA is described as "a not-for-profit organization which is engaged in saving endangered marine mammals and their oceanic environment." As has been shown in Chapter Five, harp seals are not endangered. Greenpeace USA declares its revenues for June 30, 1982 to June 30, 1983, to be $5,183,374, of which $4,458,248 was from donations.

Greenpeace Canada received $365,220 in donations in 1983 and earned an additional $139,003 from a Bingo game.

The striking success of the anti-sealing movement has been made, for the most part, in an open field. The government of Canada has proven incapable of mounting a consistent defense of the sealers because it is divided by its various constituencies. The conflict within the fishing industry has been mentioned. Some fish packers, faced with the IFAW boycott, preferred to sacrifice a $12-million industry (not their own), to save $1.6 billion in fish exports. In this, however, the fish packers show the same shortsighted "ostrich" mentality exhibited by the fur industry and laboratory-animal scientists, who fail to understand how the "victory" in the seal wars has strengthened the animal-rights movement.

As if this weren't trouble enough, the Canadian government has also been divided between officials in fisheries who do want to stand up for the sealers and others in the external-affairs department, who would like to keep a lower profile. A booklet explaining the seal industry was prepared jointly, in the spring of 1984, by the two departments, but external affairs chose not to distribute their share of the 22,000 copies printed.

An article in the London *Daily Mirror* on 7 August 1984 announced that Greenpeace is launching a campaign against fur trapping and ranching. This is the first time Greenpeace has taken on the fur issue directly.

Notes – Chapter 6

1 Cleveland Amory, *Mankind? Our Incredible War on Wildlife*, p. 210.

2 Greta Nilsson, *Facts about Furs*, p. 13.

3 Defenders of Wildlife, Washington, D.C. Its 1981 gross income was US $1,760,000. (Source: Council of Better Business Bureaus, Washington, December 1982 report).

4 Nilsson, *Facts about Furs*, p. 20.

5 Amory, *Mankind*, p. 232.

6 Amory, *Mankind*, p. 233. The mixing here in a single sentence of two ideas – *ecology* (endangered wildlife) and *cruelty* – is revealing. Spotted cats (which have been protected by trade regulations since 1970) aside, fur bearers in North America (the largest producer) are not endangered. In Canada, most species are believed to be undertrapped. Second: rhetorical value aside, presumably what is at issue here is not the "skinning" of animals, but the way the animals are caught. Blake's strange reference to "skinning" may be an unconscious reference to the key word of the baby-seal protests, that seals were being "skinned alive."

7 Amory, *Mankind*, p. 237. Amory includes a squirrel as a "trash" animal. This is not necessarily so. Three hundred thousand squirrels were trapped for fur in Canada alone in 1980 and 1981. Some squirrels, like flying squirrels, are useless for the fur trade.

8 Amory, *Mankind*, p. 237. In fact this "back-and-forth" technique, which so impresses Amory, was well-developed as a technique to establish contrast, moral isolation and distancing, when a simple "us-against-them" effect is wanted. For example, in the Nazi propaganda film, *The Eternal Jew*, "startling back-and-forths" are made between hoards of rats running through a corridor and ghetto Jews who had been herded together and then made to run, panic-stricken, before the passive, "objective" camera. *The Eternal Jew* also made use of films of kosher slaughtering; the animal-rights film, *The Animals Film*, shows kosher slaughter, too; neither film shows "ordinary" slaughter for comparison.

9 Lloyd Cook, Testimony before the federal standing committee on fisheries and forestry, 24 February 1977.

10 Paul L. Errington, "Of Man and the Lower Animals," *The Yale Review* (51): 3, March 1962. (Quoted in Shepard and McKinley, *The Subversive Science*, p. 187.)

11 Ajoy Bose in *The Guardian*, reprinted in the *Montreal Gazette*, 24 August 1983. Tigers in India's Jim Corbett National Park have doubled their numbers in ten years as a result of Project Tiger, India's most important conservation program. At least 150 people and ten thousand cattle are killed each year by tigers in India. At Dudhwa National Park, 125 villagers were killed in three years.

   Information about polar bears in northern Manitoba, which follows in the text, from personal communication with Bob Carmichael, Fur Manager, Ministry of Natural Resources, Manitoba.

12 The mid-Atlantic states are presently seeing a large increase of rabies among raccoons, especially near urban areas, where trapping is rare.

   John Gleiber, in "Apologists for the Steel Jaw Leghold Trap with Countering Views by Medical Men, Hunters, and Pet Owners," in *Facts about Furs*, pp. 158-160, has argued that trapping does not necessarily have any effect on disease control. Others, like Gary Parsons of the New York State Department of Environmental Conservation, disagree. (See Gary Parsons, "The Case for Trapping," in *The Conservationist*, September/October 1977; also February/March 1972, "The Little Foxes.")

   The point being made here, however, is not whether trapping stops disease, but only that in nature, disease is a limiting factor on populations, as is lower fertility, deteriorating quality of maternal care, lack of food and so on.

13 Quoted by Gleiber in Nilsson, *Facts about Furs*, p. 120. Gleiber claims that only the leghold trap was the target of the proposed Ohio amendment.

14 Most people fail to realize how complex is the problem of developing humane traps that will function in extreme cold and can be carried by trappers onto long, often remote trap lines. The primary mandate of the new Fur Institute of Canada is to continue the pioneering research in this field begun by the Federal-Provincial Committee on Humane Trapping.

15 James W. Goodrich, vice-president and executive secretary of the board of directors of the Wildlife Legislative Fund of America (WLFA), "Political Assault on Wildlife Management: Is there a defense?" Prepared for the 44th North American Wildlife and Natural Resources Conference, Toronto, 28 March, 1979. (Goodrich's comment, "raccoons don't vote" is taken out of context and made to look insidious by John Gleiber in *Facts about Furs*, p. 122. "Mr. Goodrich's paper ... gave the following noteworthy instructions on how to perpetuate the steel jaw leghold trap: 'Pledge to talk in terms of benefits for people. . . . Don't debate whether trapping is cruel. Talk about how trapping is necessary for people will then conclude that it is not cruel.' Then in a burst of high principles, 'Remember, raccoons don't vote.'"

16 Gleiber, *Facts about Furs*, p. 120.

17 Gleiber, *Facts about Furs*, p. 120.

18 Gleiber, *Facts about Furs*, p. 120.

19 Coish, *Season of the Seal*, p. 197. Other backers of the Ohio amendment included HSUS and Friends of Animals.

20 In the seal controversy, strict Canadian controls in 1972 didn't end protests. Instead IFAW, which had stressed the cruelty of the hunt, and Greenpeace, which had been more concerned about the ecological question of overexploitation, both moved to openly "animal-rights" positions – claiming that killing animals at all was morally wrong. Again, after Europe banned the import of "white coat" sealskins, the IFAW shifted its attack to argue that "ragged jackets" too were "babies." Presumably, if the hunt of all juvenile seals were halted entirely, the protest would move on to harp seals in general, or pregnant females, since harp seals mate soon after whelping.

(As mentioned in Chapter Five, the irony is that from an ecological standpoint, hunting "baby" seals is sound management, since a large proportion die before reaching maturity. From a humane standpoint, too, killing young pups, who are naive and relatively immobile, is probably quicker and less cruel than hunting older seals.)

The Center for Environmental Education, based in Washington, whose 1980 income was $2,210,903, was founded in 1972. The Center has begun petition drives to stop the harvest of adult ("bachelor") Alaska fur seals, on the Pribilof Islands, despite the fact that the United States government-controlled program for these seals has brought the Pribilof herd back from near extinction, in 1911, to near optimal (for food supply and mating territory) levels.

21 Threats of rabies and mice in cereal boxes, although they won the Ohio battle, do little to prepare the public for future campaigns, since they play on the same level of sentiment animal-rights groups exploit. The WLF has gone on to develop the full ecological argument since then. There are some difficulties with the WLF strategy of building as large as possible a

lobby against animal-rights initiatives. "Liberal," urban educated voters often oppose gun lobbies, and may object to the fact that gun manufacturers are represented on WLF's board (Olin Winchester and Colt Industries. It is interesting that gun manufacturers were also active in the *first* conservation movements in America.) A difficulty with applying the WLF model in Canada is that there is an inherent conflict between the interests of sports hunters and aboriginal subsistence hunters. Native trappers, as has been said, represent as much as sixty percent of Canadian trappers.

In the United States, however, the WLFA (after the Ohio campaign, the group's full name became the Wildlife Legislative Fund of America) has been notably successful in resisting animal-rights anti-trapping bills and hunter harassment tactics.

22 Clements interview. The account of the APFA is taken from this interview unless otherwise stated.

23 In April 1983, Canada proposed that the International Organization for Standardization (ISO) begin work on a standard for humane traps. Only three member countries have yet expressed interest in participating, and ISO regulations require at least five participating members before a new technical committee can be set up. (See *Consensus*, a publication of the Standards Council of Canada, Volume Two, Number 2, April, 1984, pp. 3-6.)

24 Clements interview. And yet the CBC is far from monolithic, as was revealed in August 1983, when news reporters were instructed not to wear fur coats on camera so as not to portray an "elitist" image. After strenuous protest from the Canadian fur trade, led by the Fur Council of Canada, CBC head Pierre Juneau assured the Fur Council that there was no strict policy, but that reporters' dress should suit the occasion. (Meanwhile, the original directive created the bizarre situation where reporters would remove their fur coats and put on cloth coats for the few moments they were being filmed.)

25 Clements interview.

26 A good example of the European inability or unwillingness to acknowledge the effect their ban has had on native people is shown in a letter received by Louis Bruyère, president of the Native Council of Canada, in response to his letter informing EEC members of native groups' concerns about the screening of the APFA films.

21 March 1983

Dear Mr. Bruyère,

Thank you for your letter of 1 March 1983.

The Directive adopted by the Council of Ministers on 28 February 1983 . . . contains a specific exemption for "products resulting from the traditional hunting by the Inuit."

We are not aware of any move to remove this exemption, nor would we wish to see it removed.

I think this answers the point made in your letter.

Sincerely,

Sir Henry Plumb, DL, MEP.

In fact, the collapse of the market for sealskins as a result of the EEC ban has hurt Inuit hunters worst of all, because the ringed-seal pelts they sell are so easily recognized as seals.

27 Report from the Canadian Mission to the EEC, to the External Affairs Department, Ottawa, 10 March, 1983.

28 Translation from: Hannoversche Allgemeine Zeitung, 26 January 1983.
George Clements now claims that Ressman was not a member of the APFA executive and was acting on his own in Europe, without Clements' knowledge. Clements, however, was interviewed about this time by *der Stern*, presumably on Ressman's urging.

29 *Facts about Furs*, p. 78, p. 75. See also Statistics Canada Fur-Production Reports. Many Canadian coats, moreover, are made with imported ranched mink, and much Canadian wild mink is exported.

30 These figures were compiled by the author by a survey of several of the better- and best-quality manufacturing ateliers in Montreal, where about eighty per cent of Canadian fur manufacturing is centered.
Wild mink, which are generally smaller than ranched mink, do require more pelts to make a coat. Almost all mink coats manufactured in Canada today, however, are made with ranched mink.

31 Communication with Norman Guilbeault, Fort Smith, Northwest Territories. (Guilbeault buys furs from trappers). Also with Ron Lancour, president of the British Columbia Trappers' Association, and Don McCrea, president, Manitoba Registered Trappers.
In Canada, a far higher proportion of trappers are "serious" trappers than in the United States.

32 Nilsson, *Facts about Furs*, p. 90; pp. 181-183. Cleveland Amory claims that "for every animal trapped which is wanted for its fur, two others are not even used for anything." (*Mankind*, p. 208.)

33 Even in "predator-control" programs, the furs are usually sold.

34 Anyone who doubts the importance of the food component of trapping may refer to Martin Weinstein's "Hares, Lynx, and Trappers" in *The American Naturalist* (3): 980, July/August, 1977, pp. 806-808. Weinstein shows that lynx trapped in a 220-year period in Canada, as recorded in Hudson's Bay Company records, appear to be determined not by price or by the number of lynx available each year, but by cycles in the rabbit population, upon which the trapper feeds when he is hunting lynx.

35 Colin Scott, "Production and Exchange among Wemindji Cree: Egalitarian Ideology and Economic Base," *Culture* (II): 3, 1982.

36 Two weeks later, *der Stern*, in another "exposé" on trapping, said the traps were banned in Germany in 1935. (*Der Stern*, 14 February, 1983, pp. 148-150). *Facts about Furs* chooses the middle ground, 1933, a date significant for other reasons in that country.

37 Nilsson, *Facts about Furs*, p. 141: "Each year additional nations of the world are added to those condemning its cruelty by prohibiting its use."

38 Nilsson, *Facts about Furs*, pp. 142-149. The text says there are "fifty" countries, but tables that follow list only forty-eight.

39 Nilsson, *Facts about Furs*, p. 55. The most fully developed argument against trapping is presented in this book, which was published by the Animal Welfare Institute. AWI, however, has been criticized by Peter Singer for having strong links with groups that use animals for laboratory experiments. See Singer, *Animal Liberation*, p. 231.

40 Personal communication with John Heppes, April, 1984.

41 Monica Hutchings and Mavis Caver, *Man's Dominion*, p. 90. The authors

point out that the trap ban in England is usually taken to refer only to "gin-traps" for rabbits. Larger traps, suitable for badgers and foxes, are still readily available in the countryside, they say.

42 Brazil and Chile, which have banned the leghold trap, have proved to date unable to enforce even the CITES restrictions on the export of endangered species. The total wild fur harvest of Latin America was only 3½ to 5 million pelts in 1977 to 1978, of which 3 million were rabbits and hares.

43 Canada's fur (manufactured) exports to Germany have slipped from $27 million in 1980 to $12.4 million in 1982. Part of the drop is attributable to the general slump in the German economy in this period, and especially to the relative rise of the Canadian dollar, which made Canadian furs more expensive for Europeans. But the trend has been worsened by the growth of an increasingly militant anti-fur campaign in the wake of the EEC seal ban. (Communication with the Fur Council of Canada). The exact number of aboriginal trappers is not known. The problem is complicated because most "native" trappers are Metis or "non-status" Indians, for whom no special records are kept. The figure of "sixty per cent" native trappers used in this text is taken from a letter to the author by the minister of Indian affairs and northern development, John Munro, 14 March, 1984: ". . . The Federal Government is concerned that fur trappers (some 60,000 of whom are native people) . . . would suffer in a way similar to the seal harvesters if such action (a ban on trade in leghold trapped furs) should ensue." It is commonly estimated that there are about a hundred thousand trappers in Canada, so I use the figure sixty per cent native. Further research may cause this figure to be revised.

44 Communication with Gerald Girard of the Cree Trappers' Association, Val d'Or, Quebec, August, 1983.

45 A 1977 Industry, Trade and Commerce Department (Canada) report stated that the two million muskrat trapped each year in Canada is "grossly underharvested." The three hundred thousand beaver trapped was considered about one-half the sustainable yield. Wolf, fox, bear, raccoon, ermine and mink are all underharvested in Canada. (Roy MacGregor, "Shadows of an Ancient Calling, Maclean's magazine, 16 February, 1981, pp. 46-47.)

And yet in Europe, tales of "endangered" beaver in Canada continue to circulate. In January, 1983, the powerful animal-welfare group Tierschutz (one of the first to attack the seal hunt in the 1960s) ran advertisements in Swiss publications, charging that "forty-two Canadian beavers died to make the coat in the photo" after hours of cruel torture. In fact, twelve to fourteen beaver are used for a coat (or nineteen very small beavers). Most beaver, moreover, are trapped underwater, where they die quite quickly. Tests by the Federal-Provincial Committee on Humane Trapping suggested that aquatic animals like beaver die not from "drowning" but from carbon-dioxide buildup in the bloodstream. "Called 'narcosis', it is by the most cynical definition, death from absolute euphoria . . . the trapped animal dies happily." (MacGregor, pp. 51-52.)

46 Personal communication with Richard Stardom, Fur Research Specialist, Manitoba Wildlife Management Branch, Department of Mines, Natural Resources and Environment.

47 Nilsson, Facts about Furs, p. 34. The market for raw furs (some) dropped off slightly during the severe economic recession after 1980. Prices are now (1984) rising again. Average price increases between 1970 and 1979 for

individual furs included: beaver, up 60%; bobcat, up 1150%; coyote, up 245%; red fox, up 300%; lynx, up 700%; mink, up 86%; muskrat, up 229%; and raccoon, up 643%.

48 Recorded interview with Peter Hyde, by the author, August 1983.

49 Interview with Michael Giannelli with the author. Other quotes also from interview.

50 Keats, quoted in Salt, *Animals' Rights*, p. 71. The first quotation from Salt is from p. 63 of the same book.

51 Dr. Gunnar Jorgensen, head of research, State Animal Husbandry Research Station, Hilleroed, Denmark. Quoted in IFTF Ecology Section paper: "The World's Best Cared For Domestic Animals."

52 Sven Wahlberg, general secretary, World Wildlife Federation (Sweden), and Gunnar Krantz, chairman, Swedish Federation of Animal Protection Societies, quoted in IFTF paper.

53 The only source I have found for this unpleasant bit of sensationalism is a Friends of Animals (FOA) advertisement in British newspapers, in 1969, at the height of the furor about spotted cats:

"Madam, your new tiger skin coat is ready. . . ." This tiger is lucky. He was poisoned by weed killer. If he'd been a leopard, a red-hot steel rod thrust up his anus would have done the job instead. So there wouldn't be any unsightly bullet holes in Madam's fur coat.
(Quoted in Amory, *Mankind*, p. 231)

Brian Davies, in a newsletter that accompanied his "Warning" pamphlet about kangaroo slaughter in Australia, refers coyly to the photo locked in his desk drawer that even he didn't dare print – but which he describes – of a kangaroo impaled on a fence post.

54 Testimony of John Reed, Public Relations Department, Woodstream Corporation (a major trap manufacturer) to the United States Congressional Hearings before the Subcommittee on Fisheries and Wildlife Conservation and the Environment, 17 November, 1975.

55 Godlovitch, *Animals, Men and Morals*, p. 26.

56 Consultation with trappers from the Northwest Territories via Norman Guilbeault, February 1984, Fort Smith, Northwest Territories. Lady Dowding states that this practice is used in Russia, to catch sables. (Godlovitch, *Animals, Men and Morals*, p. 27). Most Russian sables, however, are now ranched.

57 For Dowding on beating ewes with iron rods, see Godlovitch, *Animals, Men and Morals*, p. 34. Dowding adds that the finest kid leather, from India, is produced by pouring a concoction of herbs, "boiling hot, over the young goats. They are then skinned alive." (She fails to explain why skinning alive should produce finer leather.)

She also refers to the Canadian seal hunt: two observers from her organization, she says, reported that "considerable movement was observed during skinning. On several occasions, the seals' hearts were still beating after skinning was completed." (Godlovitch, p. 30.) As explained in Chapter Five, a physiological "swim reflex" can cause considerable movement, even after death. Not only must sealers ensure that seals are dead, with three blows to the head, but they must bleed the seals from the main artery between the front flippers before beginning the skinning operation.

58 Why someone who chose not to wear furs, on moral grounds, would buy a fake fur, is difficult to imagine. Presumably, "real people buy fake furs," usually because they want a real one, but can't afford it.

59 Carson, *Men, Beasts and Gods*, states that forty raccoons are used to make a coat (real figure: twenty-two to twenty-four); "an unknown number of miscellaneous animals die in traps – turtles, groundhogs, porcupines, dogs, cats, even eagles – before the forty pelts are collected." Carson also cites the favorite statistic that "for each mink coat a hundred animals are sacrificed." As his source he quotes a Friends of Animals "Actionline": "Stop, Listen – Write!" (January 1971). To discourage fur use, FOA has also offered to provide a tax-deductible receipt for the market value of furs which are sent to them – presumably to get them out of circulation. (Carson, p. 185).

On the Canadian seal hunt, Carson is unequivocal: "The cruelty is real and extinction of the species is imminent." (p. 189). The fight against fur use, he says, "is not straight humanitarianism but part of the total ecological issue," because of the "unendurable pressure on hunted fur species" (p. 189).

60 Carson *Men, Beasts and Gods*, p. 184.

61 Hutchings and Caver, *Man's Dominion*, pp. 121-122. The authors also repeat the tale about catching ermine (the winter coat of the weasel) by their tongues.

62 Surveys conducted at the author's request by Norman Guilbeault, Fort Smith, Northwest Territories. Also: communication with Ron Lacour, president, Association of British Columbia Trappers, and Jarvis Grey, of Pouce Coupe, British Columbia, a representative of United Native Nations and a trapper himself, and with a number of other Canadian trappers.

63 Bernard Rollin, *Animal Rights and Human Morality*, pp. 135-136.

64 Inside is the usual litany of misinformation: "60 mink are killed and skinned to make a single full-length fur coat" (true figure: 24 male skins; about 40 females); "25 foxes" (true figure: 12 to 18 red foxes, or 7 to 10 blue foxes); "35 raccoons" (true figure: 22-24); "50 rabbits." (Rabbit coats are not made from Canadian skins. The best rabbit skins are from France; these however are usually raised for food and not trapped at all.) The pamphlet refers to "millions" of non-target animals caught by mistake.

65 Survey of public opinions conducted in the Federal Republic of Germany, by the Dichter Institute, March to April 1983.

66 Association for the Protection of Fur-bearing Animals pamphlet.

67 University of Victoria Animal Rights Society pamphlet.

68 University of Victoria Animal Rights Society pamphlet.

69 Motion #3, carried unanimously, 22 February, 1984, by the Aboriginal Hunters and Trappers Conference, Winnipeg, Manitoba.

On June 23, 1984, at a Toronto meeting, native trappers' representatives adopted a constitution that established the Aboriginal Trappers Federation of Canada. Thus, after some four hundred fifty years of the fur trade in Canada – dating from Jacques Cartier's first visit to Quebec in 1534 – aboriginal trappers now have a united voice with which to express their own particular interests.

70 The Mathias Colomb Band, Missinippi River, Manitoba, statement to Aboriginal Hunters and Trappers conference.

71 "Notes for the Cree Trappers Association – response to proposal to ban the leghold trap."

72 Moore interview.

73 Dan Francis and Toby Morantz, *Partners in Furs: A History of the Fur Trade in Eastern James Bay, 1600-1870*. Recorded interview with Toby Morantz, by the author, September 1983.

74 I would like to thank Toby Morantz for these references from the original Hudson's Bay Company archives documents.

75 Morantz interview.

76 Furs were valued by the companies in relation to a standard for beaver pelts. Other furs were valued in multiples or fractions of beaver pelts. Thus the odd figure.

77 Brody, *Maps and Dreams*, p. 247.

78 Brody, *Maps and Dreams*, p. 97.

79 Scott interview. On August 7 to 9, 1984, close to a hundred aboriginal delegates from across Canada, as well as representatives from Alaska, the Pribilof Islands and Greenland, met in Yellowknife, NWT, to discuss strategy and set up an Indigenous Peoples' Survival International committee to deal with the threat of the anti-trapping movement. An important part of the mandate of the new committee is to communicate to the public in Canada and abroad the continued importance of trapping in aboriginal communities.

80 Brody, *Maps and Dreams*, p.212-213; see also Colin Scott, "Production and Exchange."

81 See Boyce Richardson, *James Bay: The Plot to Drown the North Woods*.

82 Brody, *Maps and Dreams*, p. 174.

83 Brody, *Maps and Dreams*, p. 274. Native leaders at the first meeting of the Aboriginal Trappers Federation on June 23, 1984, also expressed fears that the campaign against trapping was in fact intended to undermine traditional Indian culture, and would open the land to further industrial intrusion – with little control by local inhabitants, let alone any recognition of aboriginal land claims. (Author's communication with Cindy Gilday, of the Dené Nation, Northwest Territories; also with Michael Amarook, mayor of Baker Lake, Northwest Territories; Earl Danyluk, Aboriginal Peoples Alliance of Northern Ontario; Eli Weetaluktuk, of Anguvigaq Wildlife Management Inc., Inukjuak, Quebec; James Shaeffer, Northwest Territories Hunters and Trappers Federation; Joe Jalquot, Council for Yukon Indians; Ann Noonan, Assembly of First Nations; and Sterling Brass, 4th Vice-Chief for the Federation of Saskatchewan Indians.)

84 Recorded interview with Ray Demarchi by the author, August 1983.

85 Van Gelder interview.

86 Eddie Brewer, 31 October 1979. Quoted in Nilsson, *Facts about Furs*, p. 160.

87 The animal-rights strategy of taking control of a balance of power in international wildlife bodies is clearly demonstrated in the International Whaling Commission (IWC), which now includes such unlikely "whaling" nations as Antigua, Belize, Costa Rica, Egypt, India, Kenya, Mexico, Monaco, Oman, St. Lucia, St. Vincent, the Seychelles Islands and Uruguay. Canada, by contrast, resigned from the IWC because Canada no longer participates in commercial whaling – but also in reaction against

the obvious "stacking" of the voting power in the organization. A Canadian delegate to the IWC was asked by an animal-rights representative why Canada was resigning. "Because Canada is no longer whaling," was the reply. "Then why don't you vote to ban all whaling, if you don't do it anymore?" the delegate was asked. The point, of course, is that Canada was not intending to vote against whaling as long as it could be shown that proper wildlife-management controls and limitations were being respected. Rather than get another international "black eye" for defending scientific management, however, Canada simply withdrew from the IWC. The politicization of international wildlife organizations is a subject that deserves further investigation. (Sidney Holt also represents the Seychelles Islands in the IWC.)

88 As mentioned, Canada's proposals to the International Standardization Organization (ISO) have not met with sufficient response for the establishment of a new technical committee on humane traps. Meanwhile, the Fur Institute of Canada has already begun work testing trapping systems at the Alberta Environmental Centre, at Vegreville, near Edmonton. The institute employs five full-time technical and professional staff at the Centre. The Fur Institute of Canada is making a direct investment of $2.5 million for the first five years of the project (which begins in September 1984); Alberta will contribute the facilities at Vegreville, worth $2.5 million, and other provinces will contribute about the same again by supplying active trappers and by testing and refining trap designs in the field. The board of directors of the new Fur Institute includes representatives of the federal and provincial governments, industry, the retail sector, trappers and native groups, as well as wildlife and humane associations. (Source: Ron Daniel. Executive Director of Fur Institute of Canada.)

89 FOA harassment campaigns have generated a wave of "anti-harassment" legislation recently in the United States, spearheaded by the Wildlife Legislative Fund of America. The WLFA president said the strategy came in response to a large number of calls from hunters who were being harassed. In 1982 WLFA circulated a model bill that would facilitate prosecuting protesters who interfered with hunters. So far, at least ten states have passed laws that specifically outlaw harassing hunters: Louisiana, Michigan, Maine, New Hampshire, Nevada, Pennsylvania, Vermont, South Dakota and Illinois. The first state to pass such laws was Arizona. Similar bills are pending in New York, Massachusetts, New Jersey, Minnesota, Washington, Oklahoma, Wyoming, Colorado, Missouri and Montana. Cleveland Amory has called on Fund-For-Animals members to protest "these incredible bills that are being foisted on state legislatures by the gunmen's so-called Wildlife Legislative Fund."

90 To appreciate the HSUS "hard-line" on the fur industry, it is helpful to observe that HSUS itself has been under attack by more militant animal-rights groups: United Action for Animals president Eleanor Seiling accused HSUS board member Robert Marshak of conflicting interests because he was also dean at a veterinary college where tests were done on animals. Marshak is also affiliated with the National Society for Medical Research and with Biomedical Defense Fund Incorporated, set up to finance the appeal of Edward Taub, who was convicted in 1981 of cruelty to his laboratory animals. Marshak later resigned from the HSUS board. Friends of Animals president Alice Herrington has also charged that animal researchers are "infiltrating" humane societies to protect their jobs. (Source: Harvard University Study on Animal Rights).

91 Greenpeace, too, has been under pressure to radicalize its position on furs. Lifeforce, another Vancouver-based group, has criticized a report written by Patrick Moore, "Towards a Comprehensive National Policy on the Environment," which stated, "an emphasis on domestic animal-fur production and on the wool industry to replace consumer reliance on wild animal furs is supported" (Lifeforce Bulletin #2).

As this book goes to press, an article in the London *Daily Mirror* ("New Campaign to End Animal Slaughter: The Real Cost of a Fur Coat," 7 August 1984) announced that Greenpeace has launched a nation-wide campaign in Great Britain against the fur industry. "Our aim is a fur-free Britain," a spokesman said. They intend to "shame the wearers of fur coats off the streets" with a massive poster campaign.

In July 1984 the RSPCA also announced a campaign against the "international fur trade." RSPCA members also voted to recommend vegetarianism to fellow members and to the public. The RSPCA has been moving to a radical animal-rights position, especially since 1979, when radicals gained control of the twenty-three member council and secured the presidency for Richard Ryder (author of *Victims of Science.*)

92 Personal communication with George Clements, APFA, April, 1984.

93 Press release of the Woodstream Protest Committee, September, 1983. Woodstream Corporation, ironically, grew from the Animal Trap Company, an amalgam of smaller companies including, since 1925, the trap-manufacturing business of the Oneida Community – an American religious and communal group, founded in 1848 by J.H. Noyes around his philosophy of "perfectionism," free-love marriages and common ownership of property. The Oneida Community was producing and selling some seven million traps per year by 1910. (Nilsson, *Facts about Furs*, p. 115.)

94 Brigitte Bardot was in the news in Canada most recently because she sent an ivory bracelet to be auctioned for the benefit of the Quebec SPCA, which was reportedly $96,000 in debt. Canadian customs officials seized the bracelet, which contravened CITES regulations on trade in endangered species. Bardot apparently protested when she heard of it: "I didn't kill the elephant." (*Montreal Gazette*, 2 April, 1984).

95 Singer, *Animal Liberation*, p. 247.

96 In other words, about half the furs produced in Canada today are ranched. In Europe, the proportion of ranched furs is far higher: about one and a half million wild furs were harvested in Europe (1977 to 1978: Nilsson, *Facts about Furs*, p. 75,) while in Scandinavia alone, nine million mink and about one million foxes were ranched. Compare this to Cleveland Amory's mocking, "the furrier believing the 80 per cent figure [for ranched animals] is closer to 80 per cent wrong." (In the early fifties, the figure for ranched or farmed furs was indeed close to eighty per cent.) Amory smugly informs his readers that "only mink and chinchilla are widely ranched" (*Mankind*, p. 258); he has underestimated the importance of ranch-raised fox but, more important, he has failed to appreciate that "only" mink is a major share of the fur industry, as the figures reveal.

Nilsson's *Facts about Furs* states that about thirty-nine million wild animals are trapped for fur each year (1977 to 1978 figures), while about twenty-seven million are ranched (but Russian figures, which are significant, are incomplete). "Domestic" animals killed for fur – rabbits, Karakul, Persian and Swakara lambs, sheepskins, and so on – number some 237 million.

97 In 1939 there were 370 fur-manufacturing ateliers in Canada, employing 3800 people. By 1946, this had jumped to 593 shops, with 6264 employees. The value of furs produced mushroomed over the same period from $18 million to $58 million.

The peak was reached in 1949, when there were 642 shops, with 6,700 workers, producing $61 million, a volume of production which remained more or less constant until the 1970s. By 1981, the number of manufacturing ateliers was whittled back to about 300, employing a little more than 2,000 workers. Only eight "factories" in the Canadian trade employ more than 50 workers, and only 25 shops employ more than 20. These 25 factories produce about half the total product, but they also employ about half the work force.

98 *Men's Wear*, "From Sanitary Woolens to Sophistication," 19 January 1894. Animal-rights groups pretend to represent a leading edge of a changing social consensus. It is important to understand, however, that (as has been argued throughout this book) this impression is largely a media illusion. Jim Winters (until recently with Fisheries Canada) has pointed out that the IFAW's sophisticated use of computer-organized selective mailings allows that organization to achieve far higher levels of response (whether to solicit funds or to call for postcards to the EEC) than would be possible with standard blanket mailings over geographic areas. IFAW can thus create the impression that their philosophy enjoys far greater support among the general public than it actually does. (Jim Winters and Stephen Best interview on CBC Radio's "Morningside," 30 April, 1984.) See also Seth Rolbein, "Brian Davies and IFAW," in *Cape Cod Business Journal*, June 1984. According to Dan Morast, the answer to IFAW's jump in earnings after 1982 was "direct mailing expertise." Mailing lists were bought from other groups and compiled by IFAW computers. IFAW sends out about four hundred thousand pieces of mail every four to six weeks. "That's to people who've already given us a donation," Morast says. "These people are in our computer file." Computer sophistication now allows IFAW to contact people by geographic locale, by issue interest, and especially by the size and time of their last donation. In addition, there are drives for new members. In the first six months of 1984, IFAW sent out more than five million pieces of mail. Some thirty per cent of the donations received, says Morast, are "spent solely to raise and count the money."

99 The new Fur Institute of Canada will apparently allow the industry to overcome this problem for the first time. Not least important, the Institute will be able to conduct the sort of research (for example, the actual status today of spotted-cat populations) that will allow the industry to take a leadership role in the ecological aspects of the trade.

Ironically, the major challenge to the Canadian manufacturing sector may come from another front entirely. A number of East Asian countries are making a major push to take a big piece of the trade. Korea, Hong Kong and Taiwan already have fur-manufacturing plants. One in Korea produces more than $130 million in garments a year (dwarfing any Canadian operation) and employs six hundred operators (sewing with machines). Workers are paid the equivalent of about $1.10 an hour, far less than Canadian fur workers. Already a large number of Korean garments have reached the North American market, but they have been primarily low-cost garments. It remains to be seen if Asia can upgrade their product sufficiently to challenge the fine-fur markets.

The Korean workers, reportedly, receive a pep talk each morning from the owner over the PA system, and exercise periods beside the machines are compulsory each morning and afternoon. There are also compulsory sports activities during the lunch break.

Communist China, too, is attempting to enter the fur-manufacturing market. A large ultramodern fur-dressing plant has been built near Peking, but according to a recent visitor, millions of dollars worth of imported machinery designed to tan furs was standing idle and women were beating skins in the courtyard outside using primitive traditional tanning methods – apparently because no fine hardwood sawdust and oils were available to use in the machines.

A number of East European countries are also stepping up their fur exports (especially Hungary and Poland), and Greece is changing from being an exporter of fur workers and plates to being a manufacturer of finished fine fur (especially mink) garments.

On the other side of the coin: as these countries become wealthier, they may become markets for fur production; Japan has become the third-largest fur market in the world. Japan, too, has been stepping up fur manufacturing.

100 Salt, *Animals' Rights*, p. 67.

Notes – Chapter 7

1 Singer, *Animal Liberation*, p. 24. The book edited by the Godlovitches and John Harris, *Animals, Men and Morals*, preceded Singer's and mapped out the theoretical positions Singer developed (both were anticipated by Salt's *Animals' Rights*); but Singer's *Animal Liberation* has reached the larger public.

2 Singer, *Animal Liberation*, p. 24.

3 Author's recorded interview with Donald Barnes, August, 1983.

4 Barnes interview.

5 Author's recorded interview with Robert Sharpe, August, 1984. According to John Hodges, drug-information co-ordinator for Eli Lilly (Canada), Oparin was never promoted as a cure for arthritis. The drug was voluntarily withdrawn from the world market once problems were recognized. Oparin was never marketed in Canada.

Doctor Robert Dolman, director of medical research for Eli Lilly (Canada), adds that while the problem of extrapolating from animal research to humans is real and cannot be denied, he wonders if there is really any alternative. Without animal research, he says, we'd probably have no new drugs, because people are unwilling to try untested drugs. Part of the problem with Oparin, he points out, was that it became so popular and its use became widespread before its effect on elderly patients could be carefully observed. Many arthritis victims, he said, are still convinced that the drug is very good, and, in fact, a class action was initiated against Eli Lilly in the USA for having taken Oparin off the market. (The patients who organized the action were convinced the drug helped them more than anything else on the market.) Another problem, Dolman points out, is that while animal laboratory tests are carefully controlled, once the drug is on the market, manufacturers have little control over what doses patients take or doctors prescribe. In addition, many elderly patients are already taking other medications. (Personal communication with Hodges and Dolman, August 1984.)

6 Hutchings and Caver, *Man's Dominion*, p. 148.

7 Sharpe interview.

8 Sharpe interview.

9 Bernard Rollin, *Animal Rights and Human Morality*, p. 98.

10 Rollin, *Animal Rights*, p. 99.

11 Rollin, *Animal Rights*, p. 100.

12 Singer, *Animal Liberation*, p. 48.
   Similarly Ryder, in *Victims of Science* (p. 72): "We have adequate soaps, we have had them for centuries. So just how necessary is it that we should have new ones? We have adequate perfumes and face-powders, food-dyes and weed-killers; why must new ones be foisted on us? The answer is not the consumer's need but the manufacturers' desire for profits – in many cases there is no necessity except commercial greed." One wonders how Singer or Ryder would determine when "greed" begins and ends. A few lines down on the same page, Ryder informs us: "Profits mean pollution, and pollution means panic, and panic means pain – not for those who started the ball rolling, but for the unfortunate animals." (Presumably Ryder is referring to increasing consumer-group pressure for adequate testing of new products.)

13 Author's recorded interview with Doctor Harry Rowsell, director of the Canadian Council on Animal Care, August, 1983.

14 Rollin, *Animal Rights*, p. 102.

15 Rollin, *Animal Rights*, p. 103.

16 UAA "Action Alert – Research Modernization Act Introduced in New Congress."

17 Harvard University Study on Animal Rights Movement, p. 4.

18 Salt, *Animals' Rights*, p. 77.

19 Brophy, in Godlovitch, *Animals, Men and Morals*, p. 140.

20 Peters, in Godlovitch, *Animals, Men and Morals*, p. 225.

21 Brophy, in Godlovitch, *Animals, Men and Morals*, p. 144.

22 Singer, *Animal Liberation*, pp. 66-67.

23 Quoted in Singer, *Animal Liberation*, p. 66.

24 Singer, *Animal Liberation*, pp. 41-44.

25 Singer, *Animal Liberation*, p. 31.

26 Singer, *Animal Liberation*, p. 33; the Littlewood report (p. 53, p. 166). It might be noted, however, that the Littlewood report also found that "The risk of unnecessary repetition of experiments is small and the scale of duplication is not serious." (Littlewood report, Summary of General Findings, reproduced in Ryder, *Victims of Science*, p. 252).

27 Ryder, *Victims of Science*, p. 32.

28 Ryder, *Victims*, p. 246. Only a small proportion of the people surveyed knew that animals were being used for nonmedical tests. The survey reported in *Glamour*, vol. 79, p. 59 (Dec. 1981), found that eighty-four per cent of those surveyed opposed using animals to test cosmetics; sixty-three per cent opposed their use for medical purposes; and eighty-two per cent thought rats were the best animals to use as experimental subjects.

29 From S. Shuster, "Why We Need Animal Research," *World Medicine*, 13(5): 1977, p. 19; and Home Office Reports on Experiments With Living Animals, 1978. (Quoted in Marian Stamp Dawkins, *Animal Suffering*, pp. 3-4.)

30 The Littlewood report: "General Findings: (3) Public opinion generally has accepted in principle the necessity for and value of animal experiment, but cannot be assumed to assent to all that is done under the Act. (paragraph 227)." (Quoted in Ryder, *Victims*, p. 252.) According to the RSPCA survey conducted in 1973, and quoted by Ryder to prove public opposition to animal use for non-medical tests, seventy-three per cent of those surveyed opposed the use of animals to test cosmetics. Only forty-eight per cent, however, opposed the use of animals to test poisons. Seventy-seven per cent accepted using animals for medical purposes. And close to seventy per cent accepted their use for teaching medical students. More than sixty per cent accepted using animals to test drugs. (A total of 2,024 people were surveyed.)

    The survey in *Glamour* magazine found that sixty-four per cent of those sampled were against tests on animals even for medical purposes. (*Glamour*, 79, December 1981, p. 59.)

31 Singer, *Animal Liberation*, p. 31.

32 Rutgers University survey, quoted in Ryder, *Victims*, p. 35. (The survey states proportions of different types of animals.)

33 HSUS survey. (The information is from a UPI report in the Montreal *Gazette*, 2 April, 1984.)

34 CCAC, "Ethics of Animal Experimentation" for use in conjunction with "Guide to Care and Use of Experimental Animals." (November 1982.)

35 Dawkins, *Animal Suffering*, p. 124.

36 Recorded interview with Doctor Harry Rowsell, by the author, August, 1983.

37 Author's recorded interview with Leo Bustad, August, 1983.

38 Author's personal communication with Peter Hamilton, president of Lifeforce, August, 1983.

39 Singer, *Animal Liberation*, p. 137.

40 Singer, *Animal Liberation*, p. 94. The name "Kentucky Fried Chicken" is from a Lifeforce flyer, undated.

41 Ruth Harrison, in Godlovitch, *Animals, Men and Morals*, p. 17.

42 Singer, *Animal Liberation*, p. 173.

43 Dawkins, *Animal Suffering*, p. 32.

44 Dawkins, *Animal Suffering*, p. 36.

45 John Harris, in Godlovitch, *Animals, Men and Morals*, p. 98.

46 Dawkins, *Animal Suffering*, p. 36.

47 Dawkins, *Animal Suffering*, pp. 39-40.

48 Dawkins, *Animal Suffering*, pp. 42-44.

49 Dawkins, *Animal Suffering*, p. 47.

50 Dawkins, *Animal Suffering*, p. 53.

51 D. Lack, *The Natural Regulation of Animal Numbers*, quoted in Dawkins, *Animal Suffering*, p. 52.

52 Dawkins, *Animal Suffering*, p. 53, p. 75.

53 H. Kruuk, quoted in Dawkins, *Animal Suffering*, p. 49. (See also, in relation to this problem, Freud's *Beyond the Pleasure Principle*.)

54 Dawkins, *Animal Suffering*, p. 59.

55 David Cooper (best known as a counterculture "anti-psychiatrist"), quoted in Ruth Harrison, in Godlovitch, *Animals, Men and Morals*, p. 13.

56 Ruth Harrison, in Godlovitch, *Animals, Men and Morals*, p. 17.

57 Singer, *Animal Liberation*, pp. 96-97.

58 Singer, *Animal Liberation*, p. 146.

59 Dawkins, *Animal Suffering*, p. 91.

60 Dawkins, *Animal Suffering*, pp. 89-90.

61 Dawkins, *Animal Suffering*, p. 88. There are limitations to such "free-choice" models, too. Animals will sometimes choose unhealthy feed, for example, much as people will choose tobacco or sugar, even in unhealthy doses.

62 Singer, *Animal Liberation*, pp. 111-112.

63 Brophy, in Godlovitch, *Animals, Men and Morals*, p. 132. See also John Harris, in Godlovitch, p. 106: "Increased use of plant foods is the only logical solution to the world food problem."

64 Brophy, in Godlovitch, *Animals, Men and Morals*, p. 131.

65 Singer, *Animal Liberation*, p. 170.

66 Singer, *Animal Liberation*, p. 174.

67 Samuel Brody, "Facts, Fables, and Fallacies on Feeding the World Population," in Shepard and McKinley, *The Subversive Science*, p. 71.

68 Singer, *Animal Liberation*, p. 171.

69 Paul Errington, "Of Man and the Lower Animals," in Shepard and McKinley, *The Subversive Science*, p. 188: "The lessons of the lower animals could help rid us of naivetés concerning fundamentals. We could recognize that there may be more to meeting a population problem than increasing the production or improving the distribution of food or other material goods."

70 Errington, Shepard and McKinley, *The Subversive Science*, p. 190: "Ultimately live on algae? I suppose so, if that is what we must do, but why must we as rational beings get ourselves into the position of having to do it? ... A philosophy of conscientious husbandry should be consistent with a civilized and progressive attitude."

71 Brody, in Shepard and McKinley, *The Subversive Science*, p. 70.

72 Bread is the European staff of life. In other words, we have been cereal eaters. The quick increase in the North American consumption of meat in the past fifty years is in keeping with traditional American, rather than European, diet.

73 Salt, *Animals' Rights*, p. 43.

74 Quoted in Salt, *Animals' Rights*, p. 52.

75 Brody, *Maps and Dreams*, p. 55.

76 Brody, *Maps and Dreams*, p. 53.

77 Brody, *Maps and Dreams*, p. 53.

78 See Vilhjamiur Stefansson, *Not by Bread Alone*.

79 Singer, *Animal Liberation*, p. 183.

80 Brody, *Maps and Dreams*, p. 61. It is tempting to speculate that mass industrial society might one day become vegetarian: vast grain farms feeding huge centralized cities. Vegetarians like to say that abstinence from meat lessens aggression, which would be a strong argument for vegetarianism as urban-population densities increase. George Bernard Shaw, however, who was an outspoken vegetarian, wondered whether vegetarians weren't in fact more aggressive, by nature, which might be why they seek out less intense food sources.

Notes – Chapter 8

1 Giannelli interview.

2 Giannelli interview.

3 Giannelli interview.

4 Giannelli interview.

5 Moore interview, director of Greenpeace Canada, July 1983. (Patrick Moore has recently become "North America/Pacific Region representative" on the Board of Directors of Greenpeace International. Bob Cummings is now managing director of Greenpeace Canada and Joyce McLean is chairperson of the board. Douglas Mulhall is Canadian representative on the International Council. There are now national offices in Sweden, Austria, Belgium – these three new in 1983 – Canada, the United States, the United Kingdom, France, West Germany, the Netherlands, Denmark, Australia and New Zealand. Greenpeace Canada Annual Report, 1983.)

6 Duffy, in Godlovitch, *Animals, Men and Morals*, p. 115.

7 Duffy, in Godlovitch, *Animals, Men and Morals*, p. 116.

8 Duffy, in Godlovitch, *Animals, Men and Morals*, p. 117.

9 Van Gelder interview. Van Gelder suggests the fundamental unity of life processes. Eugene Marais, in his *Soul of the White Ant* (1939), says that a nest of termites resembles in every respect the organism of an animal: workers and soldiers are like red and white corpuscles; fungus gardens like digestive organs; the queen is the brain; and "the sexual flight is in every respect analogous to the escape of spermatazoa and ova. . . ." (Quoted in Robert Ardy, *African Genesis*, p. 63.)

10 Van Gelder interview.

11 Van Gelder interview.

12 Author's recorded interview with Angus Matthews, August 1983. (Greenpeace's expenditures on "whale" campaigns doubled in 1983.)

13 Matthews interview.

14 Hunter, in *Warriors of the Rainbow*, describes his "transcendental" experience with a whale. See pp. 146-148.

15 Matthews interview.

16 George Steiner, *Nostalgia for the Absolute*.

17 Matthews interview. A good example of how such anthropomorphism is actively encouraged and exploited in animal-rights campaigns is the recent Greenpeace "contest" in British Columbia to name the orca whales of the British Columbia coast. Although animal-rights groups often like to pretend that wildlife isn't managed at all, in fact all orca-whale "pods" (families) in the coastal waters are known and labeled ("B" pod, "Q" pod), and the individual whales identified and registered. As part of their campaign to prevent Sealand of the Pacific from taking two orca whales from the sea, they encouraged the public to name the individual whales – much as one does at an aquarium, ironically. Obviously, it's easier to stir public opposition if you can announce, "They're taking Molly!" than if it is reported that a whale was captured from "Q" pod.

18 Moore interview.

19 Peter Van Dresser, "The Modern Retreat From Function," in Shepard and McKinley, *The Subversive Science*, pp. 366-367.

20 "Things we can't control, we regard as sacred." Jeremy Rifkin, *Algeny*, p. 50.

21 Stanley Godlovitch, in Godlovitch, *Animals, Men and Morals*, p. 187.

22 René Dubos, *So Human An Animal*, pp. 62-63.

23 Rifkin, *Algeny*, p. 49.

24 Traue interview.

25 According to the Communications Department of Fisheries and Oceans Canada, up to eighty per cent of the mail received protesting the seal hunt is from women.

26 Germaine Greer, *Sex and Destiny: The Politics of Human Fertility*. See also Peter Singer's review of Greer's book, "Sex and Superstition," in *New York Review of Books*, 31 May 1984, pp. 15-18. Greer's thesis is certainly the logical conclusion of the animal-rights ideology. Singer, interestingly enough, doesn't address this question at all in his very critical review.

27 Van Gelder interview.

28 Tanner, *Bringing Home Animals*, p. 164.

29 Brophy, in Godlovitch, *Animals, Men and Morals*, pp. 130-131.

30 Albert Schweitzer, *The Animal World*, p. 189.

31 Schweitzer, *The Animal World*, p. 186. See Schweitzer's criticism of *Ahimsa* in Chapter Two.

32 Schweitzer, *The Animal World*, p. 131.

33 Schweitzer, *The Animal World*, pp. 191-192.

34 Schweitzer, *The Animal World*, p. 190.

35 Salt, *Animals' Rights*, p. 16; Lecky, *History*, Volume One, p. 100-101.

36 Ta T'ung Shu: The One-world Philosophy of K'ang Yu-Wei (translated by Laurence Thompson), p. 266.

37 R. Dworkin, *Taking Rights Seriously*, quoted in Rollin, *Animal Rights*, p. 73.

38 Salt, *Animals' Rights*, p. 66.

39 Quoted in Amory, *Mankind*, p. 233.

40 *Memoire Battante*, Arthur Lamothe.

41 Brody, *Maps and Dreams*, p. 280. Alan Cooke has made the very important (and rarely considered point that native people in northern Canada "gather harvests from land and seas that, through time, will be richer than any oil field." It is far from certain that the destruction of Canada's great northern wildlife habitats can be called "development" even in economic terms.

42 Greenpeace Canada in 1983 spent more than $109,000 on "whales" and "seals," but only $14,000 on acid rain, $10,000 on toxic chemicals and about $20,000 each on uranium mining and nuclear disarmament.

   Greenpeace USA spent, in 1983, $940,000 on seals; more than $400,000 on whales; $340,000 on dolphins; but only $158,000 on toxic wastes and about $140,000 on endangered species, about the only two "ecology" issues to be found on their program services for that year. Greenpeace is the most ecologically oriented of the animal-rights groups.

Bibliography

Allen, Glover M. *Extinct and Vanishing Mammals of the Western Hemisphere*. New York: Cooper Square Publishers, 1972.

Amory, Cleveland. *Mankind? Our Incredible War on Wildlife*. New York: Dell, 1974.

Brody, Hugh. *Maps and Dreams: Indians and the British Columbia Frontier*. Hammondsworth: Penguin Books, 1983.

Canadian Council on Animal Care. *Guide to the Use and Care of Experimental Animals*. Ottawa: CCAC, 1980.

——. *The Ethics of Animal Experimentation*. Ottawa: CCAC, November 1982.

Carson, Gerald. *Men, Beasts and Gods: A History of Cruelty and Kindness to Animals*. New York: Charles Scribner's Sons, 1972.

Carson, Rachel. *Silent Spring*. Boston: Houghton Mifflin, 1962.

Coish, Calvin. *Season of the Seal: The International Storm Over Canada's Seal Hunt*. St. John's: Breakwater Books, 1979.

Collingwood, R.G. *The Idea of Nature*. New York: Galaxy, 1960.

Cooke, Alan. "A Gift Outright: The Exploration of the Canadian Arctic Islands after 1880." in Morris Zaslow (ed.) *A Century of Canada's Arctic Islands*. Ottawa: Royal Society of Canada, 1981.

Cox, Bruce (ed.). *Cultural Ecology: Readings on the Canadian Indians and Eskimos*. Toronto: McClelland and Stewart, 1970.

Davies, Brian. *Savage Luxury: The Slaughter of the Baby Seals*. Toronto: Ryerson Press, 1970.

Dawkins, Marian Stamp. *Animal Suffering: The Science of Animal Welfare*. London: Chapman and Hall, 1980.

Descartes, René. *Discourse on Method and Meditations*. New York: Liberal Arts Press, 1960.

Drucker, Philip. *Indians of the Northwest Coast*. Garden City, New Jersey: American Museum of Natural History, 1963.

Dubos, René. *A God Within*. New York: Charles Scribner's Sons, 1972.

——. *So Human an Animal*. London: Sphere, 1973.

Foster, Janet. *Working for Wildlife: The Beginning of Preservation in Canada*. Toronto: University of Toronto Press, 1978.

Francis, Daniel and Toby Morantz. *Partners in Furs: A History of the Fur Trade in Eastern James Bay, 1600-1870*. Montreal and Kingston: McGill-Queens University Press, 1983.

Gelder, Richard Van. *Animals and Man: Past Present Future*. New York: Foundation for Environmental Education, 1972.

Godlovitch, Stanley and Roslind and John Harris. *Animals, Men and Morals: An Enquiry into the Maltreatment of Non-Humans*. London: Victor Gollancz, 1971.

Graham, Frank Jr. *Man's Dominion: The Story of Conservation in America*. New York: M. Evans, 1971.

Greenpeace Foundation of Canada. *Harp Seals and Hooded Seals: A Guide to the Scientific Literature.* Vancouver: Greenpeace International, 1983.

Harrison, Ruth. *Animal Machines.* London: Stuart, 1964.

Hays, S.P. *Conservation and the Gospel of Efficiency.* Cambridge: Harvard University Press, 1959.

Hornaday, W.T. *Thirty Years of War for Wildlife.* Stamford, Connecticut: Permanent Wildlife Protection Fund, 1931.

Hunter, Robert. *Warriors of the Rainbow: A Chronical of the Greenpeace Movement.* New York: Rinehart and Winston, 1979.

Hutchings, Monica and Mavis Caver. *Man's Dominion: Our Violation of the Animal World.* London: Rupert Hart-Davis, 1970.

Innis, Harold. *The Fur Trade in Canada.* Toronto: University of Toronto Press, 1970.

Jung, Carl. *Man and His Symbols.* New York: Doubleday, 1964.

K'ang Yu-wei. *Ta T'ung Shu: The One-World Philosophy of K'ang Yu-Wei.* (Lawrence G. Thompson, trans.) London: George Allen and Unwin, 1958.

Konvitz, Milton R. (ed). *Judaism and Human Rights,* New York: W.W. Norton, 1972.

Lack, D. *The Natural Regulation of Animal Numbers.* London: Oxford University Press, 1954.

Lawson, Cynthia. *Bloody Decks and a Bumper Crop: The Rhetoric of the Sealing Counter-Protest.* St. John's: Memorial University Press, 1979.

Leavitt, Emily S. *Animals and Their Legal Rights.* New York: Animal Welfare Institute, 1968.

Lecky, William Edward Hartpole. *History of European Morals: From Augustus to Charlemagne.* London: Longman, Green & Co., 1911.

Lévi-Strauss, Claude. *The Raw and the Cooked: Introduction to the Science of Mythology.* New York: Harper & Row, 1969.

Linzey, Andrew. *Animal Rights: A Christian Assessment of Man's Treatment of Animals.* London: SCM Press, 1976.

Livingston, John A. *The Fallacy of Wildlife Conservation.* Toronto: McClelland and Stewart, 1981.

Lust, Peter. *The Last Seal Pup: The Story of Canada's Seal Hunt.* Montreal: Harvest House, 1967.

Nash, Roderick. *The Wilderness and the American Mind.* New Haven: Yale University Press, 1973.

Nilsson, Greta, and others. *Facts about Furs.* Washington: Animal Welfare Institute, 1980.

Olsen, J. *Slaughter the Animals, Poison the Earth.* New York: Simon & Schuster, 1971.

Paley, William. *Natural Theology: Or Evidences of the Existence and Attributes of the Deity, Collected from the Appearances of Nature.* London: R. Faulder, 1802.

Parry, J.H. *The Establishment of the European Hegemony: 1415-1715.* New York: Harper & Bros., 1961.

Passmore, John. *Man's Responsibility for Nature.* New York: Charles Scribner's Sons, 1974.

Poland, Henry. *Fur-Bearing Animals in Nature and in Commerce.* London: Gurney & Jackson, 1892.

Prentice, Arthur C. *A Candid View of the Fur Industry*. Bewdley, Ontario: Clay, 1976.

Regan,Tom and Peter Singer (eds). *Animal Rights and Human Obligations*. Englewood Cliffs, New Jersey: Prentice-Hall, 1976.

Richardson, Boyce. *James Bay: The Plot to Drown the North Woods*. New York: Sierra Club, 1972.

Rifkin, Jeremy. *Algeny*. New York: Viking, 1983.

Rollin, Bernard E. *Animal Rights and Human Morality*. Buffalo: Prometheus, 1981.

Rosenfeld, Leonora C. *From Beast-Machine to Man-Machine: The Theme of Animal Soul in French Letters from Descartes to La Mettrie*. New York: Octagon Books, 1968.

Ryder, Richard D. *Victims of Science: The Use of Animals in Research*. London: Davis-Poynter, 1975.

Salt, Henry S. *Animals' Rights: Considered in Relation to Social Progress*. New York: Macmillan, 1894.

Schweitzer, Albert. *The Animal World of Albert Schweitzer: Jungle Insights into Reverence for Life*. (Charles R. Joy, trans. and ed.) Boston: Beacon Press, 1950.

Scott, Colin. "Production and Exchange Among Wemindji Cree: Egalitarian Ideology and Economic Base," *Culture* (II): 3. 1982, pp. 51-63.

Shepard, Paul and Daniel McKinley. *The Subversive Science: Essays Towards an Ecology of Man*. Boston: Houghton Mifflin, 1969.

Shuster, S. "Why We Need Animal Research," World Medicine (13): 5, 1977, p. 19.

Singer, Peter. *Animal Liberation: A New Ethics for our Treatment of Animals*. New York: Avon, 1977.

Slotkin, Richard. *Regeneration Through Violence: The Mythology of the American Frontier: 1600-1860*: Middletown, Connecticut: 1973.

Steiner, George. *Nostalgia for the Absolute*. Toronto: Canadian Broadcasting Corporation, 1974.

Stewart, Jean. *Traps and Trapping, Furs and Fashion*. New York: Argus Archives, 1977.

Tanner, Adrian. *Bringing Home Animals: Religious Ideology and Mode of Production of the Mistassini Cree Hunters*. St. John's: Memorial University Press, 1979.

Thomas, Keith. *Man and the Natural World: A History of Modern Sensibilities*. New York: Pantheon, 1983.

Thomas, Lewis. *Lives of the Cell*. New York: Bantam, 1978.

Turner, F.J. *The Frontier in American History*. New York: Henry Holt, 1920.

Selected Articles and Reports

Bose, Ajoy. "India's Tiger Conservation Program Too Successful; People Threatened." *Montreal Gazette*, August 24, 1983. (Reprinted from *The Guardian*.)

Boucher, Norman. "The Wildlife Trade." *The Atlantic*, March 1983, pp. 10-23.

Canadian Commentary on the EEC Commission's Report to Council on Seals, Pursuant to Article 2 of Council Directive (83/129/EEC) of March 28, 1983.

Consensus (Standards Council of Canada). "Canada Produces First Standard on Humane Animal Traps." (11)2, April 1984, pp. 3-6.

Cooke, Alan. "Naskapi Independence and the Caribou." *Recherches Amerindiennes au Québec,* (IX) 1-2, 1979, pp. 99-104.

Foote, Don. "Remarks on Eskimo Sealing and the Harp Seal Controversy." *Arctic* (20)4, 1967, pp. 267-268.

Gottesman, Dan. "Native Hunting and the Migratory Birds Convention Act." *Journal of Canadian Studies* (18)3, Fall 1983, pp. 67-89.

Grant, S.D. "Indian Affairs Under Duncan Campbell Scott." Journal of Canadian Studies (18)3, Fall 1983, pp. 21-39.

Harvard University Office of Government and Community Affairs. "The Animal Rights Movement in the United States: Its Composition, Funding Sources, Goals, Strategies, and Potential Impact on Research," September 1982. (Based on research by Phillip W.D. Martin.).

Herscovici, Alan. "Men and Animals: Building a New Relationship with Nature." (Transcript of CBC series "Ideas," November 22 - December 6, 1983). Canadian Broadcasting Corporation, Toronto, 1984.

Hollander, Ron. "The Man Who Loves Animals." *Town and Country,* March 1984, pp. 200-250.

International Council for the Exploration of the Sea. "Report of the Meeting of the Ad Hoc Working Group on Assessment of Harp and Hooded Seals in the Northwest Atlantic." 4 to 7 October, 1982.

Kobrinski, Vernon L. "On Thinking of Eating Animals—Dialectics of Carrier Social Identity Symbols." *Dialectical Anthropology:* (6)4, June 1982.

MacGregor, Roy. "Shadows of an Ancient Calling." *Maclean's,* February 16, 1981, pp. 45-52.

Moncrief, Lewis W. "The Cultural Basis of our Environmental Crisis." *Science* (170), October 1970, pp. 508-512.

Morrow, Lance. "Thinking Animal Thoughts." *Time,* October 3, 1983, pp. 47-48.

Northwest Atlantic Fisheries Organization. (Report of the Standing Committee on Fishery Science, approved by the Scientific Council.) "Assessment of Seal Stocks." June 23, 1983.

Parsons, Gary R. "The Case for Trapping." *The Conservationist,* September/October 1977.

Peter, S. "European Hypocrisy Is Alive and Well in the 1980s." *Inuit Today/Inuit Ublumi* (1): 2, 1983, pp. 9-11.

Rolbein, Seth. "Brian Davies and IFAW: The pricetag on animal welfare." *Cape Cod Business Journal,* June 1984.

Scott, Colin. "Production and Exchange Among Wemindji Cree: Egalitarian Ideology and Economic Base." *Culture* (II)3, 1982, pp. 51-63.

Shuster, S. "Why We Need Animal Research." *World Medicine* (13)5, 1977.

Der Spiegel. "Die Grosse Schlacht um Robben und Fische" ("The Battle Over Seals and Fish"). *Der Spiegel* (14) 1983, pp. 140-149.

Singer, Peter. "Sex and Superstition." (Review of *Sex and Destiny: The Politics of Human Fertility,* by Germaine Greer). *New York Review of Books,* May 31, 1984, pp. 15-18.

Taylor, Russel R. "A Review of the Structure and Economics of the US Fur Industry," PhD Thesis, University of Western Colorado, 1978.

Weinstein, Martin. "Hares, Lynx, and Trappers." *The American Naturalist* (3)980, July/August 1977, pp. 806-808.

Wenzel, George. "The Harp Seal Controversy and the Inuit Economy." *Arctic* (31)1, 1978, pp. 3-6.

White, Lynn, Jr. "The Historical Roots of our Ecological Crisis." *Science* (155)3767, 10 March 1967, pp. 1203-1209.

Zola, Judith C. et al. "Experimenting on Animals: Values and Public Policy." *Science, Technology, and Human Values,* (9)2, Spring 1984, No. 47.

Index

Cassettes of the original CBC Radio "Ideas" program, "Men and Animals: Building a New Relationship with Nature," are now available.

Order from:

Audio Products
CBC Enterprises/Les Entreprises Radio-Canada
P.O. Box 4039, Station A
Toronto, Canada   M5W 2P6